MW00834267

PALESTINIAN WOMEN
Identity and Experience

PALESTINIAN WOMEN

Identity and Experience

EDITED BY

EBBA AUGUSTIN

ZED BOOKS

London & New Jersey

Palestinian Women: Identity and Experience is published by
Zed Books Ltd, 7 Cynthia St, London N1 9JF, UK,
and 165 First Avenue, Atlantic Highlands, New Jersey, 07716,
USA, in 1993.

Copyright © Ebba Augustin, 1993

Cover designed by Andrew Corbett

Typeset by EMS Photosetters, Essex.
Printed and bound in the United Kingdom by
Biddles Ltd, Guildford and King's Lynn.

All rights reserved

The right of Ebba Augustin, the author of
this work, has been asserted by her in
accordance with the Copyright, Designs and
Patents Act 1988.

A catalogue record for this book is available
from the British Library

US CIP is available from the Library of Congress

Zed Books
ISBN 1 85649 233 8 Hb
ISBN 1 85649 234 6 Pb

Contents

Preface

Ebba Augustin

This collection of accounts by Palestinian women, narratives, research and insights into the different factors shaping the lives of Palestinian women during the Intifada, grew out of the three years I spent living and researching in the Occupied Territories. A few months after I arrived, in December 1987, the Intifada, the Palestinian uprising against Israeli occupation, started in the Gaza Strip. Within a few weeks its spirit had touched every Palestinian inhabitant of the Occupied Territories, as well as foreigners living and working with them. The empowerment generated by the popular uprising became visible in all aspects of life. People started walking with their heads held high again and everyone was energetic, looking for her or his role in popular activity and resistance. There was an increasing sense of solidarity and support.

Witnessing the Intifada shaping the life of people I was amazed by the sudden power of women. Women of all ages were at the forefront of demonstrations, they organized food, clothes and equipment for their besieged communities; with never-tiring effort they queued for papers, for stamps, for visits to their arrested menfolk and children. Women showed an amazing ability to sustain the spirit of survival in their families during days and weeks of curfew, under gas attack and siege; they comforted their menfolk and children even when they themselves needed a shoulder to lean on. Women spent long hours in sit-ins in front of the Red Cross, energetically mobilized other women, organized popular committees, cooperatives, press conferences and meetings with Israeli women – all that on top of their household duties and in confrontation not only with the army of occupation but also with their own traditional society. The women's committees more than other mass organizations played a key role in the setting up of neighbourhood committees during the first year of the Intifada, and ventured to cooperate with Israeli women activists for a peaceful settlement.

Women were key initiators of support groups and activities on the Israeli side as well. They formed specialized committees and organizations to assist the increasing number of Palestinian women political prisoners, imprisoned Palestinian minors and families of deportees. In Brussels in 1989 women from both sides met. The Israeli Reshet, a group of Israeli women peace activists, and a Palestinian coordination network emerged. The activists on both sides represented a wider range of political views than could be found in the Israeli–Palestinian dialogue among men.

Even if social developments during the uprising produced setbacks (a decrease in the marriage age of women, a rising percentage of school dropouts among girls), women were empowered – both socially and politically. Their range of movement grew, their mutual solidarity, their steadfastness and their ability to compromise. But compared to their important role in sustaining the popular uprising, women's participation in political decision-making was marginal. The political women's movement was not so much a women's movement, representing first and foremost the interests of women, as a political movement putting national liberation before the liberation of women. Its different committees were extensions of the different factions of the Palestinian national movement. In 1991 the split in the Democratic Front For the Liberation of Palestine (DFLP) led to a split in the Palestinian Federation of Women's Action Committees. Increasingly, however, the leaders of the political women's committees are insisting on being taken seriously as an independent movement; they are committing a growing part of their programmes to women's social and political concerns and are tackling obstacles to women's equality that are immanent in Palestinian society itself.

The outbreak of the Gulf War in January 1990 was a major factor influencing the course of the popular uprising. In the popular alliance with the Iraqi leader Saddam Hussein, the Intifada lost its independence and self-reliance. Following the war a period of severe economic strife and growing social conservatism set in, which still continues. Palestinians who for years had sent remittances home from Kuwait were expelled; donations made to the Palestine Liberation Organization by Palestinian workers in the Gulf were frozen. Access to the Israeli labour market was severely curtailed, leaving a majority of the 120,000 commuting Palestinian labourers without work and pay. The rate of unemployment in some communities rose to as high as 40–50 per cent. Institutions depending on Gulf money had to close or reduce their activities because of lack of funds. At the same time the different West Bank areas were sealed off from one another, which cut off labourers from their workplaces, students from their universities and families from their relatives only a few kilometres away.

The effects of the growing economic misery of the population in the Occupied Territories and the seemingly never-ending occupation are especially severe on women, who have to provide for the food and health of their families with less monetary means and under the continuing pressure of the occupation measures. Whilst hardship in the early days of the Intifada was overcome with a spirit of hope, the lack of progress towards a political solution did negatively affect the social coping mechanisms of the people and increased conservatism and the turn towards religion.

With the beginning of the peace negotiations the area of struggle shifted from the community to the level of diplomacy. Women in the community lost the power base they had been building up during the course of the uprising. They seriously had to ask the question, Why did women actively participate in the uprising and yet still do not have a place in the political power structure? The loss of the community power base helped to catalyse a major shift in the women's movement from a mainly political to a social focus. Gender issues such as legal and political rights for women and the political involvement of the grassroots are at the top of the agenda of all the different women's committees. Guidelines for the advancement of women are being drawn up and implementation is being planned.

Women lobbied for a women's Technical Committee to be formed that would be instrumental in the preparation of the structure of the future state to include women's interests. The Technical Committee, which is linked to the peace negotiations, was finally set up in 1992.

Although the position of women seems to have gone backwards, in that society has become more conservative and restrictive, and general living conditions have deteriorated, the gain of the uprising is an increased consciousness and practical understanding of gender issues on the part of the middle-class leadership and the intellectuals. With a women's agenda being worked out and a leadership pushing for political representation while closely working with the grassroots, it is to be hoped that women will have their voices heard when there is a political settlement.

This book gathers together some of the data that have been collected by the women's committees and individual researchers since the Intifada began. In addition, women from different social backgrounds present their experiences and points of view in personal accounts. Whilst the chapters presenting research are the work of their respective authors, the personal accounts are based on taped interviews I conducted. The topics covered here are by no means totally representative, but I have attempted to offer an insight into some of the problems Palestinian women are facing in a traditional society under military occupation.

Finally, this is a book on and by Palestinian women living in the Occupied Territories. Without their research work and their openness and trust it could not have been written. I am grateful to the activists of Women for Support of Women Political Prisoners for their permission to publish parts of their report, and to all my Palestinian Arab and Jewish Israeli friends for their support and encouragement.

Part One
Women in Palestinian Society and Politics

Introduction

Palestinian society in the West Bank and the Gaza Strip is hierarchical and male-dominated, with clearly defined roles and norms for men and women and gender separation. Palestinian culture, even if predominantly Muslim,[1] is influenced by various religions. Muslim and Christian women are affected by almost the same set of traditional norms, values and customs. Women are perceived as totally dependent on their menfolk for protection and maintenance. While tradition is still carefully guarded in Palestinian society, people have been affected by the rapid political, economic, cultural and social changes that have been taking place over the past twenty years. New opportunities and ways of life have opened to women, which are equally encouraging and threatening. Contact between the sexes, which in the traditional society was strictly regulated, has been opened up by increased possibilities to meet in a mixed environment. An increasing number of women make their own way, risk leaving the traditional path; others feel threatened and search for security in tradition and religion. The uprising has accelerated this process. The Intifada functions as a catalyst of social change, but at the same time puts constraints on it and turns the wheel of progress backwards.

Najah Manasra, a clinical psychologist in the Maqqaset medical school in Jerusalem, is one of the women who chose to leave the paths of traditional society. She is extremely active in women's affairs and fights constantly to remove the barriers with which her society blocks her way. The chapter she has contributed to this book – 'Palestinian Women: between Tradition and Revolution' – is a passionate coming to terms with the position of women in Palestinian society.

'The Palestine Question provided the motive and platform propelling women into a new arena as visible actors,' according to another Palestinian author.[2] The fight of the Palestinian people against colonialism and Zionism laid the ground for Palestinian women's active participation in society and politics. The white-haired, delicate woman who heads the Palestine Women's Union in Gaza proves this assumption to be true. When talked to,

Yusra Berberi quickly steers the debate away from women to the Palestinian problem. Women's activities and politics in her experience are inseparable. 'Just women?' she said. 'How can we talk about women's rights, when not even men have theirs in a life under occupation?' Sitt (title of respect for a woman) Berberi is well known throughout the whole Occupied Territories, not just as one of the most active charitable women, but also as a national figure. Consequently she has experienced all the harassment that political activism in the Occupied Territories is inseparably connected with: travel restrictions, interrogations, searches and arrests. Traditional in her outlook she is representative of the charitable women of her generation. From a bourgeois and politically active family and with opportunities for education and work (as she describes in Chapter 3), she nevertheless became one of the pioneers of the new political women's movement. Her activities helped to lay the foundation for Palestinian women's legitimate participation in all levels of social and political life.

Terry Atwan's story about her education and growing up (told in Chapter 4) is an example of the never-ending fight of intellectual, politically active women against national and social oppression. She has continually had to surmount barriers set up by her traditional society, her family and the Israeli authorities. She was obliged to fight on two fronts, and often her opponents joined forces. Israeli intelligence personnel often make use of the traditional outlook of Palestinian society towards women and put pressure on politically active girls and women through male family members, the mukhtar or the traditional elite.

After her first imprisonment, Terry was stigmatized by people of her refugee camp. She had dared to endanger the honour of her father, and the rules of the society demanded that her mother 'lose her daughter'. Whilst people are proud when their sons are imprisoned by the occupying power, girls are better kept in the house so that there is no risk that they lose their honour. But Terry proves tradition wrong. She is one of the more than 1,500 politically active women arrested before the Intifada who have helped to change the attitude of Palestinian society towards women in jail.

The Palestinian artist Vera Tamari shows in Chapter 5 that art never exists in a vacuum, but instead is inseparable from the artist's social, cultural and political environment. Arab Palestinian women have always been artistic in choosing natural pigment colours and patterns for their cross-stitch embroidery, handwoven rugs of lambs' and goats' wool, or colourful trays and baskets formed from handwoven straw. But, according to Vera Tamari, Palestinian women's expertise in painting, pottery and metalwork can be traced back only to the turn of the century; these skills were taught to improve young ladies' chances in the marriage market. Only when Palestinian cultural identity was endangered through Hashemite and Israeli hegemony, did women artists begin to picture their local environment,

Palestinian houses, landscape and folklore in order to preserve their national heritage and distinct Palestinian identity. The Intifada intensified this tendency and in the publications, logos and calendars of the political women's movement, women artists found new fields and possibilities of expression. When the schools were closed by military order, art teaching, already a secondary subject, stopped altogether. The improvised classes in neighbourhood committees focused on 'hard subjects' such as maths, Arabic and science. But at the same time teachers, psychologists, social workers and child educators in the charitable and the political women's movement more and more discovered art as a psychological outlet for children's fears, aggression and confusion. Pens, crayons and paper were distributed through the local committees and children were stimulated to paint and draw whatever was on their mind.[3]

In Chapter 6, Afaf Ghazawneh and Suha Hindiyeh Mani present basic information on the socio-economic conditions of female wage labour in the West Bank. This chapter is the product of ongoing research initiated by the Palestinian Federation of Women's Action Committees and its Women's Resource and Research Centre, which was established during the Intifada. Women activists recognized under the pressure of rapidly increasing workloads and responsibilities that new strategies for effective political mobilization, economic participation and consciousness-raising were needed. At the same time valid data on women's role and position in society, which the new strategies would have to rely on, were lacking. In close cooperation with local and foreign academics and professionals, the women activists started a series of field studies to gather basic information on Palestinian women. This chapter is one of the first reports published of this still ongoing research. It is followed in Chapter 7 by the account of Amni Rimawi, who describes the life behind the facts.

The seeds of the Intifada were sown already by the process of internal colonization that followed the 1967 Six Day War. The Occupied Territories developed into an Israeli colony, their populations economically exploited and politically, culturally and ideologically suppressed, their institutions destructured to suit Israel's interests. In response, in the early 1970s the Palestine Liberation Organization (PLO) incorporated political struggle into its strategy for national liberation and initiated an informal resistance: the building-up of a network of formal (open) and informal (underground) organizations and institutions.[4] The more that open political organizations were suppressed in the years that followed, the more the underground grassroots mass movement proliferated. Voluntary work was the purpose of one of the first open mass organizations for the mobilization of different sectors of the population, initiated by the left in the late 1960s; the concept was quickly adopted by the national movement as a whole, and has proved to be extremely successful until today.[5] Many women activists first had their interest in community work and women's issues awakened by experience in one of the voluntary work committees; such experience often has had a lasting effect on their political outlook. In her chapter Amni Rimawi gives a personal account of her experience in the voluntary work, the women's and the labour movements. Though involved in three mass organizations she is not an exception among top-level women's activists.

Western women usually find it difficult to put themselves in the place of women in traditional societies. The gulf between them seems almost too broad to cross. But women like Faten Mukarker, who grow up in both societies, must bridge it somehow. Her narration, in Chapter 8, shows how difficult it is to find and maintain one's own identity, in a Western individualistic society like Germany as well as in a collectivistic, community-orientated society like the Palestinian. To bridge the gap is only possible through compromises and tolerance on both sides. Faten Mukarker managed the difficult endeavour: her example shows that combining both cultures is possible and gives hope for women on either side of the Mediterranean.

Notes

1. The only survey (conducted in 1967) showed a Muslim population of 531,500 and a Christian population of 31,900 in the West Bank (Meron Benvenisti, *The West Bank Handbook*, Jerusalem, Jerusalem Post 1986, p. 191).

2. Rita Giacaman, 'Reflections on the Palestinian Women's Movement in the Israeli Occupied Territories', Birzeit University, May 1987, p. 2.

3. See Mary Khass, 'The Effect of Occupation on Women and Young People – Some Examples', *Journal of Refugee Studies*, Vol. 2, No. 1, 1989, pp. 147–8.

4. Samih K. Farsoun and Jean M. Landis, 'The Sociology of the Uprising: the roots of the Intifada', in Jamal R. Nassar and Roger Heacock (eds.), *Intifada: Palestine at the crossroads*, New York, 1990, pp. 15–36.

5. See also Lisa Taraki,'The Development of Political Consciousness among Palestinians in the Occupied Territories, 1967–1987', in Nassar and Heacock (eds.), pp. 53–72; and Ibrahim Dakkak, 'Back to Square One: a study in the re-emergence of the Palestinian identity in the West Bank 1967–1980', in Alexander Schölch, *Palestinians over the Green Line*, London, 1983, pp. 64–101.

1. Palestinian Women: Between Tradition and Revolution

Najah Manasra

The family is the basic unit of Palestinian society. In her family a Palestinian girl develops her social personality and gains consciousness about her gender. On marriage a woman moves from the sphere of control of her own family into that of her husband. The structure of the Palestinian family determines the role of the Palestinian woman.

Three structurally different types of family are to be found in the Palestinian society of the West Bank and Gaza Strip. Differences between families in camps and villages and those in towns reflect differences in the basis and nature of social organization. Whilst cities to a large extent are made up of a collection of individuals and families, camps and especially villages are in most cases highly cohesive structures where extended family units are still the basis of social life. The nuclear family consists of father, mother and her unmarried children. This family type is increasingly found in the towns of the West Bank, but rarely in the refugee camps of the Gaza Strip. The transitional family is a structural mixture of nuclear family and extended family. It consists of the nuclear family, uncles or unmarried aunts and one or two grandparents. This family type is found in the West Bank and the camps of the Gaza Strip. The extended family or _hamula_ consists of all the sons descended from a common grandfather, regardless of where they live, and their wives and children; five generations are included. The members form an economically closed unit headed by the eldest male. The hamula is still one of the most common family structures in the Occupied Territories but its influence on its individual members is on the decline. The decline in family cohesion varies according to location: the social influence of the hamula is strongest in villages and less in camps and towns. A wealthy hamula exercises more power and has more control over its members than does a poor one.

Relationships between families and between individual family members are dominated by religious and traditional norms and values passed on from generation to generation. Even if the shari'a laws are generally recognized in all Arab countries, their actual implementation is influenced by local

tradition and differs from country to country. This is true for the West
Bank, Gaza Strip and Jerusalem as well. In some cases religious laws and
traditional norms differ significantly.[1] In these cases elders of the particular
society decide according to the specific situation which one to give
preference to. One such difficult area is the law of inheritance described
below.

On some matters, the patriarchal tradition of Palestine gives more rights
to women than does the shari'a. The Koran demands that women cover
their bodies. Only face, hands and feet may be exposed. Palestinian society
on the other hand permits women to dress in Western fashion in trousers,
teeshirts, blouses and skirts, and to wear makeup and jewellery.

Below I take a closer look at the different stages in the life of a Palestinian
woman and describe the role expectations connected with them.

Childhood

During the nine months of pregnancy already the parents' expectations
concerning their future male baby differ from their expectations for a baby
girl. Palestinian parents in general wish for a baby boy, and the delivery of a
boy is celebrated with greater joy than that of a girl, especially if the
firstborn is a boy or the couple have daughters already. A boy carries the
name of the family and secures its future existence. In the future he will
inherit the family wealth, carry the hopes of his parents and take
responsibility for their economic survival. Even though a daughter may take
care of her parents and stand by their side, she is not expected to secure the
family income.

Families believe daughters to be a great burden on them. Girls need more
parental responsibility than boys. When a girl leaves her home to play with
her peers in the neighbourhood her parents experience constant worry. If
she returns late, she is punished regardless of the cause of her lateness. The
reason for this excessive care is the society's definition of honour. Male
honour (*'ird* or *sharaf*) is not contingent on personal achievements, but
depends on a man's ability to control the behaviour of his womenfolk. Men
are responsible for the actions of women. When girls in their early childhood
start to recognize their immediate environment, they are taught by their
parents the rules of moral behaviour and shame. The female child is
constantly observed and controlled: how she sits, walks, laughs, moves,
dresses and plays with her friends and parents. Whilst a boy can afford not
to follow the demands of his parents, a girl is expected to be obedient and
'female'.[2] She must be 'sweet', her dresses clean and in order, her behaviour
pleasant. But despite the constant parental worries and excessive care it is
widely believed in Palestinian society that girls are easier to raise than boys.

In my opinion this difference reflects the repression girls face from the moment of their birth. What girls are taught by their mothers is acceptance and endurance of their believed inferiority.

One of my students, who got married recently, mentioned her fears of childbearing. 'I don't like girls. I don't wish my girl to lead the life I do.' If she delivers a baby girl, she will certainly pass her negative feelings towards female identity on to her daughter. Then the cycle of female inferiority will have turned full circle.

The social and psychological pressure on girls to adapt to their traditional female role, which starts so very early, increases with their age and takes concrete shape when adolescent girls experience their first menstrual periods. Part of this pressure is the burden of responsibility that girls must carry from an early age. When a girl reaches the age of five she is expected to take over household responsibilities like cleaning, washing-up, the baking of bread, taking care of younger siblings, guarding the house while parents are away and caring for the babies in the family. In the refugee camps seven- or eight-year-old girls take over very responsible tasks like taking the younger children to the UNRWA [United Nations Relief and Works Agency] clinics for vaccination or medical checkups. Only girls have household responsibilities at this age. Therefore their brothers quickly develop feelings of superiority, which are reinforced daily by the behaviour of their parents.

Even in their free time girls must follow different rules to boys. Girls do not play the same games as boys of their age, like climbing up trees or walls, riding bicycles or playing sports in which they would be in danger of spreading their legs shamefully. (In the mid-1970s I was a student in the upper classes of the UNRWA school of Dheisheh camp. Again and again, worried parents filed complaints against the sports teachers and insisted that the head of the school should forbid rope-jumping for girls. The parents believed that their girls risked losing their virginity if they jumped. A ban on rope-jumping for boys was never discussed.)

The fitting environment for females is believed to be their family home. Boys, regardless of their age, accompany their parents on visits while girls stay at home. Friends of mine have twins who are four years old. When their older brothers leave the house they usually take with them the male twin; their sister is left behind. When I asked the little one why she did not go with her brothers she replied, 'Because I am a girl.'

This education of female children towards self-denial and self-sacrifice is successful. Women who are brought up to take responsibilities, to sacrifice themselves for others, accept their unjust treatment without complaints. Women, who in contrast to their brothers gain experience in all kinds of family-related matters, are denied the right of personal and social decision-making. The leading role in family and society is given to males who have never been given the chance to gain such experience.[3]

Adolescence

The degree of pressure on adolescent girls to adapt differs according to where they live. In rural areas it is higher than in towns. Adolescent girls in the cities have fewer difficulties in finishing secondary or even university education than do girls in villages or camps. The reason is not only that the latter generally have to travel further distances to reach their school or university; social fears too influence the decisions of parents. Their daughters might get to know boys, might start a relationship or, through gaining broader horizons, might no longer be willing to accept the traditional norms set by their parents and their immediate society. But gradually over the past ten years such attitudes have been changing. Inevitably, the modesty code has been gradually modified to accommodate the growing desire of parents for educated daughters.

While working in the refugee camps I learned that parents in them put a lot of emphasis on a good education, for both male and female children. This is particularly true in the camps in and around Ramallah, Bethlehem and Jerusalem, where each year since the mid-1970s growing numbers of girls have not just finished secondary school but also earned a university degree as well.

Traditional parents believe that educating girls is a waste of time because their future is determined by their role as wives and mothers.[4] Because a daughter is a burden of responsibility on the family she is married off as soon as possible, because with marriage the responsibility for her is taken over by her husband. When young girls are married off at sixteen or twenty, higher education is regarded as of minor importance. The development of alternatives to the traditional wife and mother role is perceived as a threat to society by a large section of the Palestinian population.

The different attitudes of traditional Palestinian society towards educating males and females is shown in the research of Ibrahim Ata on the Palestinian family. The mean marrige age for his male sample was 23.6 years, and the female average was 19.6 years.[5] Whilst the youngest male married at the age of fourteen, 16.7 per cent of the females married between the ages twelve and fifteen.[6] At the beginning of the 1986/87 school year the girls school in Husan village had 25 pupils in the tenth grade and 30 in the ninth. When school started again in the next scholastic year, with the exception of two girls all the girls between the ages of fourteen and fifteen had been married and therefore taken out of school.

Despite such negative examples there has been a gradual change in social attitudes towards the education of girls. This is partly a consequence of the foundation of the Palestinian universities in the 1970s and early 1980s, as well as of an increased demand for women on the labour market and of changes in the West Bank's economy. Their own economic interests influence the decision of many parents to seek a good education for their daughters. Educated women have increasingly better chances on the marriage market. If the appearance of a women does not conform to the traditional norm of beauty and her chances of getting married are slim, with a proper education she will at least have a chance to make her own living and even support her parents.

Adolescence is an important phase in the life of a woman in which her adult personality is taking shape. Conflicts between parents and daughter about socially acceptable behaviour and about the mother's efforts to inculcate in her daughter an acceptance of male authority are a daily occurrence. In my experience these conflicts centre around very simple daily matters: for example, a song on the TV. If the song deals with love or sexual symbols, which is the case with most Western pop songs, the girl will not be allowed to listen to it. Films showing love or kissing scenes are taboo for adolescent girls. Because an adolescent girl is not supposed to have her own opinions, and her individual personality usually is not taken seriously, she fights not just against the norms of her patriarchal society but also against the loss of identity.

More even than during their childhood, the behaviour of teenage girls is controlled by their parents. They are not supposed to show strong emotions, to laugh loudly or to dress immodestly. The shari'a demands that a woman show her beauty only to her husband or to family members she is not going to marry, that is, her siblings and parents. Adolescence is the time at which women are most pressured to follow religious dress regulations.

Sexuality is more than anything else a taboo topic in traditional Palestinian society. Adolescent girls are not educated about their own feelings and about how to deal with the opposite sex. Young girls gain sexual information only by talking to girlfriends (who may know little more than they), or through the secret (because prohibited) reading of books and magazines. Even talking about sexual topics is a disgrace, and information about sexual matters which reaches the adolescent girl is therefore often distorted and loaded with fear. Control of the teenager's sexuality is obtained not by informed consent but by indirect or direct threats, intended to prevent her from having pre-marital sexual relationships. Most mothers tell horror stories to their daughters, which they hope will have lasting effect. The stories tell of girls who lost their virginity before marriage and were killed by their families to avenge the disgrace. Usually the killing procedure is described in great detail. Mothers view such shock therapy as their social or religious duty, necessary to save their daughters from losing their honour, and not at all as a burden for the adolescent's psyche. In reality, honour killings are very rare, even if some cases still occur.[7] The society has developed other methods of punishment. When a young woman loses the trust of her society she is made to feel the loss in many different ways.

Society reacts with punishment not only in cases of pre-marital sexual relations but also, especially in rural areas, when adolescent girls develop close emotional relationships with boys. In extreme cases talking with boys in the street, going out for a walk or exchanging photos or letters are viewed as disgraceful behaviour.[8] Women found to be guilty are beaten, locked in their homes, prevented from studying, placed under the tight control of their family, gossiped about and married off as soon as possible. When such a young woman's former 'lover' is not available, she is married to the next suitor, often a man years if not decades older than she.

Adolescent girls in Palestinian society are therefore left to face their psychological problems alone. There is no authority to which they can turn with their questions and problems because all their society demands is unquestioning adaptation. Though the Jordanian ministry of education includes sex education in the school curriculum, many difficulties surround its teaching. Pupils are either asked to go over the relevant chapters at home or the sex education programme is dropped altogether. A sixteen-year-old girl must transform herself on marriage into a sexually, socially and emotionally mature woman. Except for the burden of daily responsibilities she has had to carry since her early childhood, the girl is not at all prepared for this difficult task. The attitude of young girls towards their families and society is therefore often negative. They feel abandoned in one of the most important areas of their lives.

Marriage arrangements

Despite the remarkable stability of Palestinian customs generally, changes have occurred in marriage customs. Nowadays in the occupied West Bank, Gaza and Jerusalem one can distinguish two kinds of marriage arrangements.

The first is the traditional marriage, which is still the norm. Here the parents and not the future groom select the bride from a circle of potential wives. By choosing their future daughter-in-law, the parents can reinforce traditional values of dependency and paternal authority. The ideal wife for a man is the daughter of his father's brother. This is expressed in the everyday saying, 'Bint il amm Hammalit Il-Jafa, Amma il Gharibe Bidda Tadlil', that is, the cousin can put up with austerity but a stranger needs looking after. (Despite a noticeable decrease in endogamous marriages over recent years, in a sample of 925 people questioned by Ibrahim Ata, 390 (42 per cent) indicated a blood relationship with their spouse.[9]) Only in a few cases is the son-in-law from outside the village or the surrounding area. A precondition for the marriage is that groom and bride see each other only on the wedding day. A future bride learns only from the descriptions of her mother what her future lifelong partner looks like, how he talks and behaves. (In the sample of Ibrahim Ata 58 per cent indicated that they had never spoken to their husband before marriage.[10]) A bride is not supposed to refuse the match her parents have arranged for her.

The strict rules of traditional marriage have been modified over the years, but without affecting the general structure of matchmaking. A young man interested in marrying inquires about a potential spouse. When he identifies one he asks a middleman or middlewoman to visit the family of the young woman and ask for her hand. Usually her parents take time to answer and consult their daughter. In villages and camps the potential groom and bride will have known each other since childhood. In the cities the woman's family will inquire about the social, religious, financial and educational background of the suitor. Boys and girls of the younger generation more and more meet privately and the future couple will have the chance to talk. Courtship takes place within the female's house, usually in the presence of other family members.

In contrast to the past, a girl today has the right to refuse a suitor and her decision is accepted by her family. But if she makes use of this right more than once or twice, by the time she reaches the age of twenty-two she may be married off by her family without her agreement. Women over the age of twenty-five have fewer chances to marry and therefore are seen as a possible long-term burden.

One of the major recent changes is that the engaged couple are able to meet each other and learn to know each other before the wedding day. Usually they meet in the company of siblings or relatives. This precaution is to prevent pre-marital sexual contact. Some parents even ask for a marriage contract at the engagement ceremony, so that they may leave their daughter alone with her future husband without worries.

In the second kind of marriage arrangement practised in Palestinian society today, young people choose their marriage partner for themselves, but this method is still not the norm. These love marriages occur mostly in the cities and camps. Of the sample investigated in Ibrahim Ata's field study, 7 per cent of women and 56 per cent of men chose their spouses themselves.[11] Social and economic changes in West Bank society over the past twenty years, the increasing number of educated women, and their active participation in social and political movements have altered the status of women and made them visible in the public sphere. Women have entered traditional male domains, girls sit next to boys in classes, male and female students struggle side by side in the student movement and against the occupation authorities, and an increasing number of women work not only on the traditional female agricultural tasks but also in factories and agencies, as teachers or in academic professions. Men and women meet, work together and in some cases fall in love. Usually a budding relationship is kept secret until both decide to get married and the man visits the woman's family to ask for her hand. If her parents refuse, she has the right to marry her boyfriend against their wishes. But she must be able to resist the social and financial pressure her parents will put on her. Couples with different religious affiliations are confronted with three options: to separate, to break with their families or to start the long task of convincing their parents and gaining their support. Some parents are able to put such an amount of pressure on their daughter that she breaks with her boyfriend; she is usually then married off in the traditional way.

In the last decade the incidence of love marriage has increased in the cities, but in the refugee camps of the Gaza Strip it is still hardly known. In my experience women in general are much more open towards this kind of marriage than even university-educated men. Even progressive men who work politically with women activists tend to marry young, inexperienced, uneducated traditional women with unquestioned social reputations.

In my own experience too, even politically progressive men are often socially conservative and live their own double moral standard. While they themselves are very much interested in having pre-marital relationships, they believe that a woman who makes use of this right for herself exceeds the bounds of socially acceptable behaviour. The relationship between the sexes in Occupied Palestine is changing, but the men in this respect lag far behind. A politically active and well-educated male friend of mine not long ago married a fifteen-year-old girl. His argument was, 'I can educate and form her according to my ideas.' For him she was like a *tabula rasa*. According to his words she was without sin, because she did not know the double standard of society. He identified as sinful women who exercised the same right as men to have a pre-marital sexual relationship (he had had one of course). His is not at all an isolated case.

The legal background of marriage

> . . . It is the family law that has always represented the very heart of the Shari'a . . . it is precisely in regard to the law of marriage and divorce that the battle is joined today between the forces of conservatism and progress in the Muslim world.[12]

Contrary to the law in Tunisia, where polygamy is banned, under the Jordanian Family Status Law a Muslim woman is bound to monogamy, whilst a Muslim man may have as many as four wives. When a Muslim couple marries, a sheikh signs the marriage contract.[13] Whilst the groom needs a guardian only if he is absent or a minor, a woman must be married in the presence of her guardian: either her father, or one of her brothers or uncles, or in absence of one of them the *mukhtar*.[14] The groom is responsible for the bride price, which is split in two parts. The first part of the *mahr*, or dowry, is paid during the wedding, the second in case of divorce. As soon as the first part of the *mahr* is paid by the groom according to article 37 of the Jordanian Family Status Law, the bride is obliged to obey her husband. If she does not accede to his demands, if she leaves their home without reason or does not fulfil her duties as wife, she loses her right to maintenance and can be punished. This right of the husband to punish physically his wife is today one of the most problematic 'rights'. It is the basis for the general acceptance within Palestinian society of wife-battering for as it were educational purposes. Even though the Koran strictly limits this right (it is prohibited to hit with one's fist, with hard materials or into the woman's face) reality is different. Because Palestinian society in general accepts that wives are beaten by their husbands, beatings are judged as matters of degree, not rejected on principle.

Even modern couples seem to find it difficult to give up old customs and habits. Whilst during the Intifada, due to the declining economic situation of the people, the bride price was fixed at a very small symbolic sum, at the same time the *mahr* for women with foreign passports increased.

Part of the *mahr* is the furniture of the newly-weds' flat. The marriage often burdens the young couple with heavy debts because their flat has to be furnished properly. Women in traditional marriages do not seem to feel responsible for the debts of their husbands and do not recognize that they have to carry this burden as well. Women in marriages that are oriented towards partnership are often employed and care together with their husbands for the household. They often take sides with their husbands against the extreme bride price demands of their families, in order to avoid burdening their marriage in advance with financial difficulties.

Women in marriage

When women marry they move from dependence on their family to dependence on their husband. Particularly in villages and camps where housing space is scarce, newly wedded couples often move into the husband's family home. Women are usually inadequately prepared to face all the sudden demands of married life. In the first years of their marriage they often suffer from a perceived discrepancy between their hopes and reality.

The prohibition against talking openly about sexuality has in my experience the worst consequences for married couples. It affects not only women but also men who are inexperienced in sexual matters and enter into married life without the necessary information. Women are ashamed to *circumcision?*

double standard

show initiative, they stay passive and expect their husband to satisfy their sexual needs. Women under these conditions are faced with almost unmanageable difficulties in becoming an active partner in their married sex life.

Household work and childrearing is in the hands of women but the authority to decide important family matters rests with the man.[15] In a traditional marriage it is her husband who decides whom his wife contacts, how she dresses, which kind of food she prepares and how she educates the children.[16] Their punishment is also the father's prerogative and women tend to lose authority over their children when they must threaten them with punishment through the father. Despite his dominant role it is usually the mother who is blamed when problems occur with the children.

In Palestinian society housewives are responsible for work in the fields, caring for the animals and the baking of bread. Modernization of households has made this work much easier, but a growing number of women perform waged labour on top of their household work. Working women carry the double burden of two full-time jobs: one as a wage-earner and one as a home-maker. A woman's entry into the labour market is not matched by a corresponding entry of her husband into the sphere of housekeeping and childcare.[17] Even in traditional marriages, where women internalize their female role, problems arise over the division of labour in the household. Even socially progressive men are rarely willing to do an equal share in the household work. Mostly their help is of a symbolic nature.

A key issue for the equality of women is the question of responsibility for household expenses. In my opinion, Palestinian society in this respect moves between two extremes. Traditional patriarchal men control the household finances tightly and their wives are not supposed to spend one dinar without their approval. Other men leave all household financial matters in the hands of their wives. Between these two extremes one can find all kinds of arrangements. But generally in the past ten years the pattern of the division of labour in the household has changed towards giving more freedom of decision to women. The reasons for this include the rising educational standard of women and, particularly during the Intifada, the growing numbers of men who are absent, whether working abroad or in Israeli factories, detained or under arrest.

Divorce in tradition and in Shari'a law

In Islamic law, marriage is not considered to be a sacrament but instead rests on a contractual basis. Therefore divorce is possible and ruled by law. But this set of laws is probably, more than polygamy, the major cause of suffering to Muslim women. A married Muslim woman lives under the ever-present threat of being divorced by her husband, without herself having the right to divorce him. Only if her right of divorce is written down in her marriage contract (only very few women make use of their right to demand equality with their husband through formulating demands in the marriage contract), or if her husband fails to fulfil his marital duties towards her can she ask for a divorce. The Jordanian Family Status Law permits a woman to ask for a divorce in exchange for payment (*al-mukhalaa*), but she must still obtain her husband's consent to the divorce. If a wife asks for a divorce, according to the law (article 49) she loses her *mahr*, the second part of her bride price, which becomes payable if her husband seeks divorce. The right to keep her maiden name acts as a constant reminder that she lives in her husband's house only so long as she fulfils her duties and obeys him.

A number of further factors pressure women under all circumstances to avoid divorce. Usually divorce is preceded by a long period of problems in the marriage and family intervention to solve them. Before a divorce is agreed, family, friends and (since the beginning of the Intifada) the local committees try to mediate. But whilst a divorced man is in a socially accepted position and able to remarry, a woman is usually blamed for the termination of her marriage. She loses the privileges of a married woman, for example her freedom of movement, becomes a third-class person and finds it difficult to remarry. Palestinian society denies her the right to live by herself – this is true for women from all social classes – so she has no option but to go back to her original home. Even for a mature woman the only choice is between seeking refuge with her family or with her brothers, who are traditionally expected to integrate her into their households. Even though most women renounce their inheritance rights in favour of their brothers, (see below), this arrangement is still usually extremely difficult.

Another reason why women try to avoid divorce for as long as possible is the question of the custody of the children. The Jordanian Family Status Law says that custody for her children should belong preferably to the biological mother (article 154). But this is so only if she is able to devote all her time to caring for her children and is able to educate them properly. Otherwise, her right to custody of her sons ends when they reach the age of nine and for girls at eleven years. Moreover, in many cases, a woman will come under pressure from her family to renounce her right of custody for her children and to leave them with her former husband, so that she will be able to remarry. The opportunities for women with children, especially daughters, to remarry are fewer even than those of childless divorced women. Another factor adds to the pressure on women. A lot of men are only willing to give their wife the divorce she has asked for if she gives up her legitimate second part of the dowry, her right to financial support and the custody of her children. Whilst a husband is able to force his wife back into their house even against her will, a wife is unable to prevent her husband from divorcing her.

The difficult position of divorced women forces many wives to stay in their marriages, even when their husbands beat them, or have love affairs, or fail to fulfil their duties towards the family. Palestinian women have sayings like 'the shadow of a husband is better than the shadow of a wall', or 'the hell of my husband is more pleasant than the heaven of my family'.

Women and inheritance

A woman's right of inheritance is guaranteed under Islamic law, although her entitlement is to only half that received by male relatives. This is seen as fair because a woman is at no time responsible for her own upkeep. But this legal right, limited as it is, conflicts with Palestinian tradition. Because women are at all times in the custody of their closest male relative, whether father, brother, husband or son, they are considered never to be autonomous. When a Palestinian women is about to marry she therefore renounces her inheritance rights in favour of her brothers. If a daughter insists on her inheritance rights and demands her money or land, she is accused of ruining her family in favour of herself. To avoid this stigma most Palestinian women behave according to tradition.

One of my women friends lives with her husband and thirteen children in a small village. His salary is very small and her life is a constant struggle. If she were to demand her rightful inheritance to a portion of the olive groves of her family, their problems could be solved. But she refuses. 'I would be ashamed to demand my share. My father wants to keep our property together and not to split it up.' Brothers too are usually unwilling to give their sisters an equal share of the inheritance, because it would invariably lower their own social status. They send their sisters presents that do not at all alter their status. Owners of olive groves send olive oil, farmers present fruits and vegetables.

City women increasingly demand their share of the family heritage, especially when it consists of cash or property. But so far this has not changed the negative attitude of society towards women who demand their rights.

Conclusion

The Intifada has changed the role and consciousness of many women. Very consciously, an increasing number of them are taking up the fight not just against the Israeli occupation but also against the restrictive norms of their own society. They fight against limiting forces outside as well as inside their own personalities, because growing up in a traditional society leaves its marks on everyone of them. We as Palestinian women experience a constant struggle between emancipated and conservative women, between traditional and progressive women, between housewives who have internalized their traditional role and believe in it and others who search for new roles and possibilities. Especially in the vanguard groups of the political women's organizations in the Occupied Territories, the Intifada has led to changes in women's roles. Whilst the political leadership of these organizations in the cities still mainly consists of unmarried and working women, more and more married housewives have made their way into the leadership.

The Intifada has changed the roles of both men and women, but in my experience it has not yet altered the traditional norms and values. Changes are still superficial. An inner struggle between men and women is taking place, but where it will lead us is not yet clear, so contradictory are the current trends in our society. During the Intifada the pressures on Palestinian society have increased. For many people, one method of coping is to 'go back to the roots', to traditional culture, to return to old, familiar customs and rites. The victims of this trend are Palestinian women. When educational institutions are closed by military order, education for girls is not a 'right' any more but becomes a luxury. People say 'Why should girls learn if even the boys can't!' One solution to this problem is early marriage. Because schools and universities are closed, girls and boys have even fewer chances to meet openly than before. The priorities of the society are shifting and long-fought-for women's rights are denounced. This tendency endangers not just the position of Palestinian women and therefore social justice in the society in general, but the very ability to sustain the Intifada. The growing numbers of women who even in centres like Bethlehem, Jerusalem and Ramallah dress in the traditional Islamic dress (whether out of their own free will, because they are pressured and threatened by fundamentalist groups or by their families, or because they can move more freely this way), are a sign of this tendency. I hope it will be only a passing phenomenon.

Fundamentalist groups, which since 1982 have gained influence in Gaza, at the universities of Najah and Birzeit, are growing in strength. They propagate traditional Islamic values and wish to resolve the present contradictions concerning the status of women in Palestinian society, by sending them back to the traditional female roles of wife and mother. The fundamentalists use the weakness of the active secular political organizations, which pay insufficient attention to growing social problems and the inner societal conflict over the role of women. To count the number of women martyrs, and speak about their important role in the fighting, without mentioning the negative developments is a dangerous policy.

The Palestinian people are more conscious about their rights than before.

But so are Palestinian women more and more conscious about their rights as women. It is wrong to believe that the Intifada is able to liberate women. It is not a magic force which fights our fight for us. We need to see that many forces are at work attempting to curtail our existing rights, not to mention the rights we are fighting for. We need to develop creativity to show that women's liberation is invariably connected with national liberation and a free society. The secular political forces must give women's issues top priority next to national liberation. We need to fight for our own self-determination. Men still are the ones who decide for us.

Notes

1. All matters of personal status for Muslims and Christians fall within the jurisdiction of the shari'a and ecclesiastical courts respectively. In the West Bank the shari'a courts use the 1978 Jordanian Personal Status Law although it does not officially apply there.
2. 'Man was created virile, venturesome, strong, aggressive and loving. Woman is submissive, emotional, fair, tender and beloved.' (Lakha and Jaffer, *Marriage, A Step Towards Fulfilment in Life*, Harrow, Matrimonial Advisory Council of the World Federation of KSI Muslim Communities, 1984, p. 26.)
3. 'Men have authority over women on account of the qualities with which God has caused the one of them to excel the other for what they spent of their property, therefore the righteous women are obedient.' (4.34) (ibid., p. 15).
4. 'She [the daughter] has to grow up, first and foremost, as a true and ardent Muslim. And then she has to be educated, trained and groomed to become a sensible wife and loving, tending, and nursing mother. This is her sacred role, and her virtues are judged in this context' (ibid., p. 28).
5. Ibrahim W. Ata, *The West Bank Family*, London, KPI, 1986, p. 50.
6. Ibid., p. 50.
7. See Rosemary Sayigh, *Palestinians: from peasants to revolutionaries*, London, 1979, p. 25f.; Laila Nazzal, 'The Role of Shame in Societal Transformation among Palestinian Women in the West Bank', unpublished PhD thesis, University of Michigan, Ann Arbor, 1986, p. 201.
8. According to research by D. Barakat and H. P. Daw (*Al-Nazihun Iqtila'wa Nafi*, Beirut, 1968, p. 46), of those leaving the West Bank in 1967, 30 per cent gave as their main reason fear of having their womenfolk assaulted by Israeli forces (quoted in Yvonne Haddad, 'Palestinian Women: patterns of legitimation and domination', in: Nakhleh and Zureik (eds.), *The Sociology of the Palestinians*, New York, 1980, pp. 147–75.
9. Ata, Table I, p. 62.
10. Ata, Table VII, p. 72.
11. Ata, Table IV, p. 66.
12. J. N. D. Anderson, 'The Islamic Law of Marriage and Divorce', in A. M. Lutfiya and C. W. Churchill (eds.), *Readings in Arab Middle Eastern Society and Cultures*, The Hague and Paris, Mouton, 1970, p. 493.

The legal texts relating to the status of women remained as they were in the Jordanian period after the 1967 war in which the West Bank fell under Israeli occupation. There are two exceptions: the Jordanian Personal Status Law, with the shari'a courts entirely outside the power of the Israeli military government, and Military Order 627 of 1976, which gives women voting and candidacy rights. (Mona Rishmawi, 'The Legal Status of Palestinian Women in the Occupied Territories', in N. Toubia (ed.), *Women of the Arab World*, London, p. 87f.

13. According to article 33 of the Jordanian Family Status Law a marriage between a Muslim woman and a non-Muslim man is not valid. The same is true of a marriage between a Muslim man and a non-Jewish or non-Christian woman.

14. Articles 9 and 10 of the Jordanian Family Status Law.

15. 'Normally a man is born aggressive and a wife should complement his effort to run their house. A man is born to lead and it revolts his mentality and damages his ego if he is ordered by his wife.' (Lakha and Jaffer, p. 15.)

16. '. . . since she is a wife, her faithfulness to him has to remain unquestionable, untarnished. In Islam, there is no permissiveness, no promiscuity. It is for this reason that a Muslim, Mominah wife would not leave the house without her husband's explict or implicit pleasure and permission, or at least without his full knowledge. This is to protect her from those situations which give rise to loose and slovenly behaviour.' (Ibid., p. 31.)

17. 'A professional woman must remember that if she wants a family life she has to sacrifice her career interest in favour of her husband and her children. By nature a woman is passive and respective psychologically. Her basic traits are shaped by her primary need – to bear children and to create a home for them. Her ego primary is based on her performance as wife and mother.' (Ibid., p. 16.)

...opments in the Palestinian ...en's Movement during the Intifada

...ugustin

The roots of the Palestinian women's movement extend back to the anti-Zionist and anti-colonial movement of the 1920s. The formation of the first Palestinian women's union, in 1921 in Jerusalem, coincided with a growing resistance to Zionist penetration of Palestine.[1] The political direction of the Palestinian women's movement was intertwined with the male-dominated national movement. As in most other Arab countries,[2] the national liberation movement became a platform for Palestinian women's participation in social and political life. Initially the Palestinian women activists were educated bourgeois women (from the urban social elite), most of whom were kinswomen of Palestinian political leaders and had the leisure time and exposure to public affairs to become socially and politically active in the Palestinian national movement. In spite of their political background, the actual work of the first and second generations of women activists in the West Bank, both under Jordanian rule and under Israeli occupation, was predominantly charitable and complementary to men's work. The basic contradictions in Palestinian society itself concerning traditional domestic roles were regarded as of secondary importance or were not questioned (even though most of the women activists considered themselves exceptions to the rule).[3]

The activities and experiences of the first two generations of charitable women activists nevertheless paved the way for the more radical women's movement which developed in the early 1970s. The new women activists had received their political education in the voluntary work committees during the early 1970s and saw themselves as an integral part of the growing mass national popular movement in the Occupied Territories. The third generation of women activists, aware of the limitations of the traditional charitable work, set up a separate political women's movement in Ramallah in 1978. This was an attempt to change radically the concept of women's activities. Within two years the movement established branches in all parts of the West Bank and fragmented into federations identifying themselves with the four main political factions of the West Bank national movement.

The Palestinian Federation of Women's Action Committees (FWAC) is ideologically affiliated to the Democratic Front for the Liberation of Palestine (DFLP), the Union of Palestinian Working Women's Committees (UPWWC) to the Communist Party; the Union of Palestinian Women's Committee (UPWC) to the Popular Front for the Liberation of Palestine (PFLP), and the Women's Committees for Social Work (WCSW) is supported by Fateh. These women's committees see themselves as integral parts of the national movement, though they differ in self-perception and ideology, organizational structure, mobilization techniques and constituency from their charitable counterparts. The charitable unions function mainly in cities, focus on charity and relief work, and tend to have a hierarchical structure with a charismatic female leader as the main decision-maker. In contrast, the new women's committees aim to mobilize women of all strata of Palestinian society, giving special attention to rural, refugee and working women. The committees have made efforts to democratize their organizational structures and seek to liberate women politically, socially and economically. However, there are significant differences among the four women's committees. Apart from their respective tactical positions within the national movement, which entail aligning themselves with the political demands of their factions, the committees also perceive key issues such as gender equality and democratic decision-making within the committees in different ways. The Palestinian women's committees have played a pivotal role in the Intifada, providing the framework for the mass mobilization of Palestinian women. This task has challenged the political women's movement in all fields of their previous activity. The internal debate on philosophy, structure and strategy of mobilization has intensified with the increasing workload and responsibility of the committees.[4]

Organizational structure: decentralization and cooperation

The Intifada increased the workload of the political women's movement drastically. The pressure mounting on the central committees came from different sides. The sheer number of women active in committee work increased considerably. The UPWWC estimated the number of its committee activists to be nearly 5,000, compared with just hundreds before the Intifada.[5] The WCSW counted a total of forty new committees since December 1987.[6] 'Our membership increased a lot during the Intifada,' a UPWWC activist in Nablus reported. 'We had lists of membership and the women paid fees. But now we have neither lists, nor is anybody paying. We have too many active women and most of them have no money. We don't necessarily want women to become members any more, but to be active.'[7]

Due to the special needs of the massive uprising, the committees had to step up some of their previous activities like teaching courses, first-aid lectures, the knitting of pullovers for prisoners, and visits to martyr's families, as well as organizing completely new ones. Public relations requirements increased considerably during the first years due to extensive press coverage. One activist of the UPWWC expresses the changes that have been taking place:

> Two years ago we moved to Jerusalem as a grassroots organization. We didn't have to deal then with bank accounts and bureaucracy like now. For a while we didn't have a headquarters, we were functioning through people's homes. Now it is a problem with fifteen day care centres, and numerous projects and new proposals. Now we have the money and bureaucracy and constantly have to adapt our organizational structure to be able to cope with all of that.[8]

Such developments forced the three leftist committees to re-evaluate their organizational framework. The growing number of grassroots committees in different regions increasingly required a specific local strategy of work. To be able to cope with this challenge the local committees had to be encouraged to make independent decisions and to be self-reliant. While the system of democratic centralism in itself was not questioned, it was nevertheless slowly undermined, giving more autonomy to regional and local groups. On the leadership level, an apprentice system developed, slowly giving qualified young cadres from various social backgrounds access to decision-making at the highest levels. A new generation of women is becoming responsible in villages and camps. These women are not necessarily academically trained and usually do not originate from a bourgeois background, unlike most of the present leading figures of the political women's movement. The WCSW is the only women's committee that has not modified its platform.

Although the central coordinating office of the UPWWC is still in Jerusalem, the UPWWC decentralized its organization. This allowed it to handle the growing workload and enabled representatives from all West Bank areas to participate on equal terms in the general planning.

> During the Intifada the activists in different areas set up their own self-administered teams of work, each concerned with one issue like: families of martyrs, families of detainees . . . the committee in Hebron for example formed a special team for the families of youth, who are chased and wanted by the occupation authorities.[9]

The UPWWC has changed its system of representation from a regional one (taking no account of the size of local memberships) to a proportional one, taking into consideration the actual size of local committees. Moreover, the committee structure was decentralized because the central committee (CC) proved unable to handle the growing responsibilities. Three regional offices were formed, each divided into specialized subcommittees for mass media and information, PR, cooperatives, kindergarten, education and studies.[10] Similarly, one activist of the FWAC reported:

> There is an increasing awareness that we have to decentralize and give the local committees more independence. We had a lot of discussions about what to do in case our central office would be closed down. We invited a Lebanese woman who talked about autonomous committees and she said that we really had to tackle this issue. The response was very positive. Nevertheless, it took one and a half years of Intifada to let the Central Committee erode the idea of democratic centralism.[11]

In July 1989 the FWAC began its decentralization with an administrative and logistic separation of the Gaza Strip from the central office in Beit Haninah. This disconnection came as a result of the increasing communication difficulties after the Gaza Strip was cut off for a long time from the West Bank. The district committees also developed a more independent stand towards the CC to cope with the different local requirements. Additionally, specialized internal units like the foreign relations committee were upgraded and others were newly created, thus defining clearly the spheres of work of each responsible specialist. This restructuring increased the possibility of pragmatic decision-making. One of the FWAC specialists described her experience:

> Increasingly we have conflicts between the responsible specialists who represent the interests of their projects and the executive committee, which makes decisions based on political considerations. The outside pressure adds to this conflict and I believe it has positive effects on our work. Groups working with us come and ask questions. When they find problems they say, 'This is mismanagement, you have to change it.' In this respect things change in a positive way.[12]

Cooperation with mass organizations

The Intifada increased the necessity of coordination and cooperation within the different mass organizations, as well as within and between the factions of the women's movement. Although cooperation has generally increased, the committees still mainly work with relief committees of their own political affiliation. Though factional competition has hampered their attempts to respond to local women's needs and in some cases had paralysed their work, the same factional structure was crucial in generating a coherent network for integrating the Palestinian communities politically in the Occupied Territories.

Parallel to the increase in cooperation, a shift in activities from theoretical political teaching to very practical work also took place. On a broader scale than before the Intifada, local women's groups organized first-aid and health lectures with workers from medical relief committees. The meetings have usually taken place either in their centres or in private homes, or even in mosques or churches. 'We don't discuss books any more, but we organize with the medical and agricultural relief committees aid, clinics and lectures, which are organized by the women locally.' Their twofold programme is expressed by two women who are active in both movements: 'The work in the agricultural relief committees is different from the work in the women's committees, but we get easier access to the women and can interest them for committee work as well as mobilize them politically.'[13] 'Our aim is to strengthen the mass organizations in general, and to create the infrastructure of the future democratic state.'[14]

The structure of the Palestinian mass movement has given rise to many cases of dual membership. Most of the thirty female agricultural assistants in the agricultural relief committee are simultaneously members in one of the leftist women's committees.[15] They are the linkage between the different mass organizations and are the best guarantee for unbureaucratic cooperation. The agricultural relief workers rely in many cases on local women's activists to distribute seeds and give instructions for planting and food preservation and guidelines for home economy. The leaflets have been distributed by their own relief workers as well as through the women's committees.[16]

Coordination of the committees: the Higher Council of Women

Since the establishment of the first women's committees, the charitable women's unions and the women's committees have met irregularly and coordinated some activities, such as organizing bazaars, demonstrations and writing petitions. This changed under the pressure of the Intifada. The active women recognized the need to coordinate their activities in order to build a solid basis for the effective grassroots mobilization of women. Political considerations were equally important. As part of the Palestinian mass movement, the women's committees were obliged to transform their infrastructure of resistance to the Israeli occupation in compliance with their possible future role in the expected Palestinian state. As one leftist activist insisted: 'We need to build a real united women's movement. We will never become strong if we don't unite. We need to become a pressure group, to extend pressure on the national movement to hear us, to draw us into the decision-making process.'

The initiative for a single coordinating body for the political women's movement resulted, in addition to a growing recognition of its necessity inside the movement itself, from three different external factors: (1) after its formation, the United Leadership of the Uprising (UNLU) called on the mass organizations to unite their efforts to enable the Intifada to continue; (2) the international women's and solidarity organizations and non-governmental organizations demanded a single body to coordinate funding and activities; and (3) Israeli women activists, who were in the process of forming a coordination network on the Israeli side, hoped for a similar Palestinian development on the eve of the 1989 Brussels meeting. Thus in summer 1989 the Higher Council of Women (HCW) was formed, composed of representatives of all four political committees as well as professional women. Charitable activists have not participated. It has been conceived of as the nucleus of a united women's movement, but based on factions. Its main functions are: coordination of activities; common representation of Palestinian women towards the Israeli organizations, as well as towards other foreign countries and their organizations; taking the initiative in conceptualizing legal issues regarding women and in the formulation of a feminist agenda; and to increase the movement's influence and independence in the national movement. Although the first steps for common work have been made by establishing the HCW, its programme still needs to be made more concrete. This will need a commitment to cooperation and considerable compromise from all committees, because their respective positions on key questions of gender liberation, basic democracy, and their role in the national movement differ considerably. The success or failure of this venture will in the long run determine the movement's social influence and political weight. How far positions can differ even among the left is illustrated by the following two comments by activists from the UPWWC and UPWC respectively. 'If we want to build a strong women's movement, expressed in the Higher Council of Women, we need to be independent from the national movement.'[17] 'The Higher Council of Women will mainly deal with the legal position of women in a future state. It is the arm of the United Leadership in all questions concerning women. The gender issue should be studied now through the Higher Council of Women. Its demands are transmitted to the UNLU which should realize them in practice.'[18]

Research and projects

The increase in workload and the time pressure on the women's committees during the Intifada mean that the committees more than ever before require a detailed knowledge about women's situation in current Palestinian society, in order to develop comprehensive strategies for political and social mobilization, to plan economic projects, and to formulate a Palestinian feminist agenda. Class consciousness and gender consciousness have been growing, both at the leadership level and simultaneously in the grassroots committees.

During our work we recognized that we had to put ourselves into the position of the women and take into consideration class and living conditions as well. Women in the cities are more organized, they can handle exact timing better. In villages and camps, on the other hand, women have been more receptive to spontaneous activities. There it has been difficult to organize activities beforehand. Their household and agricultural work depends on the weather and they don't know what will happen tomorrow. The men are in hiding. Maybe they will come and the women will have to prepare themselves, bring food into the mountains – they have to make plans to avoid the army and collaborators. According to these different needs we have to plan our activities. While cooperatives don't work in towns because women can still buy most of their needs in shops, they are needed in villages and camps. On the other hand in the villages day care centres are not needed because women rely on the extended family, unlike most city women. We more and more recognize that we can't standardize strategies. And to be able to formulate new ones we need more basic information.[19]

The Intifada in this respect has initiated a variety of research projects and schools inside as well as outside the women's movement. For example, in 1989 the FWAC set up a Women's Research and Resource Centre in the West Bank, until now the only one of its kind. In cooperation with a social researcher from the USA, the FWAC carried out a field study in the West Bank and Gaza Strip, questioning women about their conception of democracy and women's liberation.[20] During the summer of 1989 the UPWC set up a cooperative school with teachers from Birzeit University, teaching thirty-five women activists cooperative management and strategy.[21] In 1989, two professional women activists in Ramallah and Nablus started a project for the publication and translation of women's literature. They have planned regular issues of a women's research magazine and have started courses for women, teaching them the basics of social research.[22]

The political and social mobilization of women

The dramatic increase in the numbers of women activists at the beginning of the Intifada has affected the women's groups' mobilization strategies and aims. An activist in Bethlehem reported. 'What we tried to do for such a long time, to mobilize the whole population, the Intifada almost achieved. It is amazing. The circumstances supported the mobilization of women more than our work could have done.'[23] Although the women's movement has not generated the massive participation of women, it has had a major role in shaping it. The mobilization of refugee and village women has been a priority since the foundation of the movement in 1978. The uprising started in the Jabalya refugee camp in Gaza, and camps and villages continued to play a central role in the Intifada. Without the activities of more than ten years in the camps and without a network of grassroots women's committees, camp and village women would not have been able to organize as successfully in popular committees as they have done. In retrospect, the community-based character of the political women's movement has proved to be essential for the important role the movement has been playing during the Intifada. This has consequently strengthened its mass-based character.

Despite the harsh and brutal reality of the Intifada, women have shown a revolutionary spirit, and have in the true sense of the word been 'empowered'. Politics have become, more than ever before, an integral part of everyday life and struggle. The politicization of women has gone hand in hand with a loss of fear. With their men under detention, women in many cases have had to take over their responsibilities, at family and then at community level. Increasing numbers of women activists have been arrested and sentenced, slowly raising the credibility of the political women's movement. Indeed, seventeen of the nineteen Palestinian women administratively detained since December 1987 are leading figures of the women's committees.[24] A UPWWC activist explained, 'The core of our work always was political, but we could not speak with women directly. They were scared, not like now. People considered the occupation to be very strong, to have eyes everywhere – They will know about us, arrest us. This fear is largely gone.'[25] A woman in Beit Sahour said, 'In my work I feel that the women changed during the Intifada. They suggest more, have more initiative and new ideas – and they are very politicized.'[26]

The December 1989 women's demonstration made clear that psychological elements, the spirit of cooperation and united effort, have an important part to play in the mobilization for the social and political struggle for liberation. With the exception of the UPWWC, all the committees of the Palestinian political women's movement, as well as several Israeli women's groups and European peace activists, jointly organized a women's peace action. This joint Israeli–Palestinian effort brought back a spirit of hopeful resistance, which after two years of Intifada and no sign of a political solution was about to fade.

Neighbourhood committees

The women's committees more than other mass organizations played a key role in the setting up of neighbourhood committees during the first year of the Intifada.[27] Their active role changed the pattern of popular mobilization. Before the Intifada, strategies of mobilization largely aimed at increasing the constituency of the different factions. Rendering locally needed services was a means to recruit women, after an initial successful personal visit by one of the activists. The services provided, like sewing and literacy courses, cooperatives and (in cooperation with one of the medical relief committees) medical care, were usually connected with social and political lectures. The quality of the service rendered was a measure of the mobilization's success, because usually the local women needed the agreement of the menfolk, who in most cases were supportive when the community profited.

When the uprising started, the organization of the population for political struggle as well as for sheer survival became necessary. People like committee activists with organization skills and experience were needed to set up the network of popular committees. Consequently, the success of organizing local women into the different popular committees, (responsible for teaching, guarding, planting, food processing and distribution etcetera), gained priority over factional considerations. The official call of the UNLU[28] for the whole population to participate in local committees made it easier for women to convince their menfolk of the necessity of their activity. Instead of waiting for the activists to approach them, they turned increasingly more to their local women activists for organizational help and advice. Women activists were especially engaged in popular teaching, which required not only teaching and organization skills but also intensive preparation and subtle intuition. A UPWWC neighbourhood activist reported:

> When the UNLU asked for the formation of the popular committees, the women immediately responded. The women were the first to become active, the men were second. And they turned towards us to organize. We gave them first aid, which was needed most at that time. We opened popular teaching in camps and villages. Like in A'mari Camp we had teaching from the first to the sixth elementary grade. The men went quickly back to other activities after the initial responses. The women are still active.[29]

Due to their very active involvement in popular work, the women's committees were hit especially hard when popular committees were declared illegal in late summer 1988. They did not stop their work, but an important part of it was driven underground and became increasingly factionalized.

Cooperatives

In early 1988, when the UNLU called for a boycott of Israeli products and an increase of local and home production, the committees were to the forefront in organizing income-generating projects and small cooperatives. Foreign aid and solidarity funds enabled the committees to support local initiatives as well as to experiment with larger income-generating projects. Although some of the projects have not been successful, their critical evaluation offered a chance for the committees to restructure their work and set new priorities. Women's roles in household, agricultural, and paid labour have been reconsidered and reflected. The cooperatives have become an important issue for all the committees during the Intifada, and illustrate the differences among the groups in terms of ideology and work.

The UPWWC sees cooperatives as independent economic women's enterprises. One UPWWC activist working with cooperatives described her committee's approach thus:

> We have done income-generating projects since the establishment of our committee, but the way we organize them and the emphasis is totally different now. Women should learn new skills, gain experience in bookkeeping and selling, and recognize and develop their own potentials and cooperate with each other. At the same time, they are encouraged to plan the spending of their income independently from us as well as from their menfolk.[30]

The UPWWC still has some income-generating projects in food processing and sewing in which it, and not the workers, is responsible for management and marketings. But its long-term plan is for independent women's cooperatives run by the members themselves and supported financially only partially by loans and grants from the UPWWC. 'The principle of our cooperative work is that all members are able to do all steps of the cooperative work, from production to marketing. We aim at independence, the gaining of knowledge and experience.'[31]

The UPWWC was the first committee to start cooperatives in cooperation with NGOs in the early 1970s. But like the other committees it stepped up cooperative work during the Intifada, focusing mainly on rural areas and aiming at combining kindergartens with income-generating projects to mobilize women successfully. A UPWWC activist estimated the number of small food-processing cooperatives, set up mainly in the framework of neighbourhood committees, at forty. The importance of cooperative work in the strategy of the UPWWC is illustrated by its formation of a cooperative school in summer 1989. The UPWWC also views cooperatives as important elements in the national struggle for independence.[32] The emphasis on political struggle in the committee work of the UPWWC goes along with the stress on tradition. 'We emphasize the tradition and culture. We want the girls to be part of it. We don't want to destroy this moral bond between the projects and the community. We want to initiate social consciousness in the community and around the family.'[33] 'One aim of the cooperatives is to fulfil basic needs of the society, to become self-sufficient. In food production we started with items the women know. But we intend to revolutionize the structure, so that the traditional division of labour is broken. But this will be at a later stage. The cooperatives are designed to raise women's class consciousness. We need to face exploitation on all levels. 60 per cent of the coop profit is reinvestment and 40 per cent is income.'[34]

The FWAC has organized production projects in Abasan, Eisawiyeh and Hebron since 1986. It added new emphasis during the Intifada. Fifteen small-scale cooperatives were initiated by local women after December 1987 to 'offer an alternative for work in Israel, to boycott Israeli products, and allow an income for women'.[35] But the FWAC disagreed with the home economy initiative of the UNLU and has an integrated approach. 'We are against the home economy. We have to get the women out of their houses and not employ them there. We therefore argue for community-based projects.'[36] 'We don't want to have little projects like islands. We are planning a revolving loan fund to create new projects. It means the money goes back and is reinvested. This is until now in accordance with the women. They strongly link their work to the committee.'[37] Therefore, the use of the profit the women make in cooperative work is jointly decided on. They either improve their own project, start a new one, or support cost-intensive committee projects like kindergartens. As in the other committees, during the Intifada the support and revival of Palestinian culture as part of a distinct Palestinian identity became an important focus of work. As a FWAC activist said, 'We try to drop traditional women's work like embroidery or at least to cut it short. We make old designs in a new way, like the enamel project in Eisawiyeh. This way we can keep the old tradition with a new concept of work.'[38] Aware of the complexity and social effects of income-generating projects for women, the FWAC tried to develop a long-term cooperative strategy in accordance with the local needs. 'We recognized that we need a systematic system to develop the production area. We set up a complete new infrastructure, organized new production committees in the different districts and training courses for the members.'[39] The economist responsible for the training courses described her objectives. 'The women should learn to identify the needs of the community, make feasibility studies, learn troubleshooting in existing projects and management and marketing.'[40]

The WCSW started cooperative work during the Intifada. It established forty-five cooperatives in 1989. Its philosophy differs from that of the leftist committees. An activist reported, 'We find out if women are interested in work. Either we approach them or they come to us and ask for work. We give the women the material, either for food processing, knitting or sewing and tell them what to do. They work at home and when they finish their work we pick it up and sell it, for example in bazaars. The women themselves work voluntarily and the money goes either to martyr families or back to the committee.'[41] The Intifada has highlighted more than before the question of social consciousness. The movement was aware that despite women's prominent role in the uprising, their participation has been largely spontaneous and needed to be channelled more through the women's committees. If women are to be mobilized consistently and permanently, they need to be conscious about their rights and abilities. Thus strategies of consciousness-raising have increasingly become an important element of political mobilization and a central issue in the recently established women's research projects. The issue of long-term social mobilization leads to changes in ideology that are hotly debated in the women's movement and by no means finally set.

Ideology: national liberation versus women's liberation

Traditionalism and religious values
The Intifada intensified and in some committees made possible the internal debate on the relationship between the struggles for gender equality and for national liberation. The preference for national liberation has in some cases been questioned. An activist from the UPWWC argued as follows:

> A long time ago, the women's groups mostly talked politics and not about feminist issues. Now it is becoming an issue. The women's groups attack the politically active men who are stubborn and keep their women at home. But even when women are allowed to be active, they do everything in the household on top of their political work. We have to attack the issue of the division of labour. This problem was there all the time, but now it is becoming an issue.[42]

The FWAC, in a paper entitled 'The Tasks Required of the Women's Movement during the Intifada', stated that practical programmes must be adopted addressing both the feminist and the national question .

A hot internal debate has taken place even in the leftist committees. One important indicator of the interest in feminist issues was the formation of the HCW by all the four factions. That the social and legal status of women in present and future Palestinian society was an important factor in the formation of the council becomes clear in the comments of committee activists from different factions. One member of the FWAC explained:

> During the Intifada certain issues are already at stake. The society and old values are shaking and we want to benefit from it and make these changes permanent. At the same time we have to work with the women

themselves. Many of them don't believe in their equality with men. From early childhood they are taught that they don't have the same rights as their brothers. This influence is not easy to break. This is what we have to put into our feminist agenda. This was an important consideration for the establishment of the HCW.[44]

Another argued, 'Now we will work on a feminist agenda. That's why we added members of the professions into the Higher Council, because we want to work for women's liberation.'[45] Similarly a UPWWC member commented, 'We must have independent women in the HCW who want to concentrate on women's issues and who want to work through the committees to give them a voice. This is one of the main issues the HCW has to deal with.'[46]

This new emphasis on gender equality was implemented in various new projects inside and outside the political women's movement. The women's committees, even before the Intifada, had functioned as a female solidarity network. They supported women in need with legal advice, carefully intervened in family problems and tried to provide employment, independent income and childcare. During the Intifada local popular committees and women's activists intervened actively in domestic conflicts, thereby circumventing the Israeli-controlled civil courts. Women activists became more aware of the necessity of an independent support system for women. 'Today fewer and fewer women can or want to rely on the family. Especially in the cities the extended family is changing. The family structure is less close, and women are changing. I don't want to ask my mother-in-law all the time for help. I don't want to say a thousand times "please" and a thousand times "thank you". We need something other than the family support system.'[47] A house for battered women was discussed in one of the leftist women's committees, but the idea was dropped due to the absence of legal protection.[48] Inside the women's movement as well as outside, an increasing number of independent support groups have been set up to enable women to make independent decisions. In Ramallah a childcare centre has been set up, where children of working women can be taken care of after school.[49]

After a month of hot internal debate in the summer of 1990, the UPWWC formed a special committee working on strategies to 'mobilize Palestinian women to obtain their equality after independence'. The newly founded committee met in the Friends Boys' School in Ramallah soon afterwards for a working meeting with professional Palestinian women to clarify objectives and strategies. To develop a clear stand towards the existing Jordanian Family Status Law, close cooperation with the Ramallah-based lawyer's association Al-Haq was proposed. The committee finally concluded, that '. . . the women's movement has to focus more on gender issues. The national and women's liberation struggles have to be parallel and are inextricably intertwined with each other.'[50] Al-Haq itself, which during the first year of the Intifada set up a special research project on women, planned to organize a course on the legal status of Palestinian women with participants from the political women's movement and professional institutions.[51]

Traditionalism versus the requirements of the Intifada

The workload and responsibility of the women's committees increased dramatically during the uprising. Women increasingly took over activities that derive from their traditional role. For example the organization of visits to the families of martyrs, the sick and wounded is now no longer restricted to the immediate social environment. Women who had never left their village before suddenly travelled long distances for solidarity visits. A UPWWC activist from the Kaddura refugee camp reported, 'At the beginning of the Intifada, when we went to the women and asked them "let's go to Silwad and visit the family of the martyr", they refused because it had nothing to do with them. If you tell them now for example "let's go to Nahalin", we have to take a bus, and forty women come from Kaddura camp alone.'[52]

The pressure on the activists has grown, and the restrictions traditional society imposes on women's ability to move and to plan their time independently have become more problematic. Women had to reconsider the gender issue if they did not want to accept limitations on their work for the national cause. Consequently, this issue was raised more and more frequently in committee meetings. The complaint of an activist from the Jerusalem UPWWC is typical:

> We active women must be out in the streets, plan how to continue the Intifada, build relations with other groups, face the secret police, and mobilize other women, and we also have our duty at home, do all the household work, are responsible for everything. If your husband is a conservative man, he puts his legs up, reads the paper and develops himself. I can't struggle against the occupation if I need so much strength in my struggle with men. If the active women don't raise the social question, who should raise it then?[53]

The increasing and intensifying contacts with international solidarity and women's organizations have played a significant role in pressuring the women's committees to coordinate and to come up with a single feminist agenda. One activist of the FWAC expressed this clearly, 'When the four committees come together for a meeting, like this summer with the Italian women, their differences come out clearly. It is more the pressure from the outside that brings us together than the inside interest. The Italians for example raised questions like what we think democracy should look like, what about fundamentalism and religion. And we had to come up with an answer.'[54]

The feminist agenda and political power

The initial diplomatic success of the Intifada and the declaration of a Palestinian state made a political solution feasible and pressured the political women's movements to clarify their conception of a Palestinian state and women's role and legal status in it. The political women's committees agreed to the PLO declaration of a secular democratic state and equal rights for men and women. 'We don't only fight for a Palestinian state, we fight for a democratic state!'[55] Women's role in Algerian society during and after the revolution acts as a constant reminder for women's activists to formulate a feminist agenda in the Higher Council of Women and set the legal stage before the state is finally established. The leftist women's committees, therefore, started working on a list of demands to be submitted to the national leadership. The Higher Council of Women is expected to draft a new family status law to replace the present Jordanian one which basically follows patriarchal Koranic law.

Feminist claims are connected with demands for greater independence within the national movement. Especially in the FWAC and UPWWC there is an increased awareness of the need to develop an independent stand inside the national movement to enable the movement to tackle gender inequality. Therefore, some of their leading activists are demanding political power. 'We have to fight now for social issues, to be a real movement that is able to pressure the Palestinian political national movement to deal with the women not just as a baby in their womb, but as a full partner.'[56] The FWAC noted in a conference paper presented in May 1989 that 'female social emancipation must go hand in hand with political emancipation. Otherwise, women risk losing their gains after independence . . . female participation should not be limited to demonstrations and protests, but must begin to include political decision-making.'[57]

Whilst the WCSW considers itself to be the female executive of the diaspora national leadership,[58] a leading activist of the UPWWC espouses contrary demands: 'If we want to build a strong women's movement, expressed in the Higher Council of Women, we need to be independent from the national movement. And how can we be that? Only if we are democratic and women from all ages and with or without party alliance can we find a place in the movement.'[59]

Fundamentalism and traditional values

The Intifada in general made it easier for women to become active. However tendencies like the drop in marriage age, increasing segregation of women, and growing fundamentalism are threatening this newly gained freedom. On one point or another, the women's committees will need to come up with a clear position in this power struggle and confront probably not just the fundamentalists but also their own male factional establishments. While all four committees support the PLO two-state solution and a secular democratic state within this broad framework, they have extremely different policies. The committees' positions inside the national movement and their stances towards issues such as women's legal status in the Koran or the increasing influence of Muslim fundamentalists can be used as an indicator of their practical positions in the national versus women's liberation debate.

The WCSW, more than the other committees, integrates the conception of its activities smoothly into the policy of the mainstream male national movement. 'Before the Intifada it was difficult to mobilize the girls, but now the girls come to us and ask to form committees. We even had men approaching us to establish a women's committee in their village, because they saw women in other villages doing it.'[60] This happened in a Fatah-dominated village near Nablus. The project was not implemented because there was no area open for the women to work in, with the local charitable societies doing most of the social work. Other activities were not acceptable to the men.[61]

During the Intifada, Muslim fundamentalism has been on the rise, more in the Gaza Strip than in the West Bank. Islamic women's groups exist in villages, camps and cities.[62] Secular women's activists reported from the area of Tulkarm and Jenin of wives of local religious leaders who preach a return to fundamental religious and cultural values, offering a religious coping mechanism to women who are desperately looking for help and a sign of hope.[63] In 1988 the Muslim fundamentalists in Gaza, namely the Islamic Resistance Movement, Hammas, started a vicious campaign to impose the *hijab*, the headscarf, on women there. Women in Hebron, Nablus and even east Jerusalem were attacked for 'immodest' dressing and behaviour. The UNLU waited more than a year before criticizing the *hijab* campaign in leaflet No. 43 – with limited success.[64] While the issue from the very beginning was hotly debated inside the committees, none of them dared independently to issue a condemnation of the fundamentalists' actions. The Higher Council of Women finally came out with a united leaflet on the incidents.

The extent to which the different committees are able or willing to confront fundamentalism as well as traditionalism will become clearer in the following remarks. Two UPWWC activists argue, 'We can't open up a second front now. Our battle is not with men. In the context of struggling against the occupation, we have to make both the role of women and their consciousness about themselves stronger, as a guarantee for a future state.'[65] 'We believe that women under occupation suffer so much that we have to postpone questions of gender liberation till after liberation. After liberation we can tackle class and gender issues.'[66]

Similarly, a UPWWC activist argues, 'We as women are struggling for our liberation and for the liberation of our society, and we are making sacrifices. We have to take into consideration that this is not the time to make a battle with our own people. In order to change the society you have to be part of it. Therefore, you have to satisfy to some extent the point of view of the people. The full liberation of women takes place in a liberated society and it cannot take place in an occupied one.'[67] 'If we confront the fundamentalists now, we will have Palestinians fighting against Palestinians and the occupation forces will benefit. Even if they throw stones at us we don't say a word because we don't want to get in a battle with them.'[68]

Two WCSW activists agreed. 'There is not time now to open up a second front. We can't confront Hammas now.'[69] 'We believe that women's liberation means to be accepted in the society. Because we have to work with the community we accept the Koran as a foundation of our work. . . . But we have to liberate our nation first. When we have our own state, we will work on women's issues.'[70]

The FWAC formulated a similar position:

> The fundamentalists are growing stronger. For example in Sheikh Jarrah [in Jerusalem], Hammas forced women to wear a scarf. The HCW published a leaflet against it. But the policy of the committee is not to bring about religious controversy so as not to raise sensitivities. Indirectly we have enforced religious values this way. Maybe a time will come soon when we have to confront the fundamentalists.[71]

Dialogue between Palestinian and Israeli women

The Intifada has increased the number of official and unofficial contacts between Israeli and Palestinian women. Although some of the committees had contacts with Israeli women's groups and individual Israeli women before, others started a dialogue only during the Intifada. With independence no longer a pipe dream and with the Palestine National Council (PNC) declaration offering a solid base for discussion, the committees were enabled to discuss concrete policies. A breakthrough was achieved at the international conference in Brussels in May 1989, where the first constructive steps for the establishment of coordination networks on both sides were taken. The Israeli 'Reshet' and a Palestinian coordination network emerged. Together, their activists represent a wider political range than could be found in the Israeli–Palestinian dialogue among males. Activists from the political committees spoke on various occasions at meetings in Israel.

The Palestinian women's movement is mainly political. However, it ›

Israeli counterpart consists of several different groups covering a whole range of issues, from purely humanitarian to clear-cut political. Although discussion of political issues creates controversy between Israeli and Palestinian women's groups, both share common grounds in questions concerning women's issues. As an Israeli woman activist described it, 'When the Palestinian women say "We are a patriarchal society, look we have serious problems", the Israeli women suddenly agree.'[72]

Through their representation in the Higher Council of Women, which also functions as a coordination network for the Israeli–Palestinian dialogue, the four committees agree in principle on the dialogue as such, but they have different positions concerning its scope and intensity. A WCSW activist explained. 'Our standpoint is: we don't discuss politics because our position is known through the PLO. We discuss social matters like school and university closures. And we don't go inside Israel, we meet in the West Bank or in Jerusalem.'[73] A woman from the UPWC has a slightly different perspective. 'We are fully ready to meet anti-Zionist women. But we don't see an anti-Zionist women's movement in Israel, only individuals. But we cooperate in the field. The Israeli Women for Political Prisoners are the only group we work with.'[74] Two women from the UPWWC, however, believe that the opposite is true, that 'it is more important for us to sit with women from the right wing and talk with them, so that they should do something to move things in the right'. 'We have nothing against talking to Zionists. On the contrary it is very important to explain our political platform. If it comes to work, we don't work with organizations who don't accept our political view: self-determination and a PLO state.'[75] Finally the FWAC argues, 'We had contacts with Israeli women's groups before the Intifada but no joint action as now. Before that the political issue was not very clear. Now we all agree on the PNC agreement and the two-state solution. Now we talk about equal rights; before we talked about self-determination only. Now we have house and popular meetings with different Israeli groups.'[76] In contrast to the official male Israeli–Palestinian dialogue, the women on both sides did not stop their joint action during the Gulf crisis. In fact 'the dialogue became so intense that for some weeks the conference preparations [for a Women's Peace Conference on December 28–29 1990] were delayed'.[77]

Conclusion

The Intifada has fundamentally altered the structure and strategy of the political women's movement in the West Bank and Gaza. Organizationally, an increase in responsibilities and monetary means of the different women's groups became paramount. There has been a restructuring and decentralization of decision-making, and an increase in the number of persons involved

A types of Women

and in specialization. Young activists from working-class, rural and refugee backgrounds have increasingly been gaining influence.

The political mobilization of women during the Intifada has taken place within the framework of national liberation, but the Intifada made necessary a re-evaluation of priorities. The number of members recruited for a single faction was no longer the decisive point; instead the different factions were induced to place the central emphasis on effective long-term mobilization of the already active women. The women's committees played a key role in the setting up of neighbourhood committees, and later helped to set up small-scale production cooperatives for food and other necessities. The leftist women's committees conceived of the work of production cooperatives as a means for liberating women socially and economically.

Ideologically, the social and political struggle of women during the Intifada has intensified the already existing discussion on women's role in Palestinian society and politics. A special brand of Palestinian feminism has slowly taken shape. The struggle for equal rights for women is waged by members of the leftist women's committees and is strongly supported by engaged professionals, including representatives in the Higher Council of Women. This discussion has been crucially influenced by the fact that the requirements of the Intifada have come into conflict with the traditional role of women in male-dominated society. Thus problems that were latent are being discussed very openly now.

Notes

A slightly different version of this chapter was published in *New Political Science*, No. 21–2, Spring–Summer 1992.

1. Ghada Talhami, 'Women in the Movement: their long uncelebrated history', *Al-Fajr* (English-language weekly), 30 May 1986.

2. See Carolyn Fleur-Lobban, 'The Political Mobilization of Women in the Arab World,' in Jane I. Smith, (ed.), *Women in Contemporary Muslim Societies*, London, 1980: pp. 235–51.

3. See Rosemary Sayigh, 'Encounters with Palestinian Women under Occupation'. *Journal of Palestine Studies,* Vol. 10, No. 4, Summer 1981; Rita Giacaman, 'Reflections on the Palestinian Women's Movement in the Occupied Territories', Birzeit University, May 1987.

4. For a detailed analysis of the women's movement before the Intifada see Joust Hiltermann, 'Before the Uprising: the organization and mobilization of Palestinian workers and women in the Israeli-occupied West Bank and Gaza Strip', PhD thesis, University of California, Santa Cruz, June 1988.

5. UPWWC activist, Nablus, 10 July 1989.

6. WCSW activist, Ramallah, 16 April 1989.

7. Nablus, 21 June 1989.

8. Jerusalem, 26 November 1989.

9. UPWWC activist, Jerusalem, 27 November 1989.

10. Interviews with activists in Jerusalem, 19 June 1989, and Ramallah, 5 December 1989.
11. Beit Haninah, 16 November 1989.
12. Ibid.
13. Shawfat, 26 June 1989.
14. UPWWC activist, Nablus, 21 June 1989.
15. Interview with an agronomist, Beitunia, 26 June 1989.
16. Agricultural Relief Committee, Beit Haninah, 12 September 1989.
17. Activist from the UPWWC, Jerusalem, June 1990.
18. Interview with a UPWWC activist, Jerusalem, July 1990.
19. UPWWC activist, Jerusalem, 20 November 1990.
20. Interview with a FWAC activist, Al-Rahm, 3 August 1989.
21. UPWWC activist, Ramallah, 27 June 1989.
22. Interview with one of the founders, Ramallah, 8 July 1990.
23. UPWWC activist, Bethlehem, 23 July 1989.
24. 'A Nation under siege'. Al-Haq Report in *Human Rights in the Occupied Palestinian Territories*, 1989, p. 129.
25. Ibid.
26. UPWWC activist, Beit Sahour, 22 November 1989.
27. See Hiltermann, p. 401.
28. See leaflet 6, from 2 February 1988.
29. UPWWC neighbourhood activist, Ramallah, 3 December 1989.
30. Jerusalem, 27 November 1989.
31. Cooperative workers, Ramallah, 26 June 1989.
32. Ramallah, 29 June 1989.
33. UPWWC co-op specialist, Ramallah, 23 November 1989.
34. Cooperative activist, Ramallah, 23 November 1989.
35. FWAC, Beit Haninah, 10 August 1989.
36. *Al-Rahm*, 17 October 1989.
37. FWAC economist, Beit Haninah, 23 November 1989.
38. *Al-Rahm,* 3 August 1989.
39. Co-op specialist, Beit Haninah, 23 November 1989.
40. FWAC economist, Beit Haninah, 23 November 1989.
41. Ramallah, 16 April 1989.
42. Lana, UPWWC, Ramallah, 8 July 1990.
43. UPWWC, 'Women and Peace-making', 26 August 1988.
44. FWAC activist and member of the Higher Council of Women, *Al-Rahm*, 10 August 1989.
45. Beit Haninah, 10 August 1989.
46. UPWWC member in the Higher Council of Women, Jerusalem, 3 July 1990.
47. Social worker and women's researcher, Ramallah, 25 June 1990.
48. Interview, Jerusalem, June 1990.
49. Ramallah, 19 June 1990.
50. Interview with an activist, Jerusalem, 27 June 1990.
51. Al-Haq, Ramallah, 3 July 1990.
52. Ramallah, 27 June 1989.
53. UPWWC activist, Jerusalem, 3 August 1989.
54. Beit Haninah, 16 November 1989.
55. UPWWC activist, Jerusalem, June 1990.

56. Ibid.

57. 'The Uprising and the Palestinian Child: Participation of Children in the Intifada and its Social Dimensions', paper presented to the Tantur Conference, May 1989.

58. Jerusalem, 8 July 1990.

59. Jerusalem, June 1990.

60. WCSW activist, Ramallah, 16 April 1990.

61. WCSW activist, Nablus, 10 October 1989.

62. Diana Baxter's (UCLA) research, on 'A Palestinian Women's Islamic Group on the West Bank', illustrates this tendency, but at the same time shows the contradictory motivations women have entering the groups, partially not at all in accordance with fundamental cultural and religious values.

63. Interview with a woman activist, Jerusalem, 5 July 1990.

64. See Reema Hammami's article 'Women, the Hijab and the Intifada', *MERIP Report*, May–August 1990, No. 164–5 , pp. 25–6.

65. UPWWC, Nablus, 21 July 1989.

66. UPWWC, Jerusalem, 22 July 1989.

67. Jerusalem, 29 June 1989.

68. Ramallah, 26 June 1989.

69. Ramallah, 24 November 1989.

70. WCSW activist, Ramallah, 16 June 1989.

71. Al-Rahm, 17 October 1989.

72. Israeli women activists, Jerusalem, 25 June 1990.

73. Ramallah, 24 November 1989.

74. Jerusalem, 27 June 1989 and Ramallah, 5 December 1989.

75. Jerusalem, 26 and 27 November 1989.

76. Al-Rahm, 16 October 1989.

77. *The Other Israel*, September–October 1990, No. 43.

3. Active in Politics and Women's Affairs in Gaza

Yusra Berberi

I am a Palestinian, born in 1923 in Gaza city. My father owned a sesame oil factory. We were four brothers and five sisters and my eldest brother worked with my father in the factory. My second brother studied law in the American Universities of Cairo and Beirut and later became a lawyer. My third brother was educated in the University of Southern California as a hydraulic engineer. My fourth brother studied at the American University in Cairo, at Rubart College in Istanbul and the University of Southern California, where he graduated as an electronic engineer. Whereas all the boys of our family were well educated, my two step-sisters were not educated. At that time it was very difficult for girls to have a proper education in Gaza. But my elder sister graduated from Schmidt's girls' school in Jerusalem and later worked as the principal of a preparatory school in Kuwait for thirty years. Now she lives on a pension with us in Gaza. My youngest sister received her education at the primary school in Gaza and became a teacher in the women's training school in Jerusalem. I was lucky to get a good education, first in the Gaza primary school, later in Schmidt's girls' school in Jerusalem. I started my studies in social science at Cairo University, where I graduated in 1949. After that I worked as a teacher and later became the principal of the only girls' secondary school in the entire Gaza Strip. During the Egyptian regime I became principal of the preparatory school and principal of the women's training institute and public university. Then I worked as an inspector for all the girls' schools in the Gaza Strip, whose number increased during the years.

In 1967, when the Israeli army occupied the Gaza Strip, instead of continuing my work as a government employee I volunteered to chair the Palestine Women's Union, which had been established three years before.

Jews and Palestinians in Palestine – childhood in Gaza

As far back as I can remember, the Palestinian population in Palestine was in a state of revolt against British colonial rule and the growing immigration of Jews into the country. These revolts affected my life from the very beginning. There was the upheaval and revolt against the Balfour Declaration in 1919, the Palestinian revolt against growing Jewish immigration and land sales from 1936 to 1939, which culminated in a general strike. When the US President, Harry Truman promised to open the doors of Palestine to 100,000 Jewish immigrants from Nazi Germany and Europe, the Palestinians protested again – in vain. All the protests and fighting failed to prevent the partition of Palestine in 1947 by the UN.

My memories go back to one particular day when I was four years old: suddenly our house was full of women. There had been a Jewish attack on Palestinian villages and cities in the north. A lot of women from Gaza city gathered in our house and debated how to bring help to the victims. They began collecting money, and I was chosen to go around with the collection box. Before my work started they dressed me in a black dress as a sign of mourning. A sash was fastened around my shoulders bearing the words 'help the suffering families, the victims of the Jewish attack'. Even during my first school years we pupils participated in demonstrations. One of these started in front of the girls' primary school in Gaza. We had prepared a memorandum which we handed over to the governor of Gaza, who at that time was Abder Razaib Kleibo. The document was essentially political, asking the government to stop the immigration of Jews to Palestine and to stop the selling of Arab land to Zionists. The memorandum also demanded the establishment of an independent state in Palestine and an end to the British mandate.

I became politicized in my home. My second brother especially, who was a lawyer, impressed me a lot. He defended people persecuted by the British and defended Arabs whose land was confiscated by the Mandate power and given to Jews. He owned and updated all sorts of books dealing with the Palestine question. I used to read them in English and became deeply involved with our history. When I was growing up, few Jews lived in Gaza city itself. But my secondary school in Jerusalem was in the Jewish quarter and the situation became more and more tense. When the Arab revolt began in 1936, because we were in a boarding school we saw much less of the revolt than other pupils did. There was less to eat than usual, sweets were a luxury. And even though half of Palestine was covered by an umbrella of orange groves there was hardly any fruit in the markets. Often the roads between Jerusalem and Gaza were cut. We had to spend Christmas eve 1938 in the school because we were unable to return to Gaza. We could not make the ninety-minute trip back home because of the armed resistance that was being undertaken by Palestinians.

The British occupying forces at some point became unable to control the Palestinian military resistance, which used to attack the British Army on the roads. The attacks and counterattacks made travelling dangerous. During the whole time the situation in Gaza was different from elsewhere. In the Jerusalem–Hebron–Nablus area and even in the coastal area up in the North, the activists of the military resistance hid in the mountains; they never lived among the people as the activists of the Intifada do today. Women carried food and ammunition to their fighting menfolk in the mountains. And while the men were in hiding, the women had to earn their families' living. (Thus, the fact that during the Intifada women in increasing numbers have to work for their families is not a new phenomenon.) But because Gaza has no mountain areas the resistance there was different. It was organized in political committees, of a kind that was established all over Palestine, in villages and cities alike. The committees' task was not just political work: some of them organized the community, tried to maintain essential services and helped the people to cope with daily life despite the resistance, and despite the regulations of the Mandate power, economic restrictions and high taxes (whose aim was to force people to sell their land).

Even without books and advice I would have become politicized because the whole situation was deeply affected by politics. There were not only British troops: soldiers from Canada and Australia came to support the colonial power. I remember them still, knocking at the doors day and night, bursting into houses, searching all the rooms and shooting at Palestinian demonstrators. During one of our girls' demonstrations a watching relative of mine was shot and killed. Over the radio came news about attacks by the British and the Jewish underground on Jaffa and Arab villages, and details about the demolition of parts of the old city of Jaffa.

All those incidents were imprinted on my mind and I can still recollect them vividly. My political awareness grew as I grew up, and I often wondered what the relationship between Jews and Christians and Muslims was before all the trouble started. Before I was born, I was told, Jews and Arabs coexisted in Palestine. In many cases they relied on each other, helped each other. The midwife who helped my mother during my birth was Jewish. This was always a symbol for me, that my mother trusted a Jewish woman during a very important moment of her life. It became a symbol of coexistence for me, a coexistence that had existed until the mid 1920s. Until then, Arab leaders tried by peaceful means to persuade the British not to support Zionism and to grant our population a measure of self-government. But coexistence became less and less possible when the lives of Palestinians became politically, socially, culturally and economically more and more affected by massive Jewish immigration into Palestine.

After I finished secondary school, I was unable to continue my education. My family was unable to pay the high university fees, as two of my brothers were studying already. Besides that, travelling was difficult because of the political situation. The situation today reminds me a lot of fifty years ago.

There were checkposts everywhere. For three years I had to stay at home. Then I went to the University of Cairo.

During the years at home I learned to know the active women of Gaza. In the Red Cross Committee, women knitted pullovers for soldiers participating in the Second World War. And we had the Red Crescent, which was involved in charitable work. Women were active as well in women's organizations, of which at that time we had three in Gaza. The active women in these worked and served the people in social, cultural and rehabilitation activities. One of the leading figures was Mrs Shawa, the wife of the mayor of Gaza. Another was Issam Husseini and a third was Mukarram Abu Khader, who immigrated from Jaffa and refused to sell her lands. These respectable women established kindergartens, taught children, worked in rehabilitation and taught and employed women in embroidery and knitting. They collected donations and helped needy families.

Partition, war and refugees, 1947–67

When the resolution that proposed partition of Palestine was passed by the United Nations in 1947, I was at Cairo University. I remember well that all the university students demonstrated against the resolution in solidarity with the Palestinians. And, of course, as a Palestinian woman I demonstrated also. During the last month of the British Mandate presence in Palestine and at the beginning of the 1948 war Gaza was cut off from Egypt and I had to stay over the summer in Egypt. When I finally came back home a stream of refugees from the southern part of Palestine was flooding south into Gaza. Our house was near the seashore and I remember vividly the desperate refugees coming in by boat from the sea. They rushed into the streets looking for shelter, filled the mosques and schools. Despite the help of the local population many refugee families were compelled to live in the open under trees.[1] During that period there was no state control and Gazans ruled themselves. Then the Egyptian army came and took power. The first organizations that came to help the refugees were Quaker. They provided the homeless with tents and food. One of the biggest camps was opposite our house. We tried to help as much as possible: we cooked meals and distributed clothing. We had families living in our house, and forty families lived in my brother's half-finished house. We sat long hours and listened to the stories of the refugees. They were full of anger and sadness. The Jaffa refugees told us about the destruction of their city, the loss of relatives and family, the killings by the Jewish underground armies and how they had to leave their homes to save their lives.

During these hard times the charitable and women's organizations in Gaza increased their activities as much as possible. They visited the refugee families and provided them with food and clothing. They organized a guidance committee and directed new refugees to places where they could find initial shelter: to schools and mosques, because at the beginning no tents were available. The refugee camps were established only when the Quakers came.

After the short period of self-rule we recognized Egyptian control. The governor-general was now Egyptian, not British. But most Arab countries at that time, including Egypt, were governed by rulers who were puppets of Britain. Egypt was under the rule of King Farouk. Like all the other Arab armies who declared war on the newly established state of Israel, the Egyptian army came not to save and liberate the Palestinians but to occupy the land. The first order of the new governor was that the Palestinians should hand over their arms. But not everybody did.

After the Quakers came the United Nations Relief and Works Agency (UNRWA) in 1952. The refugee camps were institutionalized and being a refugee became a permanent 'status'. Immediately after the end of the war the small strip of land that was left to us was cut off from the rest of Palestine. After 1948 we could no longer travel to the West Bank or to what was now called Israel. My family had no access to their plots of land inside Israel. Through the Absent Property Law we were expropriated. Life changed in a lot of ways.

In September 1948 the Jerusalem mufti Haj Amin al-Husseini had set up an All-Palestine government in Gaza. It was recognized by all Arab states save Jordan. How seriously the Arab states had fought for the liberation of Palestine and not for their own interests became clear within a few years, when the passports issued by the All-Palestine government became invalid. The Egyptian military governor issued an Egyptian *laissez-passer* for Palestinian refugees and I carry one to this day. While the West Bank was annexed by Jordan there was still a border between Egypt and the Gaza Strip. Everybody who wanted to cross it had to apply for a permit from the Egyptian military authorities in Gaza. I used to travel by a train that connected Gaza and Cairo via the Sinai desert. But it became increasingly difficult to obtain a visa; we were usually searched for a long time and always treated as foreigners.

In 1949, when I finished my studies, I went back to Gaza, where I started working as a teacher in the preparatory school. As Gaza's first female university graduate I was respected by the people and after one year I became the school's principal. Education is highly valued in our society and people appreciate it, both for men and for women. At the same time I tried to follow the traditions of my society. Then slowly, slowly, I developed my own style of living. It was an evolution of my personal rights, not a revolution. I never allowed my behaviour to put me into a position in which I could be attacked. I chose clothes that would never be criticized by local people. I never left the house in short sleeves, I never went out without stockings. And usually I wore the full traditional costume, regardless of whether it was winter or summer.

Our school was the only girls' secondary school in the whole Gaza Strip and we had girls from Rafah in the south to Beit Hanun. But we never distinguished between refugees and residents. I taught my girls to be open to the world, but on condition that they would not overthrow or violate the traditions of our society. I was very strict in some ways, but open-minded in others. This made me acceptable to the people. With all my activities I was so busy that I never thought of getting married. Only sometimes do I have a little time to think of myself. I take language lessons in French and German. These hours are for my sake only and I enjoy them a lot.

Looking back on the twenty years we spent under Egyptian military rule I think they served us in two ways: in security and in education. Palestinian students were exempted from fees until the Camp David agreement, even in the Egyptian universities. Unlike the Jordanian policy towards the West Bank, the Egyptians never annexed the Gaza Strip. It was always considered a part of Palestine. When Palestinians from the Gaza Strip went to international conferences they represented the whole of Palestine and were identified as such. I was chosen to be a member of the Palestine delegation to the United Nations in 1963. I travelled to the US together with Dr Abdel Shafi, the late mayor of Gaza, and another delegate. The Palestinian delegation contained twenty-one members chosen from all over the world. A woman from Beirut and I were the only female delegates. All the others carried the passports of their country of residence. But we from Gaza carried the Egyptian *laissez-passer*. We used to enter the United Nations building as thieves. Only after a few days, when the guard got to know that we were members of the Palestine delegation, did he allow us in without the usual checking procedure. Our delegation only had observer status at that time. I remember that Golda Meir was at that UN meeting as well. At that time she was the Israeli minister of foreign affairs. When Mr Ahmed Shukeiri, leader of the Palestinian delegation, addressed the political committee and explained the Palestinian question and the right of Palestinians to self-determination and establishment of a Palestinian state, Meir's only comment was, 'There is no such thing as the Palestinian nation.' This apparently was proof that we did not exist: therefore there was no need to take our existence as people with a very distinct, Palestinian, identity into consideration.

At none of the international conferences did we contact the Israelis, though it was not officially forbidden. It was not easy for us as people whose land was occupied, whose people were killed and forced to emigrate, to make conversation with our enemy. It is not easy for us at all.

After my studies ended I became more and more involved in politics. In

1964 I became a member of the Palestine National Council, which was held in Jerusalem. There were many other women on the council, which was the most important representative body of the Palestinians. I was recommended to be a member of its executive committee, but they prefer to take men. I did not mind their decision at the time. As long as I could serve my people, it was fine. I was not working to reach a certain political position. According to the Palestinian Charter, we demanded a secular state where Jews and Christian and Muslim Arabs could live together. The formation of the Palestine Liberation Organization (PLO) in 1964 encouraged us a lot. Now we could take things into our own hands: the Arab states did nothing for the Palestinians, so we had to carry the burden ourselves.

In the same year the Arab Women's Union was established. There had been different women's organizations in Gaza before that, but they were all more or less under the auspices of a number of influential families. The Egyptian government did not support such organizations, dissolved them and set up an election for a General Union of Women. At that time I was already the general secretary of the Red Crescent Society in Gaza, and in the election I was chosen together with other women to form the board of the new union. The whole set-up was part of a general Egyptian scheme to establish political bodies such as trade unions and women's organizations. Because Gaza was never annexed by Egypt, unlike the charitable organizations in the West Bank we were not part of the Union of Charitable Organizations in Jerusalem. Our objectives were: to raise the social, cultural, health and economic status of women; to promote honourable options for needy women and orphans; to care for mothers and children; to promote the interests of working women and to achieve equality with men in public life; to take care of patients and their families and to cooperate with organizations sharing the same objectives. *general union of women*

We started operating from our main office in Gaza city. In the years that followed we opened new centres in Khan Yunis, Rafah and Beit Hanoun. In 1965 we founded a sewing workshop and a cooperative where the seamstresses receive 65 per cent of the selling price of the garments they produce. This programme to help women to improve their economic situation was implemented not only in Gaza but in the other three centres as well. To preserve Palestinian culture and traditional design, we founded an embroidery workshop in each of the four centres. To combat the huge illiteracy in Gaza we established ten literacy centres before the outbreak of the 1967 war. And we organized English and later – when Gaza fell under Israeli occupation – Hebrew classes for men and women. Later we set up five kindergartens, catering for more than five hundred children; we organized a nursery to help women labourers and established three libraries for women. We give aid to needy families of detainees and prisoners, provide students with scholarships, finance orphanages, and contribute to the building of mosques and to medical institutions in Gaza.

During this period, as a member of the Palestine National Council I started travelling more and more. Because I was from Gaza I was usually regarded as the president of the delegation. Since 1977 I have been unable to leave the Gaza Strip. I have been invited many times since then to conferences in the USA and to the United Nations, but each time I apply for the necessary papers I receive no answer.

Six days of war and Israeli occupation

The war of 1967 threw its shadows ahead. We learned of the stationing of Egyptian troops in Sinai and the Sharm el-Sheikh incident. The day before the outbreak of war I travelled from Rafah to Beit Hanun. I recognized that there was no army, no border guards to face the Israelis. I came back from the trip with a very severe headache. I told my family that we would certainly be defeated and occupied. And then the fighting started. Together with many other women I went to the hospitals to receive the injured. The first attack separated the north of the Gaza Strip from the south. This meant that the Egyptians were unable to send reinforcements to the northern area, and following the attack on the Egyptian airforce there was no hope of air support either. At nine o'clock on 5 June we knew that the catastrophe had happened. In the hospital we received more and more casualties. When the Israelis entered Gaza, their tanks surrounded the hospital. On the main street one of the first big tanks bore an Iraqi flag. This led the people to believe that the Iraqi army had come in support of the Palestinian people. Suddenly the people came out of their homes and welcomed the tanks. Then the soldiers started shooting. My brother had just left the house to pray in the mosque. He never returned and even today we do not know where his body is. After three days people went out to bury the dead and he must have been buried with them. Many of the people who took that risk were themselves killed.

After the occupation the Israelis imposed a curfew for a week, after which we were allowed out for just two hours. Immediately I went to my brother's house. The furniture had been smashed and there was no sign of life.

Moshe Dayan was the Israeli defence minister at that time and his policy was to crush the Palestinian resistance. If a civilian Jew was killed in one of the Arab quarters, Dayan would order the demolition of all the houses in that quarter, regardless of whether they were inhabited. The reaction to the Israeli occupation was different in Gaza from that in the West Bank. The Gaza Strip contained substantial quantities of light weapons, belonging to the Egyptian army and the Palestine Liberation Army. The resistance sought refuge in the camps, mixed with the population and hid in the orchards. In Gaza, people faced the Israeli army in the streets; there were grenade attacks, and women and men threw petrol bombs. In the West Bank, by contrast, all resistance was underground. Mines and explosives were planted at strategic places but the fighters were less involved in face-to-face fighting. The resistance was active until 1973 and during the night Gaza was ruled by the fighters' military organization. Not just in the camps, in the cities as well. In 1971, Israeli retribution reached its peak. To gain a free hand for search-and-interrogation operations, the Israeli army once again put people under curfew. More than 12,000 people were deported to detention camps in the Sinai desert; the same number were forced to leave their homes when Israeli bulldozers demolished them to clear a space for the Israeli army to move within the camps.

Despite the shock of the Israeli occupation it at least gave Palestinians in the Occupied Territories the hope that they would once more see their friends who lived within Israeli territory, and land and houses which they had not set eyes on for almost twenty years. It took a long time, but one day the Israelis opened the checkpoints on the Green Line and the Palestinians from Israel streamed into Gaza and the West Bank. But we, as occupied Palestinians, were only allowed to cross the line with a permit. The Israeli defence minister, Dayan, disagreed in this respect with the Prime Minister, Golda Meir. Dayan wanted to open the borders to enable Palestinians from Gaza to work in Israel. His aim was to corrupt Palestinian society and its political aspirations by means of an increasing standard of living. Meir, on the other hand, strictly opposed the employment of non-Jews in Israel. She was afraid that through demographic changes in favour of the Palestinians Israel would lose its character as a Jewish state.

After the Israeli occupation of the Gaza Strip the Israeli authorities tried to control all the existing institutions and change their constitutions to fit Israeli interests. I protested that this would be a violation of the Geneva Convention and left my work as a government employee in protest. Instead, I did more work for the union.

In contrast to the 1967 war, the 1973 war made the people of Gaza very optimistic. Again everybody was hoping for liberation. When Egyptian radio announced that the Egyptian army had crossed the Suez Canal we felt that the mythical invincibility of the Israeli army could be broken. But as it turned out the war brought even more destruction.

Camp David – resistance and women's activism

In 1978, the people of Gaza rejected the Camp David Accord. I was one of those elected to write the memorandum which rejected the accord. In reaction, Sadat prevented Palestinian students from enrolling at Egyptian universities. The Israelis too put a lot of pressure on the local population to accept Camp David. I believe that Camp David changed the attitude of the Israeli government. In the years from 1967 to 1978 it had tried to bring about the downfall of the Nasser regime but it was working for a real peace at the same time. But after Camp David it felt strong and the effect was that Egypt was neutralized.

In 1978 the first committee of the new Palestinian women's movement was established. During the years we have learned about each other but we are not in very close contact. Now I believe there are four committees. But I think their problem is that they are not united, that each of them relates to a political faction. This would be one reason why I could not join the Higher Council of Women. If I joined, I would have to follow its regulations and I am not ready to do this. Also, I believe we have a different conception of our tasks. But we cooperate in activities like organizing bazaars, or sit-ins.

Contrary to us those groups are not legally registered, which gives them much more freedom. We are tied to an Ottoman law dating from 1906 (with a lot of Israeli amendments) and of course we experience Israeli interference and control. We have to submit reports, we are interrogated about the origin of our donations and our archives are confiscated. Once during a search the Israeli authorities found a map of Palestine and it was confiscated. I was interrogated at a police barracks and taken to court because I organized a sewing class and an English lecture. They argue that all these activities are means to incite people. At the same time I am constantly prevented from leaving the country. I was tried once in a military court, but the military governor announced that the Israelis had frozen the accusations because of my old age.

Of course, the activists of the women's committees are harassed, jailed and interrogated as well. Therefore I believe that it is very good that we are separate and independent of each other. When our institutions are closed down they can continue serving, if they are crushed we can continue the work. Because, in fact, they do the same kind of work as we do. They organize sewing classes, kindergartens and cooperatives. Of course I cannot talk politics like they do. When I give a political statement I do it in my own name and not in the name of the union. My political ideas are not necessarily the ideas of the union. But they depend on political factions and are financed by them; this makes a difference.

Some of them started talking about women's liberation and feminism lately. I am not a follower of feminist ideas. When we have an independent state we can fight for our rights as women. But to fight for women's rights when men do not even have their political rights is nonsense. How can I fight for the rights of women at home, when the men are followed, are killed and shot, when houses are demolished and children are dispersed? I do not think now is the time for it.

I have read Simone de Beauvoir. But I believe that our traditions here in the Middle East differ from those in the West. People in the Middle East have been fighting for their freedom for more than three decades, and women are an essential part of the fight, and participate in all fields. Despite this I do not think any Arab women would dare to write a book like *The Second Sex*. There are Arab women who tackle women's issues, but in a much more covert way, not so frank and direct.

But the political tendencies of the past ten years have been working against women's liberation. Fanaticism is increasing all over the world, even in the West. I believe that wherever the economic situation is deteriorating, leaders resort to religion. When people are involved in religion they look forward to eternity in the belief that they will enjoy in heaven what they are prevented from enjoying on earth. It is the same here in Gaza. People from the bottom of society, the very poor, are the first to become religious fanatics. The reason why most of the women here in Gaza put on the shawl is that they are forced to. It is becoming dangerous for women not to cover their hair when they leave the house. Some Muslim fanatics have even threatened to throw chemicals at women not wearing a shawl. There are, of course, deeply religious women who wear a shawl out of commitment. Other women rationalize, and regard the shawl not as a part of fundamentalist Islam but as a symbolic sign of the struggle for liberation, the Intifada. And a lot of women are forced by their husbands to cover their heads.

Intifada

The Intifada is especially determined in Gaza. The birthplace of the uprising was Jabalia camp, where the demonstrations started on 9 December 1987, before spontaneously spreading to the West Bank. Israeli visitors are usually shocked at our life under occupation in Gaza. We have received many Israeli women from different organizations, both before and after the outbreak of the Intifada. Peace activists came on fact-finding missions and to express their solidarity.

Recently history has seemed to repeat itself. This time it is not US President Truman financing the immigration of 100,000 European Jews to Palestine but the Soviet Union, which is sending more than 200,000 Jews to Israel/Palestine. They say their policies are based on humanitarian concerns and human rights. But don't they see that they violate the human rights of the Palestinian people while giving human rights to Soviet Jews? Is there no way to avoid helping one people while at the same time harming others? I do not believe in a political solution which would only leave us the West Bank and the Gaza Strip. We have the same right to bring our diaspora people into our homeland as the Jews. Even if we have to have two states for a short period, in the future there will be one. And it will contain Jews and Palestinians living in peace with each other just as they lived in peaceful coexistence at the time of my forefathers.

Note

1. According to United Nations Relief and Works Agency figures of May 1950, approximately 201,000 people took refuge in Gaza (*Interim Report of the Director General of the UNRWA*, A/648).

4. Life is Struggle inside and outside the Green Line

Terry Atwan[1]

UNRWA school and student activities

My family is from inside the Green Line [the 1949 borders of Israel] from the village of Beit Maisir, which was destroyed during the 1948 war. The villagers became refugees, fleeing to the Aqbat Jaber camp in the Jordan valley, near Jericho. In 1967 when the camp was emptied and a lot of people fled to Jordan, we moved to Kalandia camp on the Jerusalem–Ramallah road,[2] where I grew up. Growing up in the years immediately after the 1967 war, as far back as I can remember, my life was always affected by politics. I was politicized in the Palestinian community, in our house, in school and later at university. It was not a matter of formal teaching: Palestinians under occupation have no non-political space to live in. My father is a nationalist and a pan-Arabist; he was a traditional political leader in our community and because of his political commitment he was imprisoned in 1969. I was only an infant then. By the time he was released he had lost all hope for change. My brother was a journalist and active in the Communist Party. He used to bring books and political literature into the house, which I read hungrily. Thus, I grew up in a highly politicized environment, even if my father did not want any member of the family, least of all the women, to get involved politically.

In the camp my father was known as a political activist and our family had a good relationship with the people of the camp. We children went to an UNRWA school in the camp, which brought us, even at that early age, into direct contact with the enemy.[3] There were always confrontations with the Israeli army during school hours or on our way to school.[4] We became involved in nationalist politics while still at school and became leaders of student activities. When the first real *intifada* started in 1976 we participated in its strikes and demonstrations.[5] Together with activists from the camps we organized activities in our secondary school.[6] I was nine years old then. Sometimes we had problems with the head of the UNRWA school, who asked us to stop our activities. When we continued, he tried to use my parents to put pressure on us. He was supported by the old people in the camp and the mukhtar. As a result, my father forbade me to leave the house when there was trouble in the camp. At first I was the only one of my family tied to the house. Then one day my brother was arrested and beaten. After his release, he suffered the same fate as I.

When I finished secondary school my parents sent me to the high school in Ramallah. Here the situation was different from that in the camp, more tense. For me it was an interesting change because the general political leadership is in the area of Ramallah. I continued my political activities in the student committee. We started to organize a student committee for all the students in Ramallah. I was the only girl on this committee. I remember feeling that the boys had wrong ideas about girls being active. They wanted girls as lovers, not as friends and activists. Many of them fell in love with me. But as I wished to be accepted as an equal partner this was not a good way to begin. It took a long time to convince them that I was an activist like them. Only then did they start to respect me; they even told me that, contrary to the traditional view of females, they wanted strong women. From that moment onwards I was expected to participate equally with the boys in all activities.

But I was handicapped by the general attitude of my society towards women activists, and by the restrictions I had to fight against. My father was very traditional. For example, I was not supposed to go out in the evenings. To be able to leave the house I had to use excuses. I would tell him that I had an extra lesson after school or that I had training with the volleyball team. I do not know how he felt about my explanations, but he accepted them. I was able to move about only on weekends, and in the holidays I was unable to leave the house. My father even forbade me to go to the birthday parties of my girl friends. These restrictions were modified over the years only because I insisted on my freedom and constantly fought for it.

My being tied to the house changed when I entered Birzeit University. With the support of my family, and especially my brother, I convinced my father that I should have a university education. The difficulty was by no means due to financial problems: one of my brothers, who lives abroad, is rich and sent us money to pay my tuition fees. Moreover, my father pushed the male members of our family to go to university, but we had to convince him to let me as a girl have a university education. The first woman in our family with a university education had been my sister, and she had been educated precisely because of my father's traditional outlook. Because her appearance is darker than mine [a possible disadvantage in the marriage stakes], his opinion was that she should get an academic degree in order to get married. Therefore she was sent to Syria to become a medical doctor.

I studied hard in order to justify my father's decision to let me study. But a lot of the activities I participated in were contrary to his beliefs and norms. And again I had to fight my way through. For example I participated in the university's Voluntary Work Programme.[7] We made trips with all the students to the coast. We would spend three or four days and nights in the villages, working during the daytime in the olive groves or on other harvesting activities. I was an active member of a *dabka* (traditional folk-dancing) group. This caused innumerable problems, and a lot of anxiety for my father. While dancing I had to put my hand into that of my male dancing partner. I remember well that my father refused to come to one of our performances in the university. He said, 'I cannot see you putting your hand into that of a man!' While he was encouraging on political matters, my social behaviour was a big problem for him.

Imprisoned

When the Israeli army came for the first time asking for me, my father tried to hide me. He said, 'If you weren't a woman I would let you go.' He was afraid that I would be raped. My losing of my honour would have in turn affected his honour and social reputation. Not long after my first interrogation I was arrested and jailed. When this became known to the people in the camp one of our neighbours came to console my mother. 'It is so sad, you lost your daughter,' she said. At that time people were proud when their boys were taken by the soldiers, but for girls such an occurrence was still very problematic. Women in jail tended to be seen as criminals, not political prisoners. My jail sentences affected not only my family but my own personality as well. My first time in jail was very scary. I was only just 18 years old and my family did not know where I was or what would happen to me. I felt myself cut off from their support. When you are arrested, suddenly you are completely on your own. You must face your own helplessness and fears, and the threats and bad conditions, by yourself. Nobody is going to take the pressure from your back. Somehow, though, I managed to cope, and came out of jail stronger than before.

The second time I was imprisoned I was held with students from Birzeit University. They were surprised to see me relaxed and without fear. We discussed a lot and even before I was released the news of my steadfastness in jail had spread around my circle of friends. I gained the image of being tough and was consequently accepted more. My third jail sentence, in 1983, changed the attitude of my family as well. They saw that I could cope with the experience, that I was obviously becoming a leading figure, and from that moment they trusted me more and I had more freedom to move. In general the jail experience made me stronger and more independent. Furthermore, the growing numbers of women in jail have affected the general attitude in our society towards the arrest of women. This has been especially true during the Intifada, in which more than 1,500 women have been jailed. It is no longer shameful for a woman to be arrested for political reasons; instead, increasingly it is becoming a source of pride for their families.

At university I was completely absorbed in my studies and in student activities. Every day there was work to be done. We were mobilizing new activists, giving political and social lectures. We used to fight on all fronts: against the administration when they planned to raise university fees,[8] against the occupation authorities when they raided the campus, arrested, killed and beat students and closed the university.[9] I believed that as a woman I was responsible mainly for organizing the female students. Therefore I and others went into the student hostels, organized gatherings and discussions to reach the women students and to get to know their problems. Many women students came from villages and camps and had absolutely no idea how to cope with life on campus. They had been thrown into a new environment with different, more open social rules. They did not know how to relate towards male students, how to live by themselves in the dorms and how to bridge the gap between the traditional norms of home and campus life. In addition to social work, we gave political lectures. All the student groups are politically affiliated and supported by their factions. This is very helpful in political work, but precisely because the emphasis is on political issues, social and particularly women's problems are neglected. This was sometimes an issue of conflict between men and women activists.

A women's committee on campus

To fill this gap, I started working with a member of the student affairs office to organize a women's committee that would contain members from all political factions as well as unaffiliated women. The politically active women students were unenthusiastic about the idea of a committee dealing with social and women's affairs only, but none of them wanted to be left out. Our first activity was to speak with women students in the hostels. We wanted them to know about our activities and that they would have somebody to turn to with their problems. Soon we had a regular discussion group.

Because it solely contained women, after a while social and sexual problems came up. Women never talked about their problems directly. They spoke about women friends or relatives. Single women generally are not supposed to talk about issues related to sexuality, it is considered '*aib*, a shame. A problem which invariably came up was how to reconcile the strict norms of Palestinian society with one's own emotions. One woman said, 'I am always under pressure when I am with my boyfriend. I have the feeling that the whole society is watching every move we make.' Most women wanted serious relationships with their male friends, but they were scared to trust them. The woman is the one who will be blamed for any relationship before marriage, not the man. Therefore a woman must place a lot of trust in her male partner: she must trust that he will not leave her or blame her in front of others. For a woman it is very easy to be accused of 'loose behaviour', and to become a social outcast. Women take a much bigger risk in confronting the norms of our traditional society than do men.

A lot of women students had sexual problems or questions and no way to solve or answer them. They were happy to talk about them, to find women who either shared their fears or could help to cope with them. I remember very well the case of one student, because it was by no means exceptional. She had grown up with her whole family in one room. Since her early childhood she had seen her parents having sexual intercourse, had seen her mother being virtually raped by her father in a very violent way. With this picture in her mind she started hating men and did not want any man to touch her. She was desperate because she did not know how to solve her problem in a future marriage.

Love and leaving

At the university I came to know my future husband and fell in love with him. Our relationship caused many difficulties. My father believed that a strong woman is a woman without any feelings, and in this respect I had come under pressure. He cared a lot about my sister and I had always felt neglected. To attract his attention I had to become as he wanted me to be, very strong. But how could I neglect the side of my personality which is very emotional? I was trapped either way. The final collision with my father came after I finished university in 1986. My father wanted to send me to Jordan, where I was supposed to get married. But because of my activities the authorities would not allow me to leave the West Bank.[10] Again my family tried to imprison me in our home. I was not permitted to leave the house, or to participate in political activity or even to try to find a job. And there was no way I could live together with my boyfriend to find out if we would fit together or not. Another problem was that he is a Christian and I am Muslim, an almost impossible combination for a Palestinian couple.[11]

The only way to solve the problem was to escape my family and country and seek refuge elsewhere. We went to Canada. But my family would not accept my behaviour. My father threatened to kill me and I know if I had been in front of him instead of thousands of miles away, he would have done so. Finally I had ruined his honour. While I was working in Canada, my sister and her husband came and tried to convince my boyfriend to convert to

Islam, because otherwise we would be unable to marry legally. We escaped to Paris and they followed us. Finally we chose the only way left to us and my future husband converted to Islam. When we came back to the West Bank months later and got married, we began the long task of winning round my parents. It took a long time and I suffered constantly, torn apart between my husband and my family. After almost a year my parents started to accept my decision. My pregnancy two years after our marriage initiated the next step of reconciliation. We were allowed to visit my parents in their house. Still, even now, they will not visit us in our home.

At present I am an active member of a committee of the political women's movement. While I was still at university I worked with the Democratic Youth Union (at that time we organized some activities, such as demonstrations, marches and workshops, jointly with the activists of the women's committees). Already at that time I considered myself to be a member of both organizations. So when one day I was asked to participate fully in the political movement's women's committee, I agreed. I am an economist and they needed a specialist for the production committee of the movement. I liked the idea because I believe that women must be independent financially before they can be liberated and lead an independent life. It is wonderful to have a job in which I am working step by step for changes in women's position in our society. Even though I work for the women's movement and I support its positions I believe that women should enter men's sphere of life and organizations in order to take up their rightful position side by side with men. Only when you mix with men can you influence them. Therefore I am still a member of the Democratic Youth Union, in which men and women work together for a free country for us all.

Notes

1. Terry Atwan is a pseudonym.
2. Kalandia camp was set up in 1949 as a tent camp. Later, the tents were replaced by permanent concrete structures with asbestos roofs. The 1983 census gave its population as 4,224. Kalandia has four elementary and secondary schools. The youth activity centre was closed indefinitely by the military government. (Meron Benvenisti, *The West Bank Handbook*, Jerusalem, Jerusalem Post, 1986, p. 185).
3. United Nations Relief and Works Agency (UNRWA) schools were set up in 1949 to serve the Palestinian refugee population. They provide schooling for the first nine years, at the elementary and preparatory levels. Some 13 per cent of West Bank and 44 per cent of Gaza Strip pupils are taught in UNRWA schools, which are obliged to use the Israeli-censored Jordanian and Egyptian curriculum. (Israeli Central Bureau of Statistics, 1988).

4. During the years of Israeli occupation schools in the West Bank and Gaza have been centres of conflict between Israeli soldiers and Palestinian pupils. Violent confrontations have occurred both when pupils were on the way to school or when soldiers raided school buildings. One method of collective punishment used frequently by the Israelis has been the short-term and (particularly during the Intifada) long-term closure of schools and universities. In addition, the authorities have punished individual student activists by arresting them shortly before their final *tawjihi* examination. (Raja Shehadeh, *Occupier's Law: Israel and the West Bank*, revised edition, Washington, 1985, p. 161ff).

5. In spring 1976, hundreds of students took to the streets in protest at Israel's confiscation of Arab property in Galilee. A number of the protestors were killed.

6. Student federations and blocs appeared openly in the early 1980s, after an initial phase as clandestine organizations, and developed into the most visible mass organizations in the Occupied Territories. They are to be found in almost every secondary school, college and university in the West Bank and Gaza. Activists in the student blocs organize demonstrations, political lectures and other social and political activities. Many of today's women activists in the women's committees and other mass organizations began their political lives as activists in one of the secondary school student blocs.

7. In 1973 Birzeit University incorporated the Voluntary Work Programme into the curriculum. Now, 120 hours of voluntary work became obligatory before students could enter the final examinations.

8. Whilst at the beginning of the student movement in the late 1970s, the major focus of the student blocs was on national politics and anti-occupation activities, in the early 1980s the increase in student fees raised the question of the social character of West Bank universities. Because students in these institutions came mainly from the middle and lower strata of the towns and from villages and refugee camps, the student movement warned against the 'elitification' of the universities, and the left student blocs fought for student participation in university policymaking and for democratization of education.

9. Birzeit University was closed by military order for the first time in 1979 for a period of two months. University closures as a means of political control, either full-time closures or closure by checkpoints, became regular practice in the eight years until the university closures of January 1987. The university was closed by military order as follows: 1980, 1 week; 1981–82, 7 months; 1983–84, 3 months; 1985, 2 months and 1986–87, 5 months. Four students were killed on campus by Israeli soldiers: in November 1984, December 1986 and April 1987. In 1987 the elected Birzeit student council president, Marwan Barghouti, was deported to Jordan. In the academic year 1986/87 alone, nineteen students were served with town restriction orders or banned from entering Birzeit, including one woman student (*The Twentieth Year: a report on the status of academic freedom and human rights at Birzeit University in the twentieth year of the Israeli military occupation*, Birzeit Public Relations Office, April 1988).

10. Released West Bank prisoners have their identity cards stamped with a triangle enclosed in a circle. Whenever they present their cards to apply for a travel permit, a job or suchlike, they are singled out; most of their requests are turned down.

11. According to article 33 of the Jordanian Family Status Law, a marriage between a Muslim woman and a non-Muslim man is invalid. The same is true of a marriage between a Muslim man and a non-Muslim woman who is neither Christian nor Jewish. A Christian man who wants to marry a Muslim woman must convert to Islam.

5. Palestinian Women's Art in the Occupied Territories

Vera Tamari

In November 1986, ten Palestinian women artists from the Occupied Territories held a collective exhibition in Jerusalem which they entitled Tallat (Outlook). The event was special, as it was the first occasion on which a group of Palestinian women artists had exhibited together. Guided by a unifying theme, the doorways and windows of Palestine, the participants portrayed aspects of their immediate environment – social life and customs, people and typical architectural elements – in a variety of moods and using a variety of effects. While local exhibitions generally focus on painting as if it were the only medium of visual expression, in this exhibition canvases were displayed alongside photographs, graphic compositions, ceramic relief panels and terracotta sculptures. The quality of the works and their display were outstanding, as one local newspaper commented:

> Palestinian women may have a long way to go in achieving parity with men in this male-dominated society. But they seem to have surpassed men in the world of artistic expression, technique and evidently art exhibition. The artists say they were not out to prove anything. . . . Their art, judged by the theme, brushwork or composition, must be considered the most presentable in any local art exhibited in more than two years.[1]

Perhaps not directly motivated by feminist issues, the participants in this show wanted simply to pool their individual experiences and talents in a joint project, sharing with each other their special outlook on life as women.

Within the context of the general art movement in Palestine, the role of women artists although still marginal, is steadily growing. Of the thirty registered members of the League of Palestinian Artists, only five are women. They have participated regularly in collective art activities and exhibitions, but none has so far taken an executive position on the board of directors of the league. There are, however, sixteen other laureated women artists (living in the West Bank, Gaza and the Occupied Territories of 1948) whose specializations may be grouped in five or six major areas: painting, sculpture, etching, art education, graphic design and ceramics. Art for most of these women does not constitute their main breadwinning career; they have to rely on other jobs to support themselves and their families, and they have only occasional opportunities to produce creative work.

Historically, an interest in art among Palestinian women can be traced only to the turn of the century. In the 1920s and 1930s, the teaching of art was confined to middle-class girls attending Catholic schools. They were offered painting and metal repoussé classes in addition to the conventional needlework and piano lessons. These subjects ensured the young ladies could be ushered into society as educated and cultured members. This phenomenon, which existed mostly in urban centres and big cities such as Jerusalem and Jaffa, conformed to a great degree to Western styles, models and taste. Having become equipped with refined skills, young women displayed their works at charitable bazaars or stored them as part of their trousseaux. It is worth noting that the quality of skills and techniques in those days was often far superior to the artistic training offered nowadays even by specialized art colleges.

Although there have been only a handful of one-woman exhibitions since the early 1950s, these exhibitions usually made a long-lasting impression. Sophie Halaby, a pioneer watercolourist, mounted several successful shows, which reflected her accurate observation and understanding of Palestinian landscapes and colours. Before the outbreak of the 1967 war, Samia Zaru held a retrospective exhibition of her work, which creatively combined oils with collage compositions, using Jerusalem and Palestinian folklore as her main theme. The author of this chapter, the only studio potter in the area, mounted two shows of her wheel-thrown vessels and relief carved panels. In her work she tried to bridge centuries of pottery tradition, combining the old with new modes of expression.

More recently other women artists have held individual exhibitions. Rihab al Nammari, a painter, displayed works demonstrating her versatility in both subject matter and techniques. The paintings of Jeanette Farah portrayed realistic scenes of Gaza, her home town, whilst Faten Toubasi showed impressionistic watercolour landscapes and oil portraits.

Some women artists have been commissioned to display their art in public places. Still vivid in many people's memories is a mural at the departure lounge of Jerusalem (Kalandia) airport. Painted in the 1950s by Fatmeh al Muhib, the painting is a pastoral interpretation of Jerusalem. The fate of this mural is unknown because the airport came under Israeli supervision and is now no longer accessible to Palestinians. Samia Zaru designed a large-scale mural at the UNRWA Women's Teacher Training Centre in Ramallah. The subject, focusing on the traditional life of Ramallah, suited the occasion for which it was made, the First Ramallah Festival of Song and Dance, which was held in 1962. A carved ceramic tile made by Vera Tamari for the reception lounge of the Notre Dame Hotel in Jerusalem portrays a village scene; it is surrounded by other plaques representing seasonal activities in Palestine. Naheel Bishara was commissioned in 1959 to decorate the newly constructed YWCA building in east Jerusalem. For this project she used combinations of drawings and ornamentations inspired by folk traditions and Islamic art.

On another level, most of the women mentioned above have been actively involved in art education, both in teaching and in the promotion of art programmes and syllabuses for elementary and secondary schools. Most prominent among them is the painter Afaf Arafat, who has worked in this field for more than twenty-five years. But art education, for both boys and girls, remains a neglected subject, especially in the absence of an official educational body that could supervise the enforcement and development of syllabuses. Art teaching virtually ceases after the fourth grade, so that the majority of Palestinian children are deprived of this creative outlet. During the Intifada, children have to an even greater extent than previously been denied the pleasure of doing art. The frequent closure of schools by the military authorities and the continual interruptions to academic work have necessitated the cancellation of art programmes and of all other extra-curricular activities in schools.

From the mid-1960s onwards, the art produced by women in Palestine started to address issues related to their national identity. Their earlier subjects had been an extension of themes practised during their academic training. Some of the topics favoured in the earlier period had included classical portraits, figure drawings, still-life compositions and landscapes. These subjects were generally devoid of either political or social context and often bordered on the romantic. Today, the art made by women is linked to an overall consciousness of issues of national significance.

Since the emergence of a national art movement in the Occupied Territories in the mid-1970s, the women artists like the men have been driven by the urgent need to preserve their much-endangered national heritage. By means of the use of symbols, they found a visual language which emphasized their attachment to the land and their aspiration for liberation and nationhood. Along the same lines, art took on a documentary role, registering pictorially images of village life and customs. Some of the most frequently painted scenes were those representing rural women carrying on with their daily chores against the typical architectural backdrop of the Palestinian home, arched doorways, domes and windows. This reflected how art in Palestine sought to go back to the roots of tradition as a way of manifesting the historical and political rights of the people to the land. The Palestinian woman, wearing the traditional embroidered costume with a soft shawl contouring her body, became for all artists the visual symbol representing Palestine, the Homeland.

In as much as the Intifada has given women in Palestine a new, dynamic role both on the political and on the social level, artistically also the Intifada motivated many women's groups to use this creative medium to help them channel their objectives, programmes and activities to others, both locally and internationally. Groups designed new logos, produced newsletters, calendars and diaries recording their outstanding achievements since the Intifada began. The new spirit of the Intifada inspired some women artists to use the dramatic and often poignant events of the uprising as major themes in their art. In a narrow, horizontal format, Faten Toubasi presented in one of her paintings a moving interpretation of a martyr's funeral, with hands and bodies obliquely stretched towards the lifted bier. In a recent three-dimensional relief entitled '. . . And They Called It Peace', Vera Tamari expressed defiance of the brutality of house demolitions (acts of collective punishment directed against families whose children have allegedly been active against the military authorities).

If in urban environments women's artistic status is now starting to find recognition and respectability within the general creative milieu in Palestine, in rural areas by contrast we are sadly witnessing a sharp decline in some of the liveliest productive activities associated with women. Peasant women were renowned for their specialization in particular crafts, such as weaving, pottery, basketry and embroidery. These skills were passed from mother to daughter, keeping intact from generation to generation a rich tradition of patterns and colour. The products combined both functional and aesthetic qualities and were generally made for immediate household use, although they sometimes found a market in nearby communities. For instance, the beautiful decorated pottery jars made by the women of Sinjil were sought in other villages where the tradition of pottery was not as strong.[2]

Village craft production suffered a marked recession in consequence of changing economic and political factors, technological advancement as well as transformations in the social structure of the Palestinian community. These led to changes in fashion and taste which in turn affected the supply of and demand for particular handicrafts. One of the most affected crafts, now almost nearing extinction, is the hand-made pottery tradition of Palestinian peasant women. With the introduction of electrical refrigerators and modern food preservation techniques, there was no longer a need for the generous storage jars which women used to make. Pottery vessels could not match or compete with more modern household containers made in enamelled metal or plastic. Moreover, modern threshing techniques leave straw stalks too short for use. Embroidery, on the other hand, has recently undergone a welcome revival. The new significance given to the embroidered costume as a means of expressing national identity has encouraged many women, in both urban and rural communities, to carry on with the skilful tradition of their grandmothers, transmitting innumerable patterns that could only be called Palestinian.

Palestinian women have gone a long way from the simple folk art of the village to the more personalized artistic expression of the present. The strength of their creativity is rising to the challenges that face them as they, like all Palestinians under occupation, struggle for freedom and peace.

Notes

1. Al-Fajr (English edition), 28 November 1986.
2. Sinjil is a small village near Ramallah.

6. The Socio-economic Conditions of Female Wage Labour in the West Bank

Suha Hindiyeh Mani and Afaf Ghazawneh[1]

After the 1948 war and the occupation of part of our homeland, the West Bank was annexed to the East Bank of Jordan economically, politically and militarily. Because the Jordanian regime focused on the development of the industrial sector on the east bank of the Jordan river, offering very limited aid to the West Bank industrial economy, annexation hindered the development and growth of several West Bank sectors, in particular the industrial sector. With the simultaneous increase of the population in the West Bank because of the influx of refugees from the other side of the 1948 border, there were insufficient production projects to employ all the labour power available.

This economic problem became even more formidable after the 1967 Israeli occupation of the West Bank. Israel's colonial occupation policies resulted in the spread of unemployment in Palestinian society. This increase in unemployment was directly related to the annexation of the West Bank economy to the more developed Israeli economy. Land confiscation was one of the cornerstone policies of the Israeli occupation, whose by-product was an influx of Palestinian farmers onto the Israeli labour market. This influx was accompanied by a process of proletarianization which expanded the structural base of the Palestinian working class. Members of the expanded Palestinian labour force from the territories occupied after 1967 did not join the productive sector of their local Palestinian economies. The occupation caused migration and economic destruction as the overall size of the labour force decreased in these local economies. The labour force decreased in the West Bank and the Gaza Strip and increased in Israeli enterprises as a result of the opening up of the wage labour market inside the Green Line.[2] In addition to internal labour migration, external migration among the youth (skilled labour and technicians) was underway. Both types of migration had a positive effect in giving women semi-relative independence, although they were still embedded within the institution of the male-dominated family. This independence was not initially the result of women's involvement in social production; it was the outcome of the prevailing objective conditions represented by male migration (internal and external) in addition to the deteriorating economic conditions. But in addition a combination of long periods of detention and the deportation of males gradually drew women into the wage labour market. But women drawn into the wage labour market were not released from familial restrictions, which extended beyond brothers, fathers and husbands (patriarchy in Palestinian society includes all males in the family). Patriarchy is internalized in Palestinian women as a result of socialization, and thus, typically, if the male is not present, the mother, mother-in-law, etcetera, assumes the role of males in the family. Thus women have remained tied to the family both socially and economically.

Almost all internal labour migrants were peasant farmers; women were left to work on the land. A look at the distribution of the female labour force in West Bank economic activity between 1983 and 1984 reveals that 57.5 per cent of female labourers worked in agriculture, 21.6 per cent in science, academic and cultural professions (with teachers and nursing most heavily represented), 9.4 per cent in the industrial sector, 8.4 per cent as skilled labourers, 1 per cent as unskilled labourers, 5.2 per cent in services, 4.3 per cent in clerical work and 2 per cent in commerce.[3] These percentages show that, with the exception of agriculture, women largely work in stereotypically female positions. Regarding agriculture, traditionally it is not uncommon for both women and men to do such work; women working in agriculture are accepted socially because they fall within the sphere of family labour.

The socio-economic conditions of female workers do not differ from the conditions of the work force in general. In capitalist societies the labour force is oppressed on the basis of class. Under occupation the labour force is also oppressed on national lines. The female labour force, however, suffers in addition from gender oppression. Marxists often argue that individual capitalists pay wages below the value of labour power to the 'semi-proletarianized' in the agricultural periphery of capitalist production. Capital, that is, pays wages below the cost of the production and reproduction of labour power, since part of those costs are met via the subsistence economy.[4] This is demonstrated in Palestinian society by the 'semi-proletarianized' Palestinians working in Israeli enterprises: the agricultural labour of the families of these workers provides their means of subsistence through agriculture. These underpaid workers become cheap labour power and an industrial reserve army.

Beechey argues that in capitalist societies married women workers are similar to the semi-proletarianized. Married women workers depend partially on their families (husbands' work) to meet the cost of production of their labour power, because their own paid wages are too low. She states that women's wages are below the value of their labour power and less than male workers' wages.[5]

The Intifada – introduction

The Palestinian Intifada has achieved much, both locally and internationally. A major achievement on the local level has been the boycotting of Israeli products, and increased purchasing of Palestinian products. The result has been an expansion and growth of the Palestinian productive infrastructure. New projects are continually being established in an attempt to cover the needs of the local market. As a result, the labour force is continually expanding in Palestinian factories, as relatively large numbers of workers are employed. Palestinian businessmen and workers have become increasingly involved in the production process with the aim of developing the Palestinian productive infrastructure.

The labour movement and the United National Leadership have taken leading roles in working for more efficient management of the national production process and in examining conflicts between employers and workers. They investigate conflicts over wages, working hours, leave etcetera, and they also draft agreements and contracts between employers and workers for the preservation of workers' rights in an increasing number of factories.

The working conditions of Palestinian workers, both male and female, employed in Israeli enterprises are far worse than those of Palestinians working in Palestinian factories. In Israeli enterprises, Palestinian workers have the lowest status, and are considered cheap labour, especially those working in Israel through brokers (their numbers are triple those who work through the Israeli labour offices). In Israeli factories, Palestinian workers receive far lower wages than Israelis for identical work. Most Palestinian workers have no labour rights and are not covered by the labour laws which protect Israelis (except those Palestinians working through the Israeli labour offices). As the national authoritative body of the Palestinians, the Unified National Leadership, is not recognized by the Israeli government, it is unable publicly and efficiently to supervise or subsidize our factories.

The United National Leadership and the regional leaderships have introduced 'laws' through the communiqués to protect workers' rights. For example, communiqués called for the exchange rate on workers' wages to be set at 4.6 shekels to 1 Jordanian dinar (as most Palestinians in the West Bank are paid in dinars, this protects them from the rapidly decreasing value of the dinar); they specified that factory workers should receive not less than the equivalent of 200 US dollars a month. The rights of women workers, however, have not yet been adequately addressed, and the conditions of Palestinian women workers in Palestinian factories are still unsatisfactory.

The conditions of female wage labour at the workplace

1. Wages and working hours

Our preliminary research found that 86.2 per cent of Palestinian women workers are unmarried; 6.9 per cent are married and 6.9 per cent are divorced or widowed. Beechey analyses the position of single women wage labourers along the following lines. For unmarried women workers, their families meet the daily costs of reproduction (housing, cleaning and feeding for example: the mother's domestic labour). Generational reproduction is not relevant to single women in Palestinian society. Hence, the economic position of unmarried male workers is similar to that of unmarried female workers. But the previous assumption suggests that unmarried women do not bear the costs of reproduction. If these women live alone, however, they are depressed into poverty. If women have children and have to meet the costs of reproduction (for the coming generation of labour power and domestic labour) from their wages, they are often depressed into severe poverty.[6]

In Palestinian factories our ongoing research revealed that factory owners prefer to hire unmarried women simply because they have fewer outside responsibilities (this was the reply of almost all the Palestinian factory owners). Married or unmarried, in addition to their wages women depend on family income. In Palestinian society, unmarried women live with their families, not as in developed industrial societies. This social tradition allows and encourages local capitalists to pay lower wages to women workers than to male workers, that is, to consider them as cheap labour. Even when women workers marry, the costs of their reproduction (housing, food etc.) is met by the family (by the husband).

The wages of male workers are on average double those of women workers in our society. In interviews with owners of mixed factories, the majority of owners stated that men receive higher wages than women first because 'they are men' and, second, because they have greater family responsibilities. Unequal wages are clearly revealed by our sample (101) of women workers. Out of 47 women working in mixed factories (containing both men and women workers), 37 (78.2 per cent) reported that equal wages were not paid for equal work. One worker replied that the nature of work was not equal, and 7 workers replied that they did not know. Two women workers (4.3 per cent) reported that wages were equal. The other 54 women in our sample worked in factories employing women only.

The entry of Palestinian women into the labour market does not represent a break with the old traditions, especially with regards to the clothing industry. Our interviews with 53 factory owners in three areas in the West Bank revealed that, of the sample of 101 women we interviewed, 82.5 per cent worked in the clothing industry. Over the entire sample wages ranged from approximately US$143 to US$250 monthly; 52 per cent of the women received US$143 or less monthly and 44.5 per cent received higher wages. Some 3 per cent of the women reported that they had only recently begun working and had not yet received information about wages or conditions. These percentages reveal the low level of women's wages, especially considering that 92 per cent of the women worked long hours (more than 8 hours a day); 55 per cent worked 9 hours or more daily.

2. Holidays and health insurance

International labour law holds that working conditions should be free of oppression and exploitation and should raise the standard of living of the working class. The results of our preliminary research indicate that the minimum appropriate working conditions specified by international law are not provided in the West Bank.

Our research found that women workers' rights were abused in respect of holidays, working hours and overtime. Several women reported that they were exploited for overtime and were often coerced into working on their day off. Interviews revealed that 36.6 per cent of the women did not receive wages for their day off; 63.4 per cent did. The latter percentage has increased because Palestinian women workers compensate for days not worked because of general strikes. The United National Leadership put forward compensation as a national demand, in order to increase production to satisfy the local market. These work days must be paid however, to be in accordance with this call.

With regard to holidays, 72.3 per cent of the women interviewed did not receive wages for International Women's Day, if taken as a day off. The remaining 27.7 per cent reported that they worked on International Women's Day. Many women got International Workers' Day, May Day, as a paid holiday. The greater concrete economic recognition of International Workers' Day may be because the right to this holiday is a matter of direct concern to men; the local labour movement struggled over a long period for this right, whilst International Women's Day has not yet received such attention. The real issues here are the absence of women from local union leaderships (with a few exceptions) and their marginalization in the unions generally. The situation does not differ significantly from that in the rest of the Arab world. The lack of rights to maternity leave that our survey revealed, and the lack of struggle on this issue, may be partially due to the high percentage of women workers who are unmarried (86.2 per cent).

Health insurance is not available to 98 per cent of Palestinian women workers. The Intifada, the Israeli restrictions on the public activity of the United National Leadership/PLO and the dispersion of the labour movement (due to deportation and massive detentions) have limited and delayed the ability of workers to impose adequate working conditions.

3. Training

As previously mentioned, the entry of women workers onto the labour market is still mainly restricted to traditional types of work. The political situation has helped women to enter the labour market and the relative expansion of women's employment; during the Intifada, the female labour force has again increased. Our research revealed that the opening of a number of factories in the last three years of the Intifada has resulted in an increase in the number of unskilled women workers joining the labour market (out of financial need). Some 68.4 per cent of our sample of women began working during the Intifada. Of these women workers, 46.5 per cent were under twenty years of age. More specifically, 6.9 per cent were under fifteen and 39.6 per cent were sixteen–twenty years old. The deteriorating economic situation and the closing of educational institutions at all age levels might be reasons for the increase in the number of young women workers. During the occupation, many families have had the number of their breadwinners reduced by martydom, detentions, or dismissals from Israeli factories. Thus, following school closures many students have entered the labour market to help meet their families' economic needs.

The restriction of women workers to traditional jobs is partially due to the absence in the West Bank of industrial vocational training schools for women. Those training programmes that exist largely focus on sewing and typing. Untrained women who gain employment in the clothing industry are often given a short training session at the workplace. In such jobs, which involve routine work, women's potentials and skills are not developed. From the sample studies, we found that 32.7 per cent of women were unskilled labourers and worked on one production line whilst 12.9 per cent undertook secondary work like folding and packing. Some 46.5 per cent replied that they considered themselves skilled labour (incorrectly – authors) because they could sew hems and seams using different machines. 4.9 per cent were secretaries and 3 per cent were cleaners.

Women's awareness of their union rights

Young women are less socially and ideologically aware than older workers and most work not for personal development or enjoyment, either current or in the future, nor as a means to achieve emancipation. Of the 101 women we interviewed, 70.3 per cent said that their incentive for work was financial; 19.8 per cent said they worked to pass time; 6.9 per cent worked because they believed in women's right to work, and 3 per cent worked because they enjoyed their job.

In liberation movements, class struggle is often marginalized temporarily until the national struggle is completed, as participation of all the classes in the struggle is felt to be necessary in this period. One question we must nevertheless deal with is that of how developed awareness of women workers is regarding their gender and class oppression and the means to struggle for their rights. Our research revealed that 94 per cent of women workers did not participate in unions because they had not heard of them, because they felt they did not have time to participate in them, or because their family did not accept their participation. Some 93.1 per cent did not belong to women's committees. These low participation rates may have several causes: many workers are young and have not completed school; many women leave work upon marriage, and their social activities are subsequently restricted as they are forced into domestic work (many women who are unionized give up their activities after marriage due to these social pressures); in addition, recruitment for the labour and women's movements is often not the main emphasis of Palestinian activists' work since they put most of their energy into the national liberation movement. The lack of women leaders in the labour movement is also an impediment to a more rapid recruitment of women. This is not to say that significant growth in both movements has not occurred, especially during the Intifada, but activists organized by these movements often focus on national issues at the expense of gender issues.

We believe that all members of our society must be involved in the national struggle, but that this must not be at the expense of women's and workers' rights. All these struggles must progress hand in hand so that women will be empowered as free and equal members in all aspects of our society, and particularly as political decision-makers.

Preliminary findings

1. Women workers are not significantly increasing their involvement in union activities and women's committees; those who are active tend to drop out of activities after marriage. Women workers are not becoming sufficiently empowered actively to demand their rights.
2. The majority of women workers are still working in traditional types of work and Palestinian factories are not significantly changing the type of work women participate in. But increasing numbers of women in the workforce is definitely a progressive step.
3. There is a great need for vocational training for women, especially in non-traditional types of work.
4. The participation of married women in the labour force is very low. This indicates strongly that Palestinian society still places pressure on women

to remain in the home as a mother or wife (even in situations of clear financial need).

5. The working conditions of women workers are very poor, and do not meet the minimum standard of workers' rights. Wages are low, and lower than those of men. Women are denied paid holidays and health insurance, and working hours are long, with women coerced into working overtime. This implies that the Palestinian bourgeoisie must be pushed to be more just in providing for workers' rights (and that women workers must be increasingly organized to demand these rights).

6. The educational level of women workers is very low – it was found that 62.4 per cent were elementary or secondary school dropouts, maybe because of school closures by the authorities, as well as the increased financial needs of families in the conditions of Intifada.

Notes

1. This chapter was written on behalf of the Palestinian Federation of Women's Action Committees and the Women's Resource and Research Centre. It was presented by the authors at the Fourth International Interdisciplinary Congress on Women, held at Hunter College, New York, on 3–7 June 1990.

2. Ribhi Katamesh, *The Palestinian Working Class in Confronting Colonialism*, Jerusalem Alzahra Centre for Studies and Research, September 1989, p. 39.

3. Ibid., p. 109.

4. Beechey, Veronica, 'Some Notes on Female Wage Labour in Capitalist Production', in Mary Evans (ed.), *The Women Question: Readings on the Subordination of Women*, Fontana, 1982, p. 257.

5. Ibid.

6. Ibid., p. 259.

7. People's Activities and Trade Union Work: a Personal Account

Amni Rimawi

I was born in 1957 in the village of Beit Rima, near Ramallah. At present I live in Ramallah city itself, together with my husband and my three children. Fidda is six, Fadi five and Saqi one and a half years old. I am a member of the administration committee of the Union of Workers in Public Institutions, in Ramallah and a member of the executive committee of the General Union of Workers and its vice-president.

Voluntary work and people's activities

The early 1970s in the West Bank were characterized by a political and cultural renaissance. People realized that the Israeli occupation was not going to end swiftly. They started to adjust to the conditions of occupation and at the same time to build an organizational infrastructure for a future Palestinian state. Mass organizations such as the voluntary work committees took hold on the West Bank. On the cultural level a political theatre and a literary movement developed. I became active in both and the experience I gained largely determined my present social outlook and work.

In the late 1960s and the mid-1970s several theatre groups were formed. Audiences seemed to appreciate their new way of expressing the issues of the time and came in large numbers. Despite their differing styles, almost all the plays these groups performed had one message in common: rejection of the Israeli occupation. The theatre was highly politicized, but it examined not only the occupation but also Palestinian society itself.

In 1975 I joined one of these theatre groups, named Dababis ('Pins' which has connotations of 'stirring up', or being critical), in Ramallah. My participation in that group stemmed from my belief that women should participate in theatre work, at a time when women's participation did not exist. Palestinian society rejects the idea that women could appear on stage. Together with a woman friend I acted in several plays in which the rest of the actors were men; we also took part in a *dabka* (folkdance) group. Our difficulties were numerous. Sometimes social pressures endangered the entire performance. For example, in one of the plays our main actress was pressured by her family into leaving the country two days before our first performance. We had to find a substitute for her, who had to learn the whole text in two days and perform largely without rehearsal. Because of this kind of social resistance, which created so many problems for active women, women were not seen as reliable partners by men.

My first acting got me in trouble with my family. Our group performed the play *Al Haq al al-Haq* (The Right is to Blame), in front of many different audiences, in Birzeit University, in Jalazoon and in the village of Eisawiyeh. I invited my family to attend a performance, but my sister-in-law, who was on a visit from abroad, initially refused to attend the play. Her argument was that it was absolutely culturally unacceptable for a woman to appear on stage. But we managed to convince her to come, and when she recognized during the play that acting does not necessarily mean improper behaviour and that our message was a political one, she changed her mind.

Our theatrical activities and my chances to improve my acting ended when the military authorities declared our group illegal and we had to disband. The military governor of Ramallah told us, in no uncertain terms, that Dababis was perceived to be almost as dangerous as the PLO. We were not the only theatrical group which had to end its activities. As a group's popularity increased, so did Israeli repressive measures. Checkpoints were set up on the roads to performances, censorship was tightened and group members were arrested and imprisoned.

In 1975 a variety of social clubs, for example cultural, scientific and sport clubs, were formed. I joined the scientific club together with five women friends. We were able to work for several months. We built a simple piece of equipment to preserve animals and issued a magazine. Then we started a study of the educational situation in the Ramallah area, during which we interviewed several school principals and the director of education. Although we finished it, the study was never published because it was censored by the school administration which was supervised by the Israeli civil administration.

The responses of Palestinian society, my family and the Israeli authorities to my involvement in popular struggle have been in many ways similar to the experiences of women activists in other sectors of Palestinian society. I first became actively involved in the struggle in 1975. At that time I was a student in Ramallah girls' school and an active member of a voluntary work committee.[1] This committee included youth from all sectors of society, students, pupils and also teachers, workers and active adults. The work was an effort towards national reconstruction and at the same time aimed to protect Palestinian land from increasing Israeli confiscations of land for settlements. For three years we were involved in various kinds of work, for example cleaning the streets of cities, villages and refugee camps, paving roads, reconstructing walls. We worked in Ramallah, Jenin and the refugee camps of Amari and Jalazoon. At the same time we did a lot of work on land reclamation, and afforestation; we laid sewage systems and helped farmers in harvesting. We picked olives in the villages of Deir Gahassaneh and Ral al Karker near Ramallah and in various villages around Jenin and we harvested vegetables in the Jordan valley. We built streets and pavements, and renovated schools. In short, we tried to help where help was urgently needed.

The voluntary work committee was the first attempt to include women in such types of work and my first experience in popular struggle. In my opinion the voluntary work groups were the most important development of the early 1970s, because they were the first framework through which people could be active. At the beginning and even during the work we faced a lot of problems. Palestinian society did not respond easily to our challenge and we were confronted by religious groups and conservative forces. Their reaction bordered sometimes on a witch-hunt. Some of our activists were accused over loudspeakers from the mosques of being communists, troublemakers and even traitors. This happened, for example, in the village of Eisawiye, near Jerusalem. But the villagers did not respond as expected to the accusations: they turned against the accusers and threw the sheikh out of the village.

Initially the percentage of women involved in the voluntary work committee was much less than that of men. However voluntary work was introduced into the curriculum of Birzeit University in 1973. That made it necessary for all students to join and the percentage of women increased. One prejudice we had to fight against was that people believed that women were incapable of doing certain kinds of work. I remember once we women were working in the Balata refugee camp on construction work. Suddenly some men approached us and tried to take the building equipment out of our hands, convinced that women were not able to handle these men's tools. But with time and because we insisted on keeping on doing such work, the men had to submit to the fact that we were indeed capable of doing the work properly; they began to recognize the importance of women taking part in all sorts of tasks.

From the very beginning it was not easy for the Palestinian women to find a place in the popular struggle. This was especially because to be effective, women had to mix with men. We had to go through much conflict with our families and our society until we were able to convince them that the way we were behaving was acceptable, even if we broke the rules of traditional society. A lot of women had to sacrifice their social ties in order to enable themselves and others to break the isolation in which we were kept. I had to inform my parents and obtain permission from them whenever I wanted to leave the area or Ramallah. I was lucky though, because my father never showed great reservations about my work, and whenever he did object it was not difficult to convince him. He himself had been active during the British Mandate and he told us a lot about his activities. Despite his tolerance I nevertheless worked hard to increase others' confidence in me. I wanted to show my family as well as our society in general that independence and mixing with men does not necessarily lead to improper behaviour, as was generally assumed (improper behaviour, in our society, meant smoking, drinking, staying out late at night and having love affairs). I was called a tomboy by many people, or 'Hassan Sabi' or accused of being a man rather than a woman (and until now, my fate, whenever we are discussing the role of women, has been that my male friends consider me one of them!). But with time I gained the confidence of my family and especially of my father, who always encouraged me. The lesson is, if the freedom of women is to be achieved, someone must toll the bell.

Being involved in voluntary work opened our eyes to the different problems women face in our society. The women in the group started meeting after our voluntary work and hotly discussed works on women's issues and the conditions of Palestinian women. The charitable organizations were active but we were not satisfied with their kind of work. Until then most attempts by young women to join the charitable societies had failed. With their elitist outlook the charitable women regarded the progressive ideas of newcomers as a threat. Our criticisms were that the number of women they were dealing with was too small, that they were reinforcing through their work the traditional role of women instead of working towards women's liberation, and that they were mostly dealing with city women. Our experiences in voluntary work made us want to involve the women in villages and camps, and close the gap between city and countryside. At the same time the women who were ready to go out and work wanted not to be exposed to men all the time. Therefore we decided to establish a women's committee which could tackle these issues and give women of all sections of society the chance to work without being dominated by men. As a group of around thirty-five active women, mostly professionals, teachers and university students between the ages of 16 and 27, we met on International Women's Day in 1978 in the Ramallah public library and announced the formation of the Women's Work Committee. The programme we decided on was a summary of our experiences over the previous years. We wanted to combat illiteracy among women, to help female students with the payment of their tuition fees, and to make women independent by means of vocational training. We wanted to link the national political struggle with improvement of the economic, social and cultural conditions of women. Therefore we immediately started building up grassroots committees in villages and camps.

I was mainly interested in the situation of working women. One of the first of our activities that I participated in was a survey of women employed in factories and workshops, which was undertaken in summer 1978 in the Ramallah area. We visited working women at their places of work and at home. Many problems were made visible through that study: working women had very low salaries, long working days, an almost total lack of holidays and no maternity leave; they worked without health or social insurance, and, above all, women were treated badly. These conditions were found by us in Israeli factories as well as in local factories. On top of those problems, women were subject to blackmail by employers and middlemen. The multiple oppression was severest for women who worked inside the Green Line [i.e. the pre-1967 borders]. They were oppressed not only socially – because they were women, or as members of the working class – but as Palestinians. Palestinian women working in Israel are subjected to the same kind of discrimination as are Palestinian men. They are employed only as unskilled labourers in seasonal agricultural work or in tailoring, as charwomen or as odd-jobbers. Many work illegally to avoid heavy taxation on top of their low salaries. But even legally employed women are deprived of their labour rights and their right to belong to a trade union.

While we conducted our research, we tried to unionize the working women we contacted. We were very successful and around one hundred women joined the union. This was a success not just for the women's movement but for the union movement as well.

Palestinian working women and the trade union movement

In 1976 I graduated from school and enrolled at the vocational school for girls of the Jam'iat In'ash Al Usra.[2] For a year I studied secretarial skills and business administration. At the same time I joined a seminar on living conditions under occupation and became a supportive member of the Union of Construction Workers and Public Institutions. I was not yet qualified to become a full member.

After I graduated I found work in a tourist agency. At that time I understood nothing about labour law. I was working without a contract and felt very uneasy about it so I became a full member of the union. My colleagues explained to me that the union would defend me if I lost my job and would provide health insurance as well. They were very enthusiastic that I as a woman was working with them because at that time for women to work in unions was not socially accepted. This was the beginning of my active involvement as a trade unionist. Even if I was not yet able to run for elections myself, I took an active part in the election campaign that started four months after I joined the union. Since then I have felt a close commitment to the labour movement and have tried to give especial support to working women, whose numbers have increased over the years without them having any laws to protect their rights.

What Palestinian women have achieved in the trade union movement today has been preceded by a long and hard struggle over the past twenty years. Before 1967 women worked only in agriculture and in housework, that is, without pay. Only a very small number of women from the upper class of Palestinian society worked for wages, in education, nursing and office work. But after 1967, the Israeli policy of destroying and merging the local economy with that of Israel led to the proletarianization of the refugee population and, by means of a policy of land confiscation, of much of the rural population. The resulting economic crisis forced more and more women to enter the labour market. But because few women were able to obtain a good professional or technical training, more than 60 per cent of them work as unskilled labourers in agriculture and small factories.[3]

Women wage-earners work under more difficult conditions than do men. Women in our society are not supposed to work outside the house when they get married. This social attitude is even emphasized by some of the factories, such as the Jerusalem Electric Company, which do not employ married women at all. Their failure to hire married women is, nevertheless, not the result of a traditional outlook; their aim, simply, is to avoid paying benefits such as maternity leave. In consequence, before 1985 married women in the workforce never exceeded 10 per cent. Now the rate is estimated to be about 25 per cent. This is mainly because during the Intifada the economic situation of families worsened considerably, forcing more and more women to look for employment. A second factor is that the opportunities now for women to find any kind of employment are getting fewer and fewer, so women tend to try to keep their work even after marriage.

Other factors are at work too. A woman usually has no right to choose her workplace: it is the right of her family alone. Furthermore, there is the tendency of bosses in the factories to isolate working women totally from the outside world and especially from the trade unions. Either women are picked up in front of their homes and brought to work and back so as to avoid contact with the rest of the society, or their work is brought to their homes and they work on a subcontracting basis. In this last case the middleman, the *simsar*, who is the connection between the Israeli factory and the Palestinian working women, takes usually half of her salary for himself. In some cases Palestinian factories act as a *simsar* themselves. They subcontract Palestinians to work for Israeli factories. The subcontracted women are paid piece rates and they receive no employee benefits at all. They are not insured and when they are unable to work because of illness or family problems they do not get paid. They are the perfect reserve labour force for Israel industry, without even recognizing it. On the contrary, most of the women believe that it is very convenient to work at home and to have extra money for the household. They are overburdened with work, because the subcontracting work is of course additional to their household and often agricultural workload. Our union tried hard to explain to women their position in the system of exploitation of labour. In the village of Beit Annan we mobilized a group of women who sewed cloth on a subcontracting basis to demand an increase in payments to make up for their loss of benefits. Their income increased slightly as a result, but in no way was this increase comparable to the loss of benefits. To gain income, in some cases women themselves act as *simsar*. When they have the facilities and the machines they use a number of Palestinian women from their neighbourhood to work for them as subcontractors.

To estimate the number of Palestinian women working in the subcontracting industry is very difficult.[4] Women are embarrassed to admit that they work in an Israeli factory or as cleaning women in Israeli households. In addition, most of them work without contracts and are therefore unregistered. Working in Israel is considered to be disgraceful because it is work for the occupying power. Therefore only women who have no options left other than to work inside the Green Line choose this employment; they are mainly women from refugee camps and border villages, women from the poorest strata of the society. We as trade unionists have only limited possibilities to help these women to achieve their rights. We try to help them at least to negotiate a fair working contract with their employer.

When women try to fight for their rights at their workplace they are usually warned not to get involved with union work. The unions are under attack from two sides: from the occupying authorities as well as from local employers. Typically, trade unionists are accused of being communists and are arrested, employers submit union membership lists to the Israeli authorities, and of course trade unions are accused of behaving improperly because they work with members of the opposite sex. Because of my involvement in the union I experienced this pressure from two sources when I was employed in my first job. I was fired after eight months when my employer got to know about my union activities. Luckily I found work in another factory shortly afterwards.

Factory work and union work – fighting on two fronts

I have experienced this contradiction between working and belonging to a union myself. Since 1978 I have worked in twelve different places and many kinds of jobs. At last, because my activities as a trade unionist were now widely known, I no longer had any chance of finding employment. In every place I worked I usually gained the trust of my fellow employees very quickly. In many instances my fellow workers became members of a union and actively involved in union work. But because of the pressure of employers and the threats of the occupying authorities, the unions have been characterized by unstable membership. When employers gained knowledge about union activists, in many cases they threatened the workers, ordering them to stop their union work or leave their jobs, and many gave in.

I was faced with the same threat when I worked in the Star soap factory in Ramallah. After only two months I gained the trust of my fellow workers and many of them became members of the union. More than once they went to the head office of the union to discuss problems they faced at work, and at that time we agreed to form the first specialized union representing only workers in chemical and pharmaceutical factories. It was called the Union of Workers in Chemical and Pharmaceutical Factories, and I became one of the members of the executive committee. In the factory where I worked at that time more than forty male and female workers, nearly two thirds of the total labour force, agreed to join the union. After a few days the director of the factory learned about the formation of the new union and became enraged. Although only a few hours before he had informed me that I would get a wage rise because of my efficiency, he changed his mind when he heard about my involvement in the formation of the new union. He threatened that unless I informed him who had joined the union I would lose my job. When I did not give in to his threats, he called the accountant to pay me all the money I was entitled to; he would not even allow me to talk to any of my fellow workers and he called a taxi to take me immediately away from my working place. After I had left, my fellow workers made many efforts to get me back to work. But all failed and the employer threatened with dismissal any worker who stayed in contact with me or with the union. In addition, our efforts to have the new union formally registered failed because it was restricted by the occupation authorities. But we gained approval to form another union under the name Union of Public Health, Civil Service and Pharmaceutical Workers a few months later.

After my dismissal I found work in a pharmaceuticals factory in Jerusalem. Again my employment did not last very long because I built very good relations with the other employees. Then I got a job in a ceramics factory. I worked there for five months, but during the summer I had to travel for one month to sit for the Beirut Arab University exams. My leave was not approved by my employer and I was dismissed because I insisted on travelling.

After I returned from Beirut I started working in a biscuit factory. Our official working hours were eight each day, but the factory worked two shifts. It was a new factory but depended on manual work and we were twenty-five female and male employees. I used to work more than ten-hour shifts, often at night, so that I would be able during daytime to do union work, such as holding meetings with the workers, visiting other factories and attending union meetings. During this time there were preparations for elections to the administrative committee of the Union of Workers in Public Institutions, to which I now belonged, which in 1979 was the only union in Ramallah. In the same year all the trade unions in the West Bank held a conference in the Electricity Company in Jerusalem. The conference came out with a recommendation to form women's committees in the trade unions. This was the initial step in the formation of such committees in the unions.

Since then the number of women workers who belong to the unions has increased continuously. Furthermore, the trend towards higher education and the rising number of women students during the 1970s in the Palestinian universities and colleges raised the percentage of educated women in the labour force and made them more inclined to join professional labour unions.[5] Male members of my union started to see the need to give way to women in the administrative committee. Together with a colleague from the Lijan al-Amal al-Nisai (the Women's Work Committees), I was nominated to be a representative on the committee. Our first activity was to implement the recommendation of the Jerusalem Conference to form a special committee to deal specifically with working women's issues. This was the first union women's committee in the West Bank. Other unions followed our example and the number of committees dealing specifically with women's work increased during the years that followed. On my election to the administrative committee, I was again dismissed from my job, and again all efforts to win me back my job failed. I at least received the compensation I was entitled to according to Jordanian law, which has applied in the West Bank since 1965. After that I started working in a plastics factory. One of the owners of the factory turned out to be a board member of the Star factory where I had worked previously. When he saw me in the factory he stopped me and told me why I had been dismissed from the Star factory. 'You were considered to be red,' he said. My reply that I was only a trade unionist defending workers' rights came too late. When I had to sit the exams for the academic year 1980/81 my application for leave was rejected by this employer too and I left work. When I came back from Lebanon this time it turned out to be impossible to find a job. It was now well known that I was an active unionist and I could not find work in any company or factory. I worked therefore for a whole academic year in a women's literacy programme in the village of Kufr Nameh. The women I taught were working in a needlework cooperative which was financed by the German Weltfriedensdienst.

While I was teaching, the Israeli authorities issued a new military law, number 825, which modified item 83 of the labour law. According to this modification the military authorities had the right to interfere in the internal affairs of trade unions. Now, the list of nominated candidates for any election as well as the list of members had to be submitted to the Israeli civil administration a month before the election. The Israeli authorities had the right to prevent any person from standing for elections on grounds of security. We considered this move to be very dangerous to us because it aimed at draining the trade unions of their national content. Therefore the new regulations were fiercely opposed by the entire labour movement. The Unified Labour Group put forward a programme for fighting the new regulations and proposed that elections should be held in the whole West Bank ignoring the new regulations. But some political groups proposed postponement of the elections for a year and an extension of the mandates of the administrative committees for a year. The reaction to the new regulations was not unified, and some unions held elections without abiding by the new law, whilst others extended their mandates. The next step of the Israeli authorities was to issue another law, requiring the General Union of Workers to dismiss the unions of East Jerusalem and other uncertified unions. But the unions also confronted this law successfully. During this period the aim of the struggle of my colleagues and myself in the Unified Labour Group was to emphasize the union's programme, presented in 1978, which included the opening of membership to Palestinian workers working in Israel and equal pay for equal work for men and women. In the beginning this programme was opposed by other unionists. But after two years it became the backbone of the union movement and was approved by the conference of the union movement in 1979/80. The union movement defeated the efforts of the Histadruth [Israeli Trade Union] to organize Palestinian labourers and make them part of the Histadruth. Legally the Arab union was not able to take Israeli employers to court. Therefore the role of the Arab unions was limited to consolidating and unifying the attitudes and positions of these workers.

Even if the union movement was growing and gaining effectiveness and influence, still in many cases workers were dismissed from their jobs when they joined a union.[6] In 1979 seven women were dismissed from their work in the Silwana sweet factory in Ramallah because of their union work. Women generally were afraid to join unions because they were afraid of losing their jobs and afraid also that they would have an even harder time to find new ones than the men. But despite the threats of employers women stayed involved in union work. In the late 1970s the union movement made a big step forward when the major political forces in the West Bank started focusing on the unions as a framework for organizing and mobilizing the Palestinian masses. The union movement gained a significant mass base during this period. But while it was vitalized, it fragmented at the same time.

Union blocs aligned to the different political forces within the national movement emerged, dormant unions were revived and new ones formed. In 1981 a women's union movement was formed in Ramallah and named the Union of Weavers, Banders and Tailoring. The role of women also became more important in the weaving unions in Nablus and Hebron where women for the first time nominated themselves for election and, in Hebron, won two seats. Particularly for Hebron, which is a traditional and conservative town, this was a big success. In 1982 women gained more influence in the union leadership. I was elected to the central bureau of the Unified Labour Group, which is its supreme body, and I have been a member ever since. More and more women became executive members in the regional committees.

When I finished my work in the literacy programme in Kufr Nameh and Beit Anan I worked for a short while in an import office and with one of the women's committees before I became a full-time union official. The role of working women in the union movement is not restricted to activities related to women and some women leaders have become prominent in the movement as a whole.

One effect of the new political emphasis on mass mobilization through unionization was growing conflict between the contending parties. In 1983 it came to a split in the union movement. Only in 1985, after many unsuccessful attempts to reunify the labour movement was the union reactivated on all levels. This did not pass unnoticed by the Israeli authorities: their reaction was a clampdown on most of the members of the executive committee. During that time active working women, although small in numbers, performed a prominent role in confronting the Israeli authorities. They kept up union work, visited the workers in their homes and at work and followed up cases.

A lot of the tasks that had to be done were not easy for women in a traditional society like ours. Visiting especially was difficult, because often it had to be done during the evenings and at night. I remember one day some of us went to the village of Deir Sudan, where we were supposed to meet workers in a medical clinic that was run by the union. When we arrived in the village I was called over by the owner of the house in which the clinic was situated to sit with her because men were approaching the clinic. After I had sat with her for half an hour, drinking tea and coffee and chatting, I told her that I came here to meet with workers and not to socialize with her. I convinced her but nevertheless she did not leave my side for the whole visit. For the next two hours she was sitting next to me, listening to the conversation. Since then she has attended all our visits with the workers.

The majority of our visits to workers' homes used to create social and communications difficulties, and invariably every time I used to find an older woman who felt obliged not to leave me alone with the workers. Once I visited the village of Arura together with three male colleagues. On the way the car broke down. It was already late at night, and two of my colleagues decided to walk to the nearby village and get help or find another car to continue our journey. When they came back they told us that they had informed the villagers that they had a woman and her brother waiting in the car. It was not at all socially acceptable that a man and a woman should stay waiting alone in a car together. When the villagers finally arrived to help us, one of them turned out to be a friend of my brother. Of course, he immediately knew that our story was not true. But luckily he was a former union activist; he knew me from a struggle in one of the factories and was ready to play the game with us.

Once we had to go to the village of Qarawet Beni Zeit and I did not know any workers there. Luckily my father had many acquaintances there. So he joined in many of our visits and introduced us to some of the workers. They were usually very surprised when they saw my father helping and encouraging me in the election campaign. In 1982 he joined in distributing the pamphlets of the Unified Labour Group during an election campaign.

Many times I have felt that I have done the work of 100 men, or at least that the work that needs to be done every day is too much to cope with as one person! To be active in household work, in family work, and in union and factory work is usually at the cost of health and private life in general. I get up early in the morning to start with the housework and usually go to bed very late. My sister-in-law helps me a great deal. Concerning my husband I am very ambivalent. On the one hand he is very supportive and accepts my union work much more than traditional men would do. On the other hand he is not willing to share family and housework equally. When I leave housework undone because I just do not have the time he does not do it instead. This of course creates a lot of tension. But I am determined not give up my struggle to make him do his share of the household work. His help depends largely on the amount of work he has to do himself. My husband is an engineer, working in an agricultural office with a plant nursery attached, so his work is very seasonal and he assists me much more when there is less work. His main help is in taking care of the children. Until they were one year old I breastfed them. I used to take them to meetings and even to work with me. When they reached the age of one I brought them in the morning to one of the kindergartens of the Lijan al-Amal al-Nasai [Women's Work Committees]. At noon I or sometimes my husband would pick them up. In the afternoon my sister-in-law takes care of them. But however hard I try to fit everything in, I recognize that my activities are somehow at the cost of the children. They are constantly demanding more time to be spent with them. Even though I am usually very tired in the evenings, I try to sit with the children, to sing and play with them. But it never seems to be enough. My youngest son is two years old. Sometimes in the night he comes to my bed and wakens me just to embrace me.

'Security measures', sorrow and success

From the beginning of the Palestinian labour movement, union activists who are politically affiliated have been subjected to harassment, imprisonment and deportation. Labour offices have been raided and material has been confiscated. We women were not spared either. Our office in Ramallah was raided twice. During increased arrests of fellow unionists, women unionists ensured that the union movement could continue and their role became more important. When it became obvious that women unionists were taking over the role of the men, the Israeli harassment was extended to women as well. I myself was subjected to 'town arrest' in the period from 31 July 1987 until 30 January 1989. The period of my 'town arrest' was extended three times, preventing me from travelling. In May 1989 I was invited to an international union meeting in Sofia, but when I applied I was denied a *laissez-passer* by the civil administration and consequently was not able to go. In addition, like other women's labour, charitable, student and grassroot activists I was interrogated by the Israeli *muchabarat*. In 1990 I was twice held for interrogation. Such interrogations are potential sources of information for the occupation forces as well as means to intimidate and threaten the person under interrogation. I was asked which factories were on good terms with the unions, about our demands and deals with the employers and about our work in general. After the interrogations the Shin Bet [Israeli Secret Police] paid visits to various factories and to the Ramallah Chamber of Commerce to inquire about me and my work.

Despite the difficulties I like my work and would not stop it for anything. And despite the harsh conditions of the Intifada we have had successes, and these keep us going. Last year we gained a major success in the Silwana sweet factory in Ramallah. It was especially a victory for the women working there (65 of the 250 employees are women). They work as unskilled labour and therefore get very low wages. The Silwana employer argued like most other bosses that women were not worth investing in. They would leave the factory when they got married and all specialized training would have been in vain. According to this argument women produce less than men and therefore deserve lower wages. But this view was contradicted by the male workers, who confirmed that women actually produced the same amount as they. For a long time we had been fighting in the Silwana factory for workers' rights, such as sick leave, yearly holidays, maternity leave, and for equal work and equal pay. At the end of 1989 the employer was willing to agree to all our demands except the one for equal pay. His argument against equal pay was the above-mentioned and that even Europe and the United States had not reached equality in this matter. But the workers and the union stood firm and told Silwana that Palestine then would be the first country where equal pay for equal work would be implemented; they said they were willing to accept the whole package deal or nothing at all. At the end Silwana gave in and on 13 November 1989 we reached an agreement in all points. Our joy about this success was overshadowed when only a short while later our office was raided and the head of our union was arrested by the military and placed under administrative detention [i.e. imprisoned]. Because administrative detention is not seen by the civil administration as a punishment there are no charges and no trials, so we can only guess what he is being punished for. The connection with our successful agreement with Silwana factory is obvious.

Working women and women trade unionists during the Intifada

The Intifada helped to make the work of women trade unionists easier. At the same time the number of women in the unions increased. Their representation in the unions had been only 2 per cent prior to 1987, but it rose to more than 10 per cent during the Intifada years. For women to leave their houses and participate in Intifada activities became more and more acceptable. Women unionists were instrumental in setting up the popular committees that were organized during the first months of the Intifada and later made illegal by the Israeli authorities. Women trade unionists, like other women and student activists, had the skills to mobilize and organize people who had not participated in organized activities before. Women workers followed the call of the United Leadership [for Palestinians] to leave work in Israel in large numbers; they tried to set up their own agricultural or home economy projects in their home towns, villages and camps.[7] For women working in Palestinian factories in the West Bank and Gaza the situation worsened considerably during the Intifada. Factory output increased but did not result in an appropriate increase in the number of women workers. Women had to work more in order to produce more but their wages stayed the same, and the women did not get compensation for strike days and for travelling expenses. The devaluation of the Jordanian dinar has been an additional burden for women and their families.

At the same time the closures of schools and universities hit girls and women especially hard because education has been one of the main factors facilitating the change of women's status in Palestinian society.[8] Girls unable to continue their school or university education because of the closures have been married off by their families, even when hardly fifteen years old. Without a proper education they will have a more problematic status in their marriage and even less chance to find an adequate job. Women who were studying before have been forced to seek employment.

This is becoming more and more difficult to find because of the growing unemployment. The decrease in tourism has hit especially hard the cooperatives and small workshops which sold their products mainly to tourists. In one embroidery cooperative in the West Bank, where formerly five hundred women were employed, now only thirty women work; the rest are now unemployed. For women working in public and government institutions, who have remained largely unorganized because of Israeli 'security' regulations, conditions are worsening day by day. Unemployment is increasing, especially among women workers in the health and education sectors because of cutbacks and layoffs caused by Israeli 'security' measures.[9] Wages have been cut drastically due to the closures of schools and universities.

Despite the worsening economic situation women confront the army just like men, participating in demonstrations, sit-ins and everyday confrontations on the streets. In the demonstrations on 1 May 1990, five women were injured. With the continuation of the Intifada the role of women and of women unionists has become even more important. The trade union movement is trying to cope with the situation and to develop programmes to counter the negative effects of the Israeli oppression of the Intifada. To do this it proposed that the following steps should be taken:

1. Professional and technical training courses should be intensified to enable working women to improve their skills in sewing, maintenance, administration, marketing, computer science etc.
2. Courses in trade union affairs should be held to help working women to understand the working classes both locally and internationally.
3. Unions should work towards giving working women leading positions in the labour movement and guaranteeing their presence in all its institutions.
4. More production cooperatives should be developed to employ larger numbers of unemployed working-class women.

We women in the trade union movement will continue our struggle for political and social liberation and equality and for a peaceful life in an independent state of Palestine.

Notes

1. The voluntary work movement emerged in 1972 from a social–literary club in Jerusalem and Ramallah. It aimed to break the barrier between manual and

intellectual labour, promote the development of a collective consciousness, help the community and improve women's rights. In 1973 the founding group expanded its activities, an increasing number of volunteers joined, and new groups in Nablus, Hebron and Jericho emerged. When, after the municipal elections in 1976, the new 'nationalist' municipalities supported their work, the local military authorities clamped down on voluntary work activities and activists.

2. The Society for the Preservation of the Family, established in El-Bireh in 1965 and headed by Samiha Khalil.

3. *Statistical Abstracts of Israel*, 1989, No. 40, Table XXVII/24 'Employed Persons and Employees, by Occupation and Sex (Judea and Samaria)'. In 1988 women were employed as: scientific and academic workers, 620; other professional, technical and related workers, 4,120; clerical workers, 850; sales workers, 210; service workers, 1,120; agricultural workers, 14,660; skilled workers in industry, 2,130; unskilled labourers, 190. The total number of registered employed women was 23,900.

4. Official Israeli data estimate the number of Palestinian women (aged 14 and over) in the labour force in 1987 to be 22,300. 17,600 worked full-time; there were 2,700 part-time workers, 1,100 were temporarily absent from work and 900 were registered as unemployed (*Statistical Abstracts of Israel*, 1989, No. 40, Tables XXVII/2 and /3).

5. The distribution of Palestinian women in professional unions in West Bank and Gaza in 1985 was as follows:

Union	% of females	Number of female members	Total membership
Dentists	12.45	33	265
Pharmacists	22.92	80	349
Engineers	2.67	44	1,645
Agricultural engineers	7.89	33	418
Lawyers	6.27	32	502
Journalists	6.55	8	122
Medical doctors	8.06	137	1,698

(*The Palestinian Working Women take Defined Place in the Labour Union Movement in the State of Palestine*, The General Federation of Trade Unions 1989, Table 3).

6. One source estimates that by the end of 1980, union membership had increased by more than 400 per cent since 1968, bringing the total number of unionized workers to 12,926 (Ghassan Harb, 'Labour Unions in the West Bank and their Role in the Development of Steadfastness', *Proceedings of the Conference on Development for Steadfastness*, Jerusalem, Arab Thought Forum, 1982, p. 14 in Arabic).

7. '. . . let us begin creating all sorts of appropriate organizational forms, committees and units in every village and city, and in every camp, so that they will link every neighbourhood and street with the aim of paving the way towards total civil disobedience as a tremendous campaign of struggle. . . . Promote the national economy and locally made national products, activate the household economy, and monitor and reduce consumption, in support of the uprising and as a step towards finding substitutes for Israeli products, which must be

boycotted.' From Communique No. 6, 2 February 1988, translated in Zachary Lockman and Joel Beinin (eds.), *Intifada: the Palestinian uprising against Israeli occupation*, Boston, 1989, p. 334.

8. 303,000 school-age children and 18,000 university and college students were prevented from attending their classes and denied access to any form of formal education. The self-learning programme subsequently distributed by some of the schools was of the least help to girls of lower-class families, who need education most, because it relied in most cases on the help of parents. In addition, kindergartens which had catered for 13,800 children in the West Bank were closed for six months in 1988, affecting negatively the situation of working women in need of childcare. Working women either had to carry the burden of private organized childcare or cut back on their working hours (*Statistical Abstracts of Israel, 1989*, No. 40, Table XXVII/49).

9. 8,000 West Bank government schoolteachers were twice placed on mandatory unpaid leave by the military authorities in 1988. 1,200 teachers with annual contracts did not receive new contracts for the 1988/89 academic year; others have been forced into early retirement. Private schools have cut staff salaries between 20 and 50 per cent. (*Palestinian Education: a threat to Israel's security?*, Jerusalem, Jerusalem Media and Communication Centre, 1989).

8.   Life Between Palestine and Germany: Two Cultures, Two Lives

Faten Mukarker

My childhood in Germany

In 1956 my mother, my father, my four-year-old brother and I left our town, Beit Jala, in the West Bank, at that time under Jordanian rule, and headed towards Germany. My father had found work as a typographer for the Arabic edition of the international magazine *Skala*. At that time I was a little baby of four months, so later I remembered nothing of my short life in Palestine.

Only years later, when I was a woman myself, did my mother tell me about her life in Germany. Especially at the beginning it was very difficult for her. She found the German language completely alien and was not even able to go shopping on her own. My brother was sent to a kindergarten and within two months he learned the language so well that my mother took him with her when she went shopping. She told him *chubbes* and he asked for *Brot* (bread). She asked for *halib* and he asked for *Milch*. Wherever she went he was her translator. But she hardly went anywhere. She stayed at home, prepared the meals, cleaned the house and took care of us children. How could she have learned German under those conditions? She hardly had contact with other women who could have taught her at least the basic words. My mother never thought of participating in a language course. She was an Arab woman and therefore belonged in the house.

Unlike my mother I learned German like all the native children, in the kindergarten, in the neighbourhood and later at school. At home my mother spoke only Arabic, to which we responded in German. German was the language which flowed more easily from our tongues. We could understand almost everything she was telling us but could speak Arabic only a little.

When eventually my mother had learnt some German it became easier for her to make contacts. She got to know our neighbours, though at the beginning it was difficult and there were many cultural misunderstandings. When my mother felt sufficiently able to communicate in German she invited our neighbours like she used to in Beit Jala. Her first attempt failed and doors were virtually slammed in her face. Only when the whole block of flats had a washing day and my mother offered our women neighbours our balcony on which to dry their laundry was the ice broken. But she had to take the initiative. In Germany you have to take the initiative if you want to get to know people. Otherwise you live next door to each other but could be on another planet. Germans are suspicious and believe you want to bother them. Here in Palestine it is different and in this respect much more free. You invite somebody – 'Please pass by if you are in the area' – and people take the invitation seriously and come. If you say to a German, 'I have invited you so many times, why don't you come?' most of them are suspicious and try to find out what could be the reason for you inviting them.

My parents lived a very cut-off life in Germany. As an Arab woman my mother was not used to articulating her own demands. She had to take care of the household and behave as if she was not living thousands of miles away from Palestine. My experience is that Arab men consider their home to be an island of their own culture to which they return every evening like a traveller from overseas. To try to change the traditional environment at home means to challenge a whole concept of life.

Thus some Arab fathers are 'more pious than the Pope' when it comes to the traditional education of their daughters or to following the traditions. My father has lived in Germany for more than three decades. I do not see that there is a big difference between him and any other man from Beit Jala who never left the country. He might in some respects be a little more moderate than men of his age in Beit Jala, but things have changed in Palestinian society as well and the young men are much more open than my father. He grew up fifty years ago when the social taboos separated the sexes from each other almost completely. Men and women lived strictly separated, and personal freedom for girls was almost nonexistent. The man was everything. On top of this attitude my father was not willing to accept anything new because in his eyes everything Western was alien and bad. He had to protect his identity in a strange world and therefore he relied on centuries-old norms and values. The people in Beit Jala on the other hand could be open to new developments without necessarily endangering their identity. My father travelled with the experience of his childhood to Germany and closed himself up to almost everything new. In this respect I think he is more conservative than many Beit Jalis who never left the country.

My mother was not necessarily more open to new values, but she was ready to make compromises towards us children and help us when we took other than the old-fashioned path. In Germany when I came home after seven or eight in the evening my father would be furious. So, many times my mother covered up my lateness and told my father that I was already upstairs doing my homework. When I eventually returned she would open the back door and I could sneak into my room.

In my first year in school, I was the only foreigner in our class in Schwarzrheindorf, a small village close to Bonn. I think I was very much accepted. I was elected the class spokeswoman and later even as a school spokeswoman. I never had problems as a foreigner, maybe because there were only a few of us. Now, with sometimes more than 50 per cent foreign pupils in one class it is of course much more difficult.

My parents did not interfere in anything concerning my education. The German language and the German education system were strange and incomprehensible to them. I was totally responsible for my education and my parents had scarcely any idea what my school life was like. Sometimes that led to instructive encounters. Once when I was going on a trip with the ninth form to Berlin my father brought me to the station. The whole class was waiting there, and when we approached my schoolmates on the platform my father suddenly stopped and stared, astonished. 'But there are boys as well!' Immediately he wanted to take me back home. I asked him, 'Did you only now realize it? These are my classmates and we are going to travel to Berlin!' Then my teacher intervened and tried to explain to my father that girls and boys would sleep in separate houses. It took quite some effort to convince him to let me go. A few years later, when I was already in college I was walking with my father past the college. A boy on my course who was standing in the courtyard recognized me and said, 'Hello, Faten.' My father was embarrassed. 'Where does he know you from and how does he dare to address you like this on the street?' I did not know whether to cry or to laugh because I was already seventeen years old. But I had to take my father's reaction seriously because it was up to him whether I left the house or not. He could lock me in if he wished to.

This difference between my life and the life of my German girlfriends was one reason why later I chose to live in the home town of my parents, in Beit Jala in the West Bank. At school I was fairly independent of my family's traditions. But I wanted to go to the disco, the cinema, to birthday parties and to the swimming pool. Our school organized a youth-disco, but I was not allowed to go there though that does not mean that I did not go. In fact, my whole life developed into a kind of hide-and-seek. Officially, when school was over I was only allowed to go straight back home, and I was sometimes not even allowed to go to the birthday parties of my girlfriends. I well remember that I was once invited to a party by my girlfriend. My father wanted to pick me up afterwards. When I heard his car in the yard I hid myself. He must not find out that boys were invited as well. My girlfriend told him that I had left already and off he went again. And of course I was not supposed to invite boys to our home.

These restrictions were not connected with my age. In Germany you can reach an age at which things that were prohibited before are allowed. But according to Arab customs, for certain kinds of freedom women never reach the appropriate age. A girl aged from six to seven years onwards is treated like a woman. When I had my own children I remembered my suffering and tried to support my daughter. When she reached the critical age of six, she was not allowed to move her body like she wanted to. My husband exhorted her always to sit decently. From the age of five until she grows old, a female human being is a 'woman'. This was my situation in Germany. There was no possibility of waiting until I reached a certain age at which I would be free to decide myself. Approaching the age of twenty, I was as dependent and limited in my actions as a small girl.

As far back as I can remember, I was always taught that a girl's honour is the most important matter in the world. My father told me, 'The honour of a girl is like a piece of glass. If it is broken you will never be able to glue it together again.' I was obliged to think always of Beit Jala and the fact that my father had to be able to hold his head high walking through the streets of the town. If I behaved dishonourably in Germany my family would never be able to live in Beit Jala again. I had to understand that my personal honour and that of my family were directly linked with a town 4,000 miles away on the other side of the Mediterranean.

My father had always told me, 'Don't ever think that I will let you marry a German.' In his opinion German men were not husbands for a lifetime. Too many German couples got divorced, whereas I was supposed to marry for a lifetime. I had my own ideas about this. I was sure that my husband could never be an Arab. If the discussion got round to the topic of marriage and my parents insisted that I marry an Arab I threatened suicide.

I finished school and started training to become a medical assistant. But I was not happy with that because my dream was to obtain a university education. Then, on top of all my inner turmoil about what to do and how to narrow the cultural gap between my home and the society around me, my father decided to drive to Beit Jala on summer vacation. And of course I had to go with the rest of the family. Since my early childhood, every second year we had made for six weeks the long journey to the Middle East. My parents visited their families and for them it was always a special occasion. Not so much for me. I considered these visits to be terrible. There was always more stress, restraint and fuss than in everyday life in Germany.

When I had been in Beit Jala two years before, in 1972, the first thing I had been obliged to do was to lengthen my skirts. And even after all the sewing, according to the customs of Beit Jala they were still not long enough. One incident is carved into my memory. My father went with me and my uncle to visit some relatives in the town. I was wearing a skirt which was already much longer than it had been before our arrival. When my uncle saw my outfit he turned to my father and said, 'I am not willing to cross the streets with your daughter in a skirt like this. She has to go home and change.' My father obeyed and sent me back home. But I refused to change. I asked my father bitterly, 'Why am I allowed to wear this skirt in Germany and you never complain, and here I am supposed to change it?' My father answered, 'We are not in Germany and I have been living abroad for too long. My brothers know better how to behave in town and so they have to decide.'

Another time I wanted to visit a girlfriend in Beit Jala and my father gave me permission to go. When I was just about to leave, I bumped into my father and my uncle in the yard (whenever we went on holidays to Palestine we stayed in the house of my grandparents and all the bachelor brothers of my father). When my uncle saw me leaving he stepped into my path and forbade me to go. I answered him furiously, 'My father allowed me to go. Mind your own business.' Then he started hitting me, while my father watched without moving a finger to help me. I shouted at him, 'But you are my father.' He answered, 'I can't do anything. I have nothing to say in this house. We don't live here. If I give you permission, when we leave afterwards to go back home, your uncles are left with the gossip. While we are here we have to obey my family and respect their opinions.'

All these experiences did not help to make me feel comfortable in Beit Jala or to come willingly. We never came as tourists. We never went on any sightseeing tours or outings to the shores of the Mediterranean; once we had arrived we stayed at the same spot. For my parents it was a wonderful time, for me a difficult one. I would rather have travelled to England or France, and the most interesting part of the whole trip for me was the journey from Germany to the Middle East and back. All these experiences only strengthened my determination never to marry an Arab. The idea of being tied to a man who would prohibit most of my activities like the men in my family did made me sick.

Marriage and a new identity

Thus, in the summer of the year of my nineteenth birthday we travelled again for the usual six weeks in Beit Jala. A few days after our arrival we were invited by relatives to a baptism. I did not want to go, but my mother insisted. She argued that I had to learn to know my relatives and I obeyed. When we came back home later, my mother disclosed to me that the same evening a potential suitor would visit us. Caught by surprise I asked her, 'Who is coming?' and she answered, 'A young man saw you in church during the baptism.' This was a shock. Spontaneously I said 'By no means can he come, and I am not going to marry an Arab anyway. And no way am I going to marry somebody I don't even know, who didn't even speak with me.' My mother replied, 'The customs prohibit you from rejecting a potential suitor in advance. Let him come, have a closer look at him and if you don't like him you are free to say no.'

I thought the whole subject over and secretly said to myself, 'I can risk it, forget about my boredom and have fun.' There was not much else I could do. But deep inside I was determined to reject his offer. During the rest of the day only one thought was in my head: what kind of man could he be if he could court a woman after only a first glance. I was trying to work out who he could have been in the sea of faces I had seen during the baptism. All of them were unknown to me and it was difficult to recall them. I tried to remember any man who could have given me some hint, some sign to attract my attention, who could have smiled, waved or winked. But none of the faces were special. Then I became furious. Why didn't he try in church to chat with me? He had said not even one 'Hello, how are you?' I was puzzled.

In the evening the anxiously expected visitor came. He arrived with his mother, grandmother and uncle at the house of my grandparents. He took a seat next to me and we started talking with each other. What happened then was something like love at first sight. Inside I was in turmoil; there were so many arguments against him, I had been so furious in the afternoon, but suddenly my rage was gone. He appeared to be nice, and, as we talked he became nicer and nicer. We spoke about religion and politics. What helped to make him even more sympathetic in my eyes were seemingly unimportant details – like that he had studied for three years in Sweden, and that he liked mayonnaise. Not one other Arab I knew had heard of mayonnaise. And he knew and liked many pop stars and singers whom I idolized at that time.

Suddenly things started changing inside me. If I ever thought of marrying an Arab it should be someone who had left the country at least once, so that he knew what I was talking about. And I enjoyed chatting with my suitor more and more.

The next day I was expected to give an answer. I was stunned! How could somebody expect me to decide on a husband after only one date? I was not won so easily and asked for a second chance. Again his whole family came with him. My grandparents' house contained only one large room and a kitchen, so our intimate date took place under the watchful eyes of both our families. Even if we had tried hard to achieve some measure of closeness by means of talking we could not learn to know each other under so many watchful eyes.

Despite the difficult circumstances we liked each other more and more. After our second date I knew certainly I was expected to give an answer. I was trapped. My parents, who had seen me smiling and obviously happy, were already certain. They tried to convince me. 'He is a good man. He has a lot of land and dunums of olive trees.' This was a symbol of wealth. 'And he comes from a good family. You are already twenty years old. Who knows when you will next come back to this country. The older you get, the worse a husband you have to expect.' Then my father turned to my mother and complained, 'I can't take her back to Germany. It would be irresponsible to travel with a nineteen-year-old girl to Germany. Until now I could take care of her, but who knows how much longer I will be able to do so.'

For the past month I had been trying to think myself and my future prospects through. I was confronted with a single choice: either to marry here, or to leave home as soon as I returned to Germany. I could not go on living like this. Under the pressure of this choice I asked for a third meeting. This was too much for his family. Enraged, they asked, 'Are we not good enough for her? Are we to come three times? When is she going to decide?' Only because I was considered a foreigner was I given the privilege of a third date. Already the opposition to me was growing in the other family. I had grown up in Germany and was therefore in their eyes irresponsible. Only a short while previously the brother of my suitor had obtained a divorce from his Swedish wife. They had separated after fifteen years of marriage. The reaction of his family when they heard about their younger son's choice of wife was 'Not a foreign woman again.'

By the time the third date was over I was definitely in love. But I was still not willing to get married and live in Beit Jala. I wanted to learn to know my suitor better and the only way to do that was to get engaged. Even once engaged it was still possible to say no to marriage if I decided against him, and I thought it would be easy to find an excuse shortly before our departure.

After we became engaged we were able to see each other every day and had the chance to be alone. We sat on the balcony and talked. I explained to him my conditions: 'I want to visit my parents once a year.' He agreed. 'I want to work.' He nodded, and he agreed as well on all the other preconditions I set. In reality things turned out different, but that was because of the circumstances, because we did not have the money for a flight, or because my written Arabic was not good enough to get me a job.

After our chats I started to compare my life in Germany with Beit Jala. In Beit Jala suddenly I had a place in life, a position in society. Most girls get married sooner or later and if you compare life in Palestine and life in Europe from the point of view of a married woman things look different. In both societies you have to take care of the household and the children, you have to get up early in the morning, to clean the house and to work as a housewife if you do not work outside the house. If I got married here I would be somebody, I would have a social position and status, and my future husband seemed very nice. There was no way back to my old life in Germany anyhow. To live my life according to my wishes and hopes would have led to a split with my family. How long could I have been happy under those circumstances? And if I had thought about living a free life without my family, why had I not done it before? Wasn't it better to live in an unfree country with more freedom than average than to live in a free country unfree?

There was not much time for consideration, only the one week of the engagement. Everything happened so quickly, at breathtaking speed. Only years later did I recognize that I had had to make one of the most important decisions of my life under such pressure from outside.

There was barely time for the wedding preparations because my parents were about to leave to travel back to Germany. Palestinian custom does not permit the couple to see each other in the week before the wedding. But because we had only got engaged a week before, the time during which we were not allowed to see each other was reduced to the last two days before the wedding. There was so much work to be done anyway. According to tradition a woman has to bring tablecloths and bedcovers as part of her marriage dowry. All these things and my wedding dresses I had to buy, on top of all the bedroom furniture. All wedding expenses are paid by the future husband. After these wedding preparations were finished, my fiancé and I went to buy gold and make-up. I had a disagreement with my mother-in-law, who wanted to buy the biggest rings and necklaces instead of nice small ones, but I gave in. For Muslims this gold is part of the *mahr*, the bride price, but Christians follow this custom as well.

Time was flying and my wedding day was close. All the questions an Arab woman usually asks her fiancé before the marriage, like: Where and with whom are we going to live? What are you going to buy me as wedding presents? How do you plan our life? I forgot to ask them! I was caught up in a dream I had no influence on.

On the last day before the wedding both our families had a big party in the house of the groom. There was Arab music and the man with the *tableh* [small drum] set the rhythm. The older women started dancing and pulled the young girls into the centre of the impromptu dance floor. According to their different characters they shyly moved their hips just twice and sat down again or performed virtually a *Thousand and One Nights* belly dance. One performance followed another; each time another dancer took over the place in the centre, surrounded by the rest of the women. Men were present only in the distance. They glanced at us from afar as interested spectators. It is an unwritten rule that men and women celebrate separately.

The next morning I got married in the church of Beit Jala. We had two witnesses to the marriage, the man was chosen by the family of my husband, the woman by my parents. Just married, we drove off for three days' honeymoon in Ramallah, a town ten miles north of Jersualem. These days flew by like all the days before and still I could not catch my breath. Back home in Beit Jala our two families welcomed us with a huge dinner and a parade of relatives bearing presents. Most of them gave us money. It was a strange ceremony I had never seen before. My mother stood next to me with a huge shawl around her neck, its two ends crossed in front of her forming something like a cotton basket. One by one our guests stepped in front of my husband and me. They lifted the hands holding the money, touched first the forehead of my husband, then moved to mine and at the very end dropped the money into my mother's shawl.

The next day we celebrated *imbarakeh*, the congratulation ceremony. The parents of the bride come and offer the newly-weds fruits, sweets, and a whole sack of nuts and congratulate the groom. Nuts served in huge bowls are offered as well to the wedding guests. The leftovers are supposed to be thrown onto the floor as a sign of happiness. All the female wedding guests are presented with a little sack of nuts, handed to them with the sentence, 'We hope there will be a wedding in your house soon as well.'

After so much celebration and the beginning of a completely new life, I needed some time for myself to think everything over, but still there was none yet. I moved into the house of my husband's family and started living together with his mother, his two brothers and one sister-in-law. The whole first week I was not allowed to see my parents. After seven days my parents invited my parents-in-law to the traditional farewell dinner for me. As a sign of mourning I wore a black dress. The farewell from my parents was final. As if to underline it the next morning they left for Germany. I stood in the middle of the street, waving and following the departing car with my eyes until it disappeared behind a block of houses. I imagined myself running, following the car, while in reality I stood motionless on the street. Suddenly everything seemed unreal. Why was I not sitting in the car like so many times before, driving back home? The man next to me was a stranger. I was married to him, but did it make a difference? I had known him less than two weeks. This country seemed strange to me even if I had been born here twenty years before. The same was true of my numerous relatives, whose language I could understand but hardly speak. I could not even communicate without problems with my husband. I felt empty and at the same time burdened with a responsibility which seemed too much to bear. Turning around silently I walked back to the house.

Starting a new life – cultural brainwashing and metamorphosis

The first days without my parents were difficult. I started to compare my life in the West Bank with the life I was used to. In Germany the table was set carefully with a lot of little decorative things. Here everything was just thrown onto the tablecloth. In Germany everybody knocked at the door first before entering one's room, now all the family members just burst into my privacy. All these differences piled up within a few days to make a burden which was too much to bear. I could not go on any longer. I told myself that I had chosen to live here, therefore there was only one way left. I closed the window shutters. In the dark I began brainwashing myself. 'You are born again today. There is no connection to the past. From now on your daily experiences and the people here will be your basis of life. Germany does not exist any more.' To live thus became a matter of survival.

From my 'brainwashing' onwards I led a double life. I behaved as much in line with the demands of my family and Palestinian culture as I could, I became brave, nice and obedient. This metamorphosis oppressed my own personality. I was wearing a mask on my face which slowly became a second skin, part of myself. Even if deep inside I knew that in reality I was different, I performed a role which my new family believed to be the real me. And all my frustration and sadness was buried deep inside so as not to be shown on the outside.

To keep up this image I never asked my new family to leave me some privacy and never locked the door of my room. To do so would have been to accuse them of potential robbery. And I accepted without complaint that my mother-in-law woke my husband with a cup of coffee. For six years, every morning when I opened my eyes I heard the voice of my mother-in-law next to me, found her sitting on the edge of the bed at my husband's side and talking over with him the affairs of the coming day. There was never any privacy for us. During the day it would have been improper to be in the bedroom together. In the evening the whole family gathered in front of the TV and to excuse ourselves before them would have been improper behaviour too. All those years I dreamed that one day my husband would wake me up, take me in his arms and kiss me good morning. There was no way to explain to him or his mother how I felt. I knew that she thought she was doing us a favour in offering us morning tea.

Similar problems occurred in the kitchen. Together with my mother-in-law every day I had to prepare one of the time-consuming Arab meals, even if I, left to myself, would at least once in a while have cooked something easy. Constantly under pressure lest I do something wrong, I never learned how to cook properly.

The education of my children became a problem too in the extended family household. I hardly had any influence on them. Everybody in the house was educating them their way. Therefore my plans to bring them up with German as their second language failed. I was ashamed to speak German in front of my family and when we finally had our own flat it was too late; my German was rusty and they were used to Arabic.

In the first year of our marriage we started building our own flat on top of the first floor of the home of my parents-in-law. The more the end of construction was delayed, the more I suffered. After six years finally we moved into our own flat. And a lot of problems caused by the closeness and permanent social control of the extended family household vanished as if they had never existed. Suddenly I was able to cook properly and could compromise with my husband about the kind of meals we ate. I had more control over my children and, at last, some privacy. There was a door which could be closed and only opened from the inside.

The first year of my self-imposed brainwashing was very hard. I tried to push Germany out of my mind. After I had given birth to my first child my parents invited me to come to visit them. But before I could travel I got pregnant again and so luckily had an excuse for not being able to make the long journey. I was afraid that if I met my old friends in Germany again, I might decide not to come back to Beit Jala. Because of this fear I kept finding excuses and postponed the trip to Germany for more than ten years. Finally I went and it was a shock for me. I visited my girlfriends and found them involved in married and family life. Their former independence was gone and they were involved in the same household responsibilities, the same everyday rhythm of children, school, cooking, shopping, cleaning and supervision of homework that I was. And on top of that most of them worked. I recognized that in some respects I even had more freedom than they, more support from my family, was more closely integrated into a caring social fabric than they. Now I really had the choice of going back or staying. There was no way my husband, being thousands of miles away, could impose on me his will to have me back. But suddenly I started looking forward to going back home to Beit Jala and I did soon fly back. When I was home again in our flat and both of us were sitting close to each other on the sofa I told him, 'For the first time I feel that this is the place where I belong. For the first time I have really come back home.'

This feeling changed my life radically. I felt independent, self-assured, I started going out, participated in the activities of the Lutheran church in Jerusalem and got to know German women I could speak their and my language with. Now after so many years I was happy that my parents had educated me according to the norms of Palestinian society. If I had grown up with European norms I would never have been able to cope with the first six years and keep on living in the West Bank.

When I visited Germany a few years ago I became aware of how much I had internalized the norms and values of Palestinian society. As I saw young women walking hand in hand with their boyfriends, I was unable to put myself into their position. When we went swimming and a woman next to me sat topless in the sun, I felt embarrassed. How could people kiss openly in the streets, when kissing was something very private. I was unable to understand behaviour I had found absolutely normal ten years before and even desired for myself. This was a sign that I had already made a choice. I would not now be able to go back to Germany, even though I still believe it was a blessing to be able to live in two cultures and to try to take the best out of both. One aspect of European culture that I admire a lot is the democratic way of dealing with children. I try to educate my children as far as possible in this spirit, to teach them to build on their own opinions, decide for themselves, bear responsibility and offer a helping hand in the household – boys or girls alike. That my boys have to help in household work is very unusual in male-oriented Palestinian society and consequently I meet a lot of resistance from my relatives. My sons are teased by their uncles. 'Psurra, psurra' they say, 'quick quick, your mother is calling, she needs a helping hand to do the washing-up or to make the beds.' My sons are of course furious, but they know that I am not willing to compromise on this matter. They are responsible for their rooms like the girls. I do not want to raise husbands for my future daughters-in-law who are as uninterested in helping in the household as my husband.

In Germany I learned that wives are equally able to act according to their own beliefs about child education and matters of daily life as men. This is normally not the case in Palestinian society, where a wife is responsible for the household and the child-rearing and a husband for work and the upkeep of the family. But because I kept pushing for my rights in this respect we take a lot of decisions together.

In the eyes of a woman from a Western culture Arab societies might seem very close-knit and restrictive of women. But they have a lot of positive aspects which are substituted in Western societies by social welfare systems. Family ties are very important and are relied upon. You are never on your own but consequently never lonesome. When a family member gets sick, there is always somebody to take care and to cheer the invalid up. Last year I was immobilized as the result of a foot operation and was confined to my bed for more than two weeks. My family hardly felt my absence in the household because my relatives took over my work. When there are problems between husband and wife, the wife can turn to the older male members of the family for help and her husband will usually not turn their advice down.

I try especially hard to pass on my experience of living between two cultures to my daughter. I am afraid that she will marry at the age of sixteen. According to the norms of our society a woman is not supposed to refuse too many suitors. If she is favoured by a lot of men, it will be difficult to let her finish school and study. Apart from that I want to give her all the freedom she can have in this society. It will be less than in Germany but she is probably going to live here, so she has to learn to live in accordance with the rules of this society.

Occupation and Intifada

The main difference between Germany and Palestine is life under occupation. For the first two years of my marriage I did not move outside our small town, so I did not feel the depressing atmosphere that much. The cities were not so much under military observation and affected by army raids as the villages and refugee camps. I hardly saw soldiers in the streets. Jerusalem was the only place where I stood eye to eye with soldiers controlling Palestinians who walked into the old city. I always felt a cold rush going down my spine and was afraid that one of their Uzi submachine-guns would go off. Then, in the early 1980s, paying the taxes for our sewing workshop became virtually impossible. The occupation authorities increased taxes whenever they wanted to and my husband got more and more desperate. Then one day in 1982 strangers in civilian clothes knocked at our door, entered without being invited and started turning the contents of all the drawers in the house upside down, searching for tax papers. They arrested my husband and took him with them to prison. They set a date by which I had to bring the exact amount of money they asked for, otherwise my husband would stay in jail. I was almost hysterical, and spent a whole day borrowing money from all our relatives until I had gathered the amount together. Immediately I took my children with me, went to the jail and waited until my husband was released. From that day on I could not ignore the occupation. It had become reality and it would reach me even if I wanted to escape it. From now on I followed the daily news carefully, listening to the reports from Lebanon and the Occupied Territories.

My second key experience was in 1983 when one of our relatives, who had been working for a long time in Saudi Arabia, came back home and invested all his money in a furniture shop on the Jerusalem–Hebron road. One night only a short while after his successful start as a merchant, the army came in the night to his house and arrested him. It turned out later that the night before, fedayin had used his flat roof to fire from onto patrolling soldiers. He was accused of having opened the door to them. For one full week we did not hear from him. Then suddenly he stood outside our door, his arms swollen and his body dotted with cigarette burns. He did not answer a single word to our questions about what had happened. The next day he went to the military government and applied for a *laissez-passer*.[1] 'I am unable to live in such a country,' he said. One month later he left with his family to Peru, where he was shot by robbers just a few months ago. His family, who applied at the Israeli embassy in Peru for entrance papers to be able to travel back home to the West Bank were denied the necessary documents. They were told by embassy personnel, 'Peru is much more beautiful than Israel, you should stay here.'

The Intifada changed our lives in a lot of different ways. My children were without school for a long time.[2] It is exhausting to have children at home all day. I tried quite unsuccessfully to teach them, but because nobody else was having regular lessons they later refused even to open their school bags.

Popular teaching classes were organized by women's groups and neighbourhood committees. In some areas they were successful, in others not. When the popular committees were made illegal in mid-1988 a lot of them, ours as well, stopped. The teachers were afraid. We had to stand by and watch the basic school knowledge of our children go down the drain. The greatest effect was on the very small ones in the first three and four years of primary school. I could see it happening in front of my eyes to my youngest son, who had just finished his first year. After one year without school, he had forgotten almost everything he had learnt in the first year.

The constant fear of army raids is a second factor which makes our lives more difficult. The soldiers come during the night when everybody is fast asleep; they knock at our doors and call the men out of their beds to paint out the new slogans on the walls. With soldiers pointing guns at their backs, the men cover the slogans either with paint or with dirt from the streets. We have to be very careful about the colours of the material we have in our sewing workshop. Whenever packs of green, red, black and white cotton, the colours of the Palestinian flag, are found next to each other, even accidentally, people can be jailed.

The Intifada has in some ways changed the distribution of work between the sexes. I would not dare send my boys shopping; even at night, when usually women would stay at home. I would rather send my daughter than one of my sons. Girls and women are still harassed less by the army.

After my experience with the army and the arrest of my husband, I looked for a way to become active. One day I discovered that opposite the house of my parents, a women's group met regularly in the Orthodox club. It was ideal for me. I could leave the little ones with my mother and participate in the group. We meet once a week, organize lectures, courses and visits, collect schoolbooks, clothes and household equipment for poor families and have discussion groups. Fashion, festivals and parties play no part in our activities since the beginning of the Intifada. There are no wedding parties any more and no big social events. One of my friends remarked, 'Nowadays weddings and funerals can only be differentiated because the coffee at weddings is sweet and at funerals it is bitter like death.'

Through the committee I came into contact with more women, and learned to know their problems, which were astonishingly similar to mine. I became more self-confident and active and could breathe more freely. It was as if in leaving my home I had left a prison, a prison that I myself had set up. We discussed politics and I learned to understand more about political developments. The women were much more politicized than my family and put aside other topics of less interest for politics.

Soon the women's groups became something like a task for a lifetime. All of us have become more active and self-confident during the Intifada. We organize solidarity visits to families of martyrs or people who have family members in jail, detained or injured. At the moment we knit pullovers for the detainees, because in the winter it becomes icy cold in the desert. Through our work, we have learnt that women can only join forces and work in their own interest in women's organizations. As individual women we are too weak, only together are we strong. I hope that one day I will live in a Palestinian state, a state where men and women of all the different religions live in equality and in peace with each other.

Notes

1. Palestinians from the officially annexed eastern part of Jerusalem have to apply for this permit to leave the country through an Israeli airport or harbour, at the Ministry of Interior. Palestinian inhabitants of the Occupied Territories have to fill out their application in the military government building.

2. After several short term closures and army occupations of the schools in the West Bank, they were finally closed on 4 February 1988 by order of the Israeli defence ministry. The closure affected all 1,194 primary and secondary schools, including all the private and government schools, all UNRWA schools, colleges and the six universities of the West Bank. Consequently 300,000 pupils and 18,000 students were without education. In mid-July 1989 the schools were reopened following growing international pressure, only to close by the end of November 1989 for two months of 'holidays'. The universities are still closed. (Briefing paper, September 1989, No. 1, Public Relations Office, University of Birzeit).

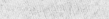

Part Two
Women in the Intifada

Introduction

The Palestinian Intifada is not a transitory phenomenon but the acceleration of an ongoing process of resistance against Israeli hegemony. By means of collective action Palestinians in the West Bank, Gaza Strip and East Jerusalem – women, men and children alike – practise 'politics by other means' to achieve an end to the Israeli occupation. The Intifada is a Palestinian answer to Israeli military colonial policy in the Occupied Territories and its character has been shaped by twenty years of resistance.

> By creating a web of 'popular sovereignties – institutions, social relations, and ideology in response to Israeli colonial oppression – the Palestinian natives wove an opposition 'fabric of hegemony' through which collective action could be mobilised and sustained and Palestinian society could be restructured and preserved in the face of Israeli colonialism. But having won the war of position in a long and difficult struggle, the Palestinians were prepared to initiate a new strategy – 'the war of maneuver' – an uprising that needed only a precipitous trigger.[1]

This precipitous trigger was pulled in December 1987 in Jabalya refugee camp, in the Gaza Strip.

Life in the refugee camps of the Gaza Strip had for twenty years been marked by a constant chain of local uprisings against the occupation. Confrontations and clashes with soldiers from the Israeli army posts, which were sited permanently at refugee camp and UNRWA school entrances, were a daily occurrence in most of the refugee camps of the Gaza Strip. The pressures of existence were increased by the extremely bad living conditions of the population. The camps resemble townships. Their population density is that of towns, but they lack the attributes of civic life, such as infrastructure, social services and employment opportunities. The youth especially is hard hit. Hundreds of young people, unemployed and with few prospects for the future, spend their time in coffee shops and on the streets. There are no facilities for community life. Through the sheer lack of other opportunities for meetings, the mosque is the focal point of community action. Many families depend more or less on UNRWA's social welfare. Housing conditions in the Gaza camps are the worst in the entire Occupied Territories.

Thus it was that the initial spark that ignited the Intifada came out of a Gaza refugee camp. Jabalya was later renamed by its inhabitants *Mu'askar al-thawra*, camp of the revolution. Things began when three men from Jabalya died in a car crash with an Israeli army tank. Their funeral the same night turned into a huge demonstration. Like a bush fire, the following day Jabalya's demonstration set ablaze the whole of the Gaza Strip. The upheaval, centred on the refugee camps, brought tens of thousands onto the streets waving flags, carrying symbolic coffins, closing camp entrances with stone barricades and shouting nationalist slogans. 'We want a state, we want an identity,' was heard all over the Strip. But this time the uprising did not cease after a few hours and days. It continued, and spread within days to the camps of the West Bank; within weeks the whole of the Occupied Territories were burning.[2] From January 1988 onwards the spontaneous and massive resistance of the population was channelled and structured by a clandestine United Leadership of the Uprising (UNLU). In its Communiqué No. 2 of 13 January 1988, the UNLU referred to the initial role the people of the refugee camps played in initiating the Intifada by enumerating them: 'In escalation of our people's glorious uprising . . . we promote the revolutionary epics written by the sons of Jabalya, Balata, al-Bureij, Kalandia, al-Am'ari, Rafah, Khan Yunis, Al-Shati', Tulkarem, and all the camps, towns and villages of Palestine.'[3]

The Gaza Strip differs markedly from the West Bank in its isolation, which enables the Israeli military to clamp down on the population more easily. Consequently there is much higher pressure on Gazans, especially on the inhabitants of the overcrowded refugee camps. The imposition of the lengthy curfews became a characteristic Israeli measure against the camps, and they were enforced very strictly. 'People in the refugee camps in Gaza are really tough, they suffer most,' West Bankers often admit. In order to counter Israeli hegemony and limit its influence on Gaza society a 'culture of refusal' had emerged during the twenty years of Israeli occupation and conservatism increased in the Strip. Women were seen as preservers of the Palestinian heritage. 'The fear of loss of control over the female sector, of sexual revolution, of emancipation on the Israeli model (with mini-skirts and pre-marital sexual relationships falsely equated with "emancipation") have added new dimensions to the "women Problem"', Rosemary Sayigh observed in 1980.[4] The traditional Palestinian family structure was one of the few institutions that survived the dislocation of occupation; consequently, women were increasingly confined to the home and their honour had to be guarded carefully. But pure economic necessity forced more and more women to look for work. Women in the Gaza Strip increasingly had to walk the tightrope of leaving the house for work whilst avoiding risking their family's reputation.

Pressure on women has increased during the Intifada. Whilst women's sphere of action increased through their active participation in community action, their workload grew as well, because of the extreme living conditions. Israel's indiscriminatory mass arrests, the massive use of tear gas and increasingly violent military action put additional psychological pressures on women, who fear for their husbands as well as for their children. Whilst women's important role in community action during the Intifada has to some extent had a liberating effect, more and more people retreat from depressing political reality into Islamic fundamentalism. The Muslim fundamentalists in Gaza, namely the Islamic Resistance Movement or Hammas, started a vicious campaign to impose the *hijab* (headscarf) on women. As a result of constant threats and violent attacks, by December 1988 even the most courageous activists of the leftist women's committees did not dare to move in Gaza without their heads covered. The UNLU waited more than a year before criticizing the *hijab* campaign in its Bayan [communiqué] No. 43 – with limited success.[5, 6] The pressure on women to wear the *hijab* does not necessarily restrict them in their ability to move and be active. But the campaign was a crucial test of priorities for the UNLU and it showed that women's rights are still secondary, despite propaganda to the contrary.

I met Iman Jardallah from Bureij camp in the Gaza Strip in a discussion initiated by one of the leftist women's committees in the West Bank. Approximately thirty young women from West Bank and Gaza were talking about sensitive issues such as: What should a Palestinian state be like? What is democracy? What attributes would your ideal husband have if you could choose yourself? The concept of choice turned out to be difficult to grasp, particularly for women from Gaza, whose lives are very much dominated by social expectations and the pressures of Israeli occupation. The discussants nevertheless found that women's ability to make their own decisions had increased from the generation of their mothers to their own. None of their mothers would have travelled unaccompanied the long and unsafe journey by taxi and bus from Gaza to Jerusalem to attend a mixed meeting in a secular political women's commitee, but all the young women present evidently had. The change that has taken place in women's lives in Gaza during the last twenty years is evident in the story of Iman and her mother told in Chapter 9, even if the lives of both are dominated by their fight for survival under Israeli occupation.

Villages like Kufr Malik are spread throughout the West Bank. Hidden in the valleys of the central mountains their desert beige houses are hard to distinguish from the surrounding stone-dotted mountain slopes. By mid-

December 1987, the uprising had already spread from camps and villages in Gaza to a few villages in the West Bank. Israeli's military countered the uprising by isolating areas of 'riots' and by a policy of 'more of the same, but much more',[7] that is, a dramatic increase in repressive measures. The villagers reacted by forming popular committees for the supply of food, which provided supplies for the besieged camps in their vicinity. In the following weeks a specialized underground network emerged, mainly composed of the new generation of politicized village youth, which had recently emerged to threaten the hegemony of the traditional village elders. Popular committees were organized out of pure necessity. The *shebab* of the guard committees erected stone barricades on the streets leading to their villages to prevent the army from moving around freely and from entering. The local *shebab* also raised Palestinian flags over areas declared 'liberated zones'.

The Israeli Defence Minister, Itzhak Rabin, reacted by declaring an 'economic war' against the uprising. In spring 1988, electricity and water supplies and telecommunications were cut off in a lot of villages. The villagers, who in large numbers had neglected their farmland in the previous twenty years in favour of wage labour in Israel, returned to the land. Popular committees for agriculture were formed, which coordinated with the agricultural relief committees in the towns for seeds, fertilizer and know-how. Village women, who previously had relied on highly processed Israeli-made or imported food and who had forgotten traditional ways of food preservation, contacted the women's committees for help. The agricultural relief committees and the women's committees distributed seedlings, and leaflets giving planting and food preservation instructions, and organized lectures.

During this massive clampdown on the West Bank population not even the remotest villages were left out. But the internal information network was functioning better and better, and villages that previously scarcely anyone even in the Occupied Territories had ever heard of became famous overnight. The village of Beita, for example, became a symbol of resistance against the provocation by settlers after, in April 1988, a Jewish settler from Elon Moreh shot and killed two Palestinians from Beita and a girl member of his own group. The reaction of the army was a clampdown on Beita: fourteen houses were demolished, more than one hundred olive trees were uprooted, six Beita residents were deported to Lebanon and hundreds of others were arrested for interrogation.

When Jordan cut its legal and administrative ties with the West Bank on 31 July 1988, thus finally terminating the option that the West Bank might be integrated into Jordan, Israel reacted by declaring a 'new strategy'. Through a systematic military campaign, 'combing' through besieged localities, the uprising was finally to be quelled. A comprehensive field study on a sample of eight villages later estimated that the total financial losses of villages hit by the army raids were US$7 million.[8] The raids almost always followed a certain pattern, especially targeting remote villages, that had declared themselves to be 'liberated zones'. A curfew would be imposed, and electricity and water supplies would be cut, while the Israeli army searched houses for suspected activists.

The clampdown on the villages reached its climax when the PLO at the Palestine National Council meeting in Algiers declared the establishment of the Palestinian state on 15 November 1988. A curfew was imposed on the entire Gaza Strip and thirty-one areas in the West Bank, imprisoning more than 1 million people in their homes.[9] Whilst the curfew in the cities was soon lifted, people in villages and camps continued to be imprisoned in their homes. In Chapter 10 Suha 'Adi reports on the fifty-three days her village, Kufr Malik, spent under curfew following the Palestine National Council meeting in Algiers. She represents the new active female members of the emerging community leaderships of the Intifada. Despite her relatively young age and her difficult status as an unmarried woman, she is trusted by the village community and people turn to her for help and advice. When one of the agricultural relief committees in Jerusalem sought someone in Kufr Malik to coordinate the agricultural relief work in the village, the local leadership recommended Suha. For seedlings, equipment and advice the villagers now turn to her. Suha is not politically involved, not a member of any of the political factions and she was not mobilized through their political lectures, but she is deeply concerned with the survival of her community and outraged by the injustice done to all of her people. Her active work for the community is a living example of the empowerment of women in times of crisis. Deeply affected by the use of indiscriminate violence against the people who are dearest to her, Suha, like a lot of Palestinian women during the Intifada, is successfully challenging the male-dominated local resistance.

In 1989 the West Bank town of Beit Sahour made international headlines by staging a successful strike against an arbitrary Israeli tax policy initiated in yet another attempt to quell the uprising by means of economic measures. Mordechai Bareket, department head of Customs and Excise, declared in *Ha'Aretz*, 'If I were to try to apply within the boundaries of the Green Line, even a portion of the measures I have used to step up the collection of taxes in the Occupied Territories, I would be hanged in Zion Square.'[10] The steadfastness of Beit Sahour, a largely Christian town which had been able to generate substantial wealth in its factories and workshops, and whose inhabitants therefore really had something to lose, became a symbol of peaceful resistance throughout the entire Occupied Territories. The refusal of the entire citizenry of the town to pay taxes to the occupation authorities succeeded because the people refused to let Israel create a conflict between their individual interests and their collective determination for national liberation. The community network of popular committees helped to share the town's economic resources with more than two hundred households and workshops attacked by the tax collectors. Beit Sahour's Christian majority and Muslim minority are dedicated to a non-sectarian community life, and their successful struggle became a national symbol of opposition to Israel's policy of divide-and-rule, which had been used against the non-Jewish population since the establishment of the Israeli state.[11] Miriam Rishmawi describes in Chapter 11 her experiences during the tax campaign of 1989. Her family life is dominated by her community's fight against occupation. People develop a lot of creativity in the course of events, and Miriam herself decided to leave the boundaries of Beit Sahour and to write an appeal to the world. There is no island left in the Occupied Territories where Miriam Rishmawi and her family could live a peaceful private life. The illusion of 'benevolent occupation' is long gone. Israel's indiscriminatory and massive clampdown on the Intifada, on villages, camps and towns alike, has united the whole population and forced even traditional Christian women, grandmothers such as Miriam Rishmawi, to leave their private spheres and to use their imaginations not for petty concerns and household matters but for national liberation.

In recent years a new generation of political and socially active women has emerged in the women's committees movement and is already influencing its programmes and strategies for mobilization. In'am Zaqut is one of them. While the present leadership of the four main committees still consists of the movement's founding activists, who set the programme and the tactics for the past ten years of women's activities and all are now in their forties, the new generation is already stepping out of their shadow, struggling for acceptance, influence and change. They come from all social levels of Palestinian society, from refugee camps, towns and villages. Through their active participation in voluntary work, the student movement and trade union work, they have gained a lot of practical experience in organization and mobilization. They know Palestinian society from the grassroots upwards from endless counselling trips to the committees, even those in the remotest corners of the West Bank. Women activists like In'am started pushing for feminist demands out of pure necessity: they felt constantly limited and hindered in their activities by the traditional outlook of their society. Like a lot of top-level women activists, In'am married a progressive, politically active man. Their life is determined by their activities and from the very beginning they have had to cope with innumerable difficulties. Her husband Majed's deportation, the worst scenario they both could envisage, is one of the hardest situations to bear and it continues still. In'am's account in Chapter 12 gives an idea of life in the pressure cooker of occupation, with no way out.

The formation of popular committees in the second phase[12] of the Intifada, and the organization of the entire population in such a short time, was made possible by experienced activists of the existing mass organizations.[13] Even before the UNLU called for people to 'participate in the national and popular committees and the specialized committees',[14] activists of the women's, student, and political groups had started organizing people in neighbourhoods, camps and streets to cope with the difficulties that local communities were facing as a result of the Intifada. These voluntary popular committees, together with the groups of the Palestinian mass organizations, form the organizational network of the Intifada and are designed to become part of the infrastructure of the future Palestinian state. The activities of the popular committees are planned, organized and carried out in groups, and independent decision-making is needed if groups are to be able to adjust quickly to rapid changes in Intifada daily life. Rana Salibi's account, in Chapter 13, of popular work shows the difficulties the activists have to cope with: there is enthusiasm and empowerment as well as hesitation, fear and traditional belief. Her description shows the important role the women's movement has played in organizing the popular committees, though she criticizes its factionalism. She shows clearly that Israel's attempt to quell grassroots organization by making the popular committees illegal was partially successful. The neighbourhood committees declined as a result, thus putting more organizational responsibilities on the shoulders of the medical and agricultural relief committees, as well as the student and women's committees.

As the December 1987 uprising gathered momentum and the empowering spirit of the Intifada began to change everybody's lives, Palestinian writers immediately started to put down on paper what was happening in front of their eyes. Their short stories and poems dealt with the daily fight for survival in camps and villages, with the courage of Palestinian children confronting the Israeli Goliath with stones and slogans, and with feelings of grief and pride over the daily death toll of Intifada martyrs: women, men and children sacrificing their lives for national liberation and freedom. The history of the Palestinian literature of resistance goes back to the foundation of the state of Israel in 1948. Since then Palestinian poets and writers have focused in their work on the Palestinian people as at the same time audience and theme. Following Sartre's concept of *littérature engagée* they have tried to raise their people's consciousness about their alienated life under occupation to enable them to join forces for liberation. Despite their small number, Palestinian women writers have an important place in the Palestinian *littérature engagée*. Three of them originate from Nablus: the famous poet Fadwa Touqan, Hannan Mikha'il Ashrawi and Sahar Khalifeh, who sharply criticizes and analyses the internal contradictions of

Palestinian society, its dependence on the Israeli occupying power and the problematic role of the left, which preaches but does not act. Known to be one of the few Palestinian feminists, she focuses in her writings on all the forces limiting Palestinian women's abilities, talents, freedom, consciousness and life – the Israeli occupation policy as well as the traditional class structure of Palestinian patriarchal society. 'Women writers are progressive already, to pass the obstacles of "to want to write" and "to write", while men writers – even leftists – are still bound by the traditional role of women. . . . Real-life women are never represented [in their work].'[15]

The ties of traditional society, which differ from one social class to another, but in all are nevertheless equally limiting, are a theme in Hannan Mikha'il Ashrawi's short story 'A Pair of Shoes'. But here the Intifada offers strength and enables the woman, after experience of deep suffering to throw off her bondage. The writer depicts here the very spirit of the Intifada and its effect of liberating its participants from fear – fear of male violence and of oppression in general. In her stories women are conscious individual human beings with their own feelings and ability to determine their lives. These women of the Intifada challenge the conservative view of women as obedient wives, romantic lovers or all-providing mothers (this last image is used in the Palestine-as-woman concept in literature and art).[16] Hannan Mikha'il Ashrawi, who is at present Dean of the Arts Faculty at Birzeit University, wrote her doctoral thesis in 1982 at the University of Virginia, on 'The Contemporary Literature of Palestine: poetry and fiction.' Her study is known by scholars on that topic to be the basic work on Palestinian literature; it places its history, themes and motives in the context of the experience of the Palestinian nation as a people whose identity is denied. During the Intifada Hannan Mikha'il Ashrawi has become one of the leading internationally known Palestinian national figures, playing a prominent role in the peace talks with the Israelis.[17]

'The Israeli authorities don't even have to imprison me, all they need to do is spread nasty rumours about me which reflect on my sexual reputation as a woman.'[18] Nadira Shalhoub Kevorkian, a sociologist and researcher in the department of criminology at the Hebrew University of Jerusalem, inquires in Chapter 15 into this delicate matter. Both actual sexual harassment and the fear of sexual harassment by Israeli soldiers, border police and members of the *mukhabarat* (the intelligence service) 'have become a serious problem', she finds. That women's fear of sexual abuse and assault is by no means groundless is demonstrated in the 1990 report of the group Women's Organization For Political Prisoners. Its findings and the testimonies of two political detainees reprinted in Chapter 16 provide solid evidence for Nadira Kevorkian's conclusion. The motive for sexual violence against women (and men) is less sexual lust than the urge to demonstrate power.[19] In an uncontrolled situation of hierarchical power, therefore, women are inevitably victims of sexual assault. In the case of Palestinian women, sexual assaults by the occupation forces can additionally be seen as part of an Israeli policy to control women's activism by exploiting the rules of shame and honour in Palestinian traditional society. This policy was fairly successful until the beginning of the Intifada and it remains so, despite shifts in social values. It affects women's activism on the personal, family and society level by raising the level of individual fear among women, by pressuring parents and husbands to restrict the movement of their females, and by creating suspicion and resentments among Palestinian society that may force women activists to terminate their projects.

Notes

1. Samih K. Farsoun and Jean M. Landis, 'The Sociology of the Uprising: the roots of the Intifada', in Jamal R. Nassar and Roger Heacock (eds.), *Intifada: Palestine at the crossroads*, New York, 1990, pp. 15–35.

2. See Anita Vitullo, 'Uprising in Gaza', in Zachary Lockman and Joel Beinin (eds.), *Intifada: The Palestinian uprising against Israeli occupation*, Boston, 1989, pp. 43–57; Adil Yahya, 'The Role of the Refugee Camps', in Jamal R. Nassar and Roger Heacock (eds.), *Intifada: Palestine at the crossroads*, New York, 1990, pp. 91–106; David McDonald, 'A Profile of the Population of the West Bank and Gaza Strip', *Journal of Refugee Studies*, Vol. 2, No. 1, 1989, pp. 20–25.

3. Communiqué No. 2, 13 January 1988, reprinted in Lockmann and Beinin (eds.), p. 329.

4. Rosemary Sayigh, 'Encounters with Palestinian Women under Occupation', *Journal of Palestine Studies*, Vol. 10, No. 4, Summer 1981, p. 26.

5. The clandestine UNLU, the United Leadership of the Uprising, comprises Fatah, the Popular Front for the Liberation of Palestine (PFLP), the Democratic Front for the Liberation of Palestine (DFLP), the Communist Party and the Islamic Jihad. The UNLU communicates with the people of the Occupied Territories by means of *bayanat*, leaflets containing announcements, calls to action, strike instructions etc. Hammas is not part of the UNLU.

6. Reema Hammami in her article 'Women, the Hijab and the Intifada' gives a detailed and interesting account of the *hijab* campaign in the Gaza Strip (see *Merip Report*, May–August 1990, Nos. 164–5, pp. 24–25. For further information on women in Gaza see Susan Caroll Rockwell, 'A Study of Palestinian Women Workers in the Israeli-occupied Gaza Strip', BA thesis, Harvard, Radcliff College, April 1984; Isobel Mc Connan, 'A Dual Challenge – Women and Activism in the Gaza Strip', *Spare Rib*, No. 183, October 1987, pp. 10–11; Mary Khass, 'The Effect of Occupation on Women and Young people – some examples', *Journal of Refugee Studies*, special issue, *Palestinian Refugees and Non Refugees in the West Bank and Gaza Strip*, Vol. 2, No. 1, 1989, pp. 147–9.

7. Ramallah, Al-Haq, *Punishing a Nation*, 1988, p. 5.

8. *The Siege of Agriculture: examples of Israeli sanctions against agriculture in the Occupied Territories during the Palestinian uprising*, Jerusalem Media and Communication Centre, October 1988, cited in Husain Jameel Bargouti, 'Jeep Versus Bare Feet: the villages in the Intifada', in Nassar and Heacock (eds.), pp. 107–25.

9. Bargouti, p. 121.

10. *Ha'Aretz*, 31 October 1989, quoted in the B'teselem report, *The System of Taxation in the West Bank and the Gaza Strip as an Instrument for Enforcement of Authority During the Uprising*, Jerusalem, February 1990.

11. See Salim Tamari, 'Factionalism and Class Formation in Recent Palestinian History', in Roger Owen (ed.), *Studies in the Economic and Social History of Palestine in the 19th and 20th Centuries*, London, 1982.

12. The phases of the Intifada are analysed by the Palestinian sociologist Salim Tamari in his article 'The Uprising's Dilemma', in: *Merip Report*, No. 164–5, May–August 1990, p. 5.

13. See the Introduction to Part I on Amni Rimawi.

14. Communiqué No. 3, 18 January 1988, cited in Lockmann and Beinin (eds.), p. 333.

15. Literary critic Mohammed Batrawi in 'The Image of Women in Palestinian Literature', Flavia Pesa, *Al-Fajr* (English-language), 15 March 1985, p. 11.

16. See Ilham Abu Gahazaleh, 'Women in Intifada Poetry', *Al Kateb*, No. 110, June 1989, p. 25ff.

17. Verena Klemm has my gratitude for her inspiring analysis of contemporary Palestinian literature.

18. Quoted in McConnan.

19. Dianne Herman, 'The Rape Culture', in Jo Freeman, (ed.), *Women: a feminist perspective*, Palo Alto, 1979, pp. 45–7.

9. We in Bureij Camp and the Intifada[1]

Iman Jardallah

(I) I am eighteen years old and all my life I have lived in Bureij camp in the Gaza Strip.[2] My family is originally from Saba, near the Negev (Naqab). They became refugees in 1948 and since then they have lived in Bureij.

Our camp is very small compared with others but it is still extremely populous. My family and I live in a house with four rooms, an entrance hall, kitchen and bathroom. The members of our family living in the house comprise my mother and father, my brother, his wife and his two sons and four daughters, my sister and her two daughters and two more of my sisters, each with two boys, and one brother. A month ago my younger sister was still living with us, but she got married and moved to live with her husband.

We have mattresses piled up in one corner of the room during the day, and these are spread on the floor for the night. In the winter time, when it rains, we must all stay in the house, cook, read and watch TV, together. When I want to do my homework I go into one of the bedrooms to find a little space for myself.

(M) At the moment I am the only one responsible for the household. I take care of all the children and of the adults. Iman can hardly bend her arm as a result of being beaten by Israeli soldiers and she cannot do heavy work. In the morning I make two big pots of tea and gather the children together. By the time their parents wake up the youngsters have already had their breakfast. The smaller children stay in the house the whole day because we do not have a kindergarten in the camp. They usually play by themselves because none of the adults is free to play with them.

My daughter is living here with us because her husband left to work in Abu Dhabi. He left her and the two boys. It is our custom that when a husband leaves his wife she goes back to her family. At the moment our family is completely responsible for taking care of her and the children, because her husband sends no money. And he has not divorced her either, to

This chapter is the translation of interviews with Iman Jardallah and her mother. Their remarks are differentiated by a preceding (I) for Iman and (M) for her mother.

set her free. At the moment he comes every few months as a guest. But we cannot force him to divorce her or criticize his behaviour. He does not live in his homeland any more. Always he stays only for fifteen days, and it would take at least a year to take him to court. He only has his old mother here in the Gaza Strip. She is very unhappy about him but she has no influence on him and can do nothing because she is a widow. What can we do? These are the traditions. For a divorced woman it is very difficult. Who will marry a woman with two children by another man? Sometimes if a woman is divorced she refuses to get married anyhow, because usually she can only get a husband much older than she. That is our tradition and it is not good. But what can we do?

(I) I am not as pessimistic as my mother. Tradition changes through time, but we have to work for it. It is a long and difficult struggle but we have to start it. I already move around much more than my mother, and even leave the Strip. Things are changing, but there are people who try to turn the wheel back.

My father earns the money to support our family by means of his flock of thirty sheep. My father himself, my smaller brother and my sister go out with the flock into the fields, and I help when I come back from school. We milk the sheep and sell the milk together with their wool and the lambs. When we have curfew the sheep stay in the pen. We always feel bad during curfew because sheep, donkeys, cows and chickens have been killed by the tear gas. So you never know how many might be alive the next day. Tear gas canisters are dropped from helicopters, shot from jeeps into the crowded camp or are thrown by the soldiers themselves directly into the houses. This way nobody is safe from the tear gas, and neither are the animals. We have chickens as well as sheep, which lay about ten eggs a day. My mother takes care of them.

We have curfews often. Sometimes they last a whole month, sometimes only for a few days.[3] Whenever we feel that the situation is getting more tense and clashes are happening we go immediately and buy food. We hate the curfews but we have got used to them. If my brothers or my father are in the house when the soldiers come in the morning, they are ordered out to clean the streets; if they refuse and sit on the floor, they are beaten or sometimes jailed. Last year we were under curfew for three and a half months. Many young people were killed because they went out to get food to save their starving families.[4] It was girls mainly who went out, because they have the biggest chance to make it, and they got shot too. We lost around 7,000 Jordanian dinars because some of our sheep and goats died, from hunger and tear gas.[5]

(M) We were allowed to go out for one hour a day, but that was not enough time to lock the children in the house and buy food. Sometimes the army announced by loudspeaker that we were only allowed out for half an hour and that only the women were allowed to go out. Some young men could not stand to be trapped in the house for such a long time – houses are often very crowded. They broke the curfew and were beaten up very hard. When we were allowed to leave the house, we could only go to a few shops which were licensed to bring food into the camp. The shops were very crowded because everybody had to buy food at the same time, and in a lot of cases there was nothing left in the shops. Bottled gas and flour were the most difficult things to get. Flour especially is a problem. Bread is the most important food in a Palestinian kitchen. So most of the time we lived on tahini, ful, sha'ria, flour and spaghetti.[6] When we did not have flour for *khubz* we cooked sha'ria for the children.

Almost every second night there was no electricity, and very often we ran short of gas because we could not refill the bottles. In such cases families in the neighbourhood helped each other, and people shared what they had. When one of us wanted to go over to one of our neighbours the girls were sent to the roof and had to keep watch to see if there were soldiers in the streets. When everything seemed clear, the small girls, aged between five and seven years old, would run quickly to the door of the neighbour. The soldiers know by now that the small girls are sent on purpose because they run the least risk of being beaten, shot or jailed. So when they see the small ones running they call them and beat them to teach them a lesson. But they are still the ones with the least chance of getting jailed or killed.

Once my little daughter was beaten when she was outside in the street to get some food. We could hear her cries and I rushed out of the door.

'What are you doing here,' I shouted at her and then I turned to the soldiers. 'We didn't know that she was out. She slipped out without us recognizing it.'

'Shut up,' the soldier shouted at me, and he continued beating my little girl. 'The next time I will do the same to you.'

But I managed to pull my daughter into the house and to shut the door behind her. When the door slammed I started shouting behind the door so that the soldiers could hear me. 'Why did you go out? You know very well that it is forbidden.' Then when we felt that the soldiers had gone away we calmed her and the other children, who were panicking. The rest of the day she was stiff, quiet and thoroughly frightened.[7]

The children talk a lot about this incident. They put it into games and play soldiers and *shebab* ('youth', but sometimes used to mean young fedayin). In their play they take the guns from the soldiers and beat the helpless soldiers like they are beaten by them. But the fear is still in their eyes. When they hear the soldiers outside the house, they all huddle in one corner or rush towards one of the adults for security. But when the initial shock is over they react in astonishingly different ways. Some start crying, some shout and some are not afraid at all. But all of them ask the same questions: Why are they coming? What are they doing here? We try to explain that the soldiers are our enemies, that they took our homeland and that now they are trying to take our sons also.

The curfew is very hard on the children. They hate it. They shout all the time. Sometimes they are so full of energy and so much under pressure that they start hitting each other. Other times, when they sit without moving and stare into empty space, I am scared. Usually when the army announces a curfew the older children remain in the rooms, each group in the room where they sleep. The younger, courageous ones used to go up to the rooftop and gather round the soldiers if they were on the roof in order to control the streets. They quickly find out if these are soldiers one can deal with or not. Before the Intifada the kids were not afraid of the soldiers. But once the army came into our house and beat their uncle in front of their eyes, and since then they panic when they see the soldiers. So I take the small ones in my arms when they cry, and try to calm them down.

A big problem under curfew is the tear gas.[8] There is no way to escape it when it comes into the house because, of course, you cannot leave. You are not even supposed to open the windows. Once five tear gas canisters entered the house. Ever since that day our four-year-old, Abdur Rahman, has suffered from chest pain. He inhaled too much of the gas. When he sleeps you can hear a strange noise in his lungs. We took him several times to a doctor but he told us only that the affected lung might be better when he grows up.

When tear gas canisters are thrown into a room all you can do is run out as quickly as possible. If there is gas everywhere we use onions or eau de Cologne. When this does not work, and since the beginning of the Intifada it almost never does, we use bicarbonate of soda. We dissolve it in water and wash our faces and the faces of the children with it when they start burning, and we breathe through pieces of cloth dipped in sodium bicarbonate solution.

Usually the soldiers come each day in the morning. Yesterday they took five men who were on their way to work and arrested them for nothing. They shot into the air to frighten people. We all ran up to the roof to see what was happening but the five had already been taken away in the jeep. This is the usual morning routine: the soldiers come, enter some houses without knocking and take the men and boys away. We try to be quicker than the army and as soon as we hear the warning whistles from the guarding *shebab* at the edge of the camp, we women go out onto the roofs and give signs to the *shebab* in our area that they have to run away. We signal to them from which direction the soldiers are coming.

This is one of the new roles of women during the uprising. And we see it as our duty to defend the camp like the men do. Many times as well we have had to defend our men. Like last week, when the army attacked the mosque during prayers and started to throw tear gas inside. The men inside were soon unable to breathe and they ran out of the mosque. Then the soldiers started shooting. We women heard the shooting, went outside to see where it came from and took our children and started running towards the mosque. All of us started throwing stones at the soldiers to distract their attention so that the men could run away. They were shooting at us but we were thinking only of our men. We did not care any more about the danger, not even about the danger to the young children with us. You get in a funny state of mind in which you become absolutely wild and furious about what is happening, and you react without thinking.

A few months ago they wanted to arrest my son. I ran with my two little girls out of the house and we began to shout at the soldiers to leave him. But they did not listen and wanted to hit the girls. The smallest one hit the soldier who held my son back and by accident, maybe because he was stumbling already, the soldier fell to the ground. He became furious and started to beat the bigger girl. I think he was a big shot in the army. While he was on the ground, all of us managed to escape in the confusion.

Before the Intifada a lot of things were different. The soldiers did not come every morning, and they did not attack houses so much. Before the Intifada children did not worry about the soldiers. They were just part of everyday life, like something you see and ignore if possible. Now it is different. If the children see a jeep they begin throwing stones at it. Also the boundaries of violence have drifted. Formerly, soldiers did not beat and curse women like they do now. I learned to curse back at them and sometimes I curse even worse than they do.

In the winter especially, but in autumn and spring as well, the house is very cold inside. When we are under curfew and confined to the house we are freezing cold. So when the soldiers are not in sight, we sit on the flat rooftop of our house to catch some warmth. The rooftop has an area of at least 30 square metres, and we have a little hut with some chickens and pigeons. It has a metre-high wall around it, so we have some shelter and at the same time we can see what is happening in the camp. But we have to be very careful that we are not seen by the soldiers. Under curfew we are not even allowed to switch on the radio.

We have a good relationship with all our neighbours, and the Intifada has brought us even closer together. Once we and our neighbours all went out in the curfew. The soldiers came and rushed into the houses and broke everything they could lay hands on and took the men away with them. Whatever they break in the house, including things needed for household work, is now very difficult to replace because we do not have the money. Now if there is a curfew only we women go out. We are not afraid. But if the soldiers arrest boys and men when there is no curfew still we all of us go out onto the streets.

During a curfew the women have to take care of the household; they try to cook with what they have in the house and to occupy the children. Some of the men are not afraid to go out even in the curfew and they visit neighbours. But more and more the fear of the entire population of Bureij camp is vanishing, so we go out very often during curfew. When you are not even safe in your own house, *where* you are beaten up becomes unimportant.

(I) Recently the soldiers came to our house. They had been looking for my twenty-year-old brother Ashraf for several months, but without success, since for quite a while he has only very occasionally slept in our house, knowing he is wanted. Instead, he sleeps under the trees outside the camp, or with friends with whom he feels safe.[9] That night at six in the morning the soldiers came. They hammered at the door and shouted 'Iftah al bab' [open the door]. The children in the house started crying because they were afraid and even though Ashraf was not at home my sixteen-year-old brother was sleeping in his room. My mother opened the door.

'Where is Ashraf? Where are you hiding him?' the soldier shouted and rushed into the house.

'He is in Israel working,' my mother answered.

'You are a liar,' the soldier shouted and started hitting me and my mother. Then they started searching the house and ran into the room where my other brother was sleeping. My mother shouted, 'This is my small boy, not the big one.'

'No, he is a donkey,' the soldier burst out and pulled my brother out of bed. 'Come with us.'

So they took him instead of Ashraf. My brother was trying to put on his shoes, but he had only managed to get one on when the soldier pulled him out of the room. We were trying to prevent them from taking him and we took hold of his arm. 'He has his exams in school tomorrow,' my mother said.[10] 'He has to go.'

'No, you take it for him,' one of the soldiers answered. While some of the soldiers were taking my brother the others kept searching the house. They found my father and started beating him at the same time as they were handcuffing him.

We were mad. We dressed quickly, put on our shawls and ran out of the house. We went looking for my father and brother, and the *shebab* and our neighbours told us where the soldiers had taken them. We had to make our way outside the camp. There they were with a lot of soldiers. We ran towards them and started shouting at the soldiers. 'You can stay for hours, you won't get them,' one of the soldiers replied. And then they started hitting me. When my father saw that, he shouted, 'Go home, go home, you will only be beaten, go home!' We obeyed him and left, but on the way home we ran into a group of soldiers and my other brother, Ashraf, who had been staying with a friend who was also wanted. The army had surrounded him. They had put him against a wall and were hitting him harder and harder. He was already bleeding – there was blood everywhere – and he was hardly able to stand. He was blindfolded and all the time he could see nothing, not even that we had come. We ran to the soldiers and tried to tear them away from my brother. As they tried to fight us off, one of them took the blindfold from my brother's eyes and ordered him to tell us to go home, otherwise we too would be beaten. So he told us to leave. But we would not go. We wanted my brother and my father. There was nothing at home to go to. So we refused to leave the wall. Then one of the soldiers pointed the gun at us and said: 'If you don't leave we will kill your brother in front of your eyes.' We answered, 'You can kill all of us, we won't go.' And as an answer I sat down on the ground in front of the wall. 'Shoot me if you want, but I go only with my brother and my father.' The soldier hit me in the face and another used his gun to hit my sister very hard in the back. But still we showed no sign of giving in. So the soldiers took Ashraf to the army post where my father and my other brother were and released them. They got Ashraf, which was what they wanted.

Last year the soldiers crushed my elbow. Even now after more than a year and three operations I cannot bend my arm. It was in March 1988. I was in my school, which is outside Bureij camp. Suddenly in the middle of a lesson a *shebab* burst into the classroom and told us that a man from our camp had been killed by the soldiers. Immediately everybody jumped up, we left the classroom and wanted to leave the school. All of us have had more than enough experiences with the soldiers. We have an army camp right next to our school grounds and many times the army has raided our school and we have been badly beaten up. On this day we ran out of the school and towards the camp. Suddenly we saw two big military vehicles coming towards us. One was full of about ten settlers with sub-machine guns and the other was an army vehicle. They stopped when they saw us coming out of the school and the men inside jumped out. We ran for cover, trying to escape between the olive trees. One settler, still driving the car, accelerated and tried to run me over. I managed to reach the trees, where he could not follow, but the soldiers were still behind us. It was a rainy day, and the ground was slippery. While trying to escape I slipped and fell. In a second the soldier was over me, raising his baton. Instinctively I raised my arm to protect my head. The blow hit my elbow very hard and even though he must have seen that it was smashed he hit it twice more with full force. Then he left me in the mud.

Some of my school friends saw me bleeding on the ground and carried me to the school. A teacher took me to the camp and later on to hospital. All the time the soldiers were looking for me. My elbow was crushed completely and I had to go to the Nasser Hospital in Khan Yunis. I stayed there for three months and had three operations but still I could not move my hand. They tried physiotherapy for six months but still it would not move. So I was transferred to the Makkaset Hospital in Jerusalem. There they told me that I would have to have another operation. I stayed there for another month and they opened the wound and rebroke the bones. After that my arm was straight but still I could not move my hand. More physiotherapy did not work either. So they operated on it again. Now it is getting better and I can bend my elbow a little bit again. But I still have pain in my shoulder.

But now I am no longer afraid. They have hit me so many times. If they want to kill me, okay. You get used to their violence or they break you.[11] My brother was in jail but he said nothing even though they hit him many, many times. He knows as well as I that it makes no difference whatever he says.

I have recently finished my *tawjihi*[12] and I am studying Arabic, history and geography in order to become a teacher. That is not my first choice of career. I would very much like to become a doctor, but all the universities are closed and my family just does not have the money to enable me to leave the country and study somewhere else. So I started with languages. I still dream of studying medicine and becoming a doctor but who knows if my dream will ever come true.

When I finish my studies I want to get married. But I am going to convince my husband to let me work. This is what I have been doing with my brother and my father. I do not love anybody yet and I am trying to avoid it. I see a lot of young men, but I am afraid to fall in love with anyone in case I can't marry him because my father and mother refuse.

My sister is now sixteen. She married a few weeks ago. My father married her off because we have no money. It is a shame because she was the cleverest girl in school and always dreamt of completing her studies. But my father is already paying my tuition fees and he cannot afford to let both of us finish our education. But she has managed to reach an agreement with her husband that she can finish her studies at home.

(M) We are fighting for our own independent state and we want to compensate for all the young men we have lost by having new sons. During the Intifada women have had more children than before. We need to make up the losses.

Nothing will stop the Intifada. It would be a waste of all the years of struggle if we failed to achieve a solution. We know that it is impossible for us to have all of Palestine. We only demand the territories of 1967.[13] We are now also struggling as women not to have zero status in our state. We want to have a position equal to that of the men. Even though I am a Muslim woman I do not want to live in a Muslim state such as Iran. But I do not want a state without religion. We should have a state where Muslims and Christians can live together with the same rights.

(I) I dream that we will have a Palestinian state in the West Bank and Gaza, that we will get our freedom. This is a dream not only for me but for all the Palestinian people. But nevertheless I love the camp. If we gain our freedom I will still live in the camp. I was born there, and it provides me with my food and drink. I love the people there. They stick very much together, even more so since the Intifada. You can rely on them, and I do not want to live without my friends and neighbours for too long. Even though I am willing to go and study medicine anywhere in the world, I would come back to the camp.

Notes

1. The interviews with Iman Jardallah and her mother took place in Beit Haninah and in Bureij camp, on 30 November and 1 December 1989. I would like to express my thanks once again to Fadia Daibes for her wonderful translation job in Bureij.

2. More than 200,000 refugees moved to the Gaza Strip after the 1948 Arab–Israeli conflict. The Gaza Strip itself, located in the south-western part of Mandatory Palestine, is only 40 kilometres long and 6–10 kilometres wide. Through natural increase, the Strip now has one of the highest population densities of the world, at about 1,800 persons per square kilometre. About 70 per cent of the population of 650,000 are refugees, and of these 55 per cent, or 255,831, according to figures from December 1988, live in the eight refugee camps of the Strip. Bureij camp is located in the central area. Its original refugee population of 13,000 in 1949 has grown to 17,000 people. (United Nations Relief Works Agency – UNRWA – information sheet on Palestinian refugee camps.)

3. According to UNRWA statistics, between 31 January 1988 and 31 August 1989 Bureij camp was under curfew for seventy-nine days.

4. In the first twenty months of the uprising, 11 residents of Bureij camp were killed and 1,436 were injured, half of them by beatings (UNRWA information sheet on Palestinian refugee camps).

5. In 1988 the Jordanian dinar had a value of roughly US$2–2.50. After King Hussein announced on 31 July 1988 that all 'administrative and legal ties between Jordan and the West Bank would be cut' the dinar dropped in value. This trend continued after the economical and political upheavals in spring and summer 1989.

6. Tahini is ground sesame seeds, *ful* is a dish made from brown beans, lemon and garlic and is usually eaten with *khubz*, the flat bread. *Sha'ria* are small noodles which are fried briefly in hot oil and then cooked and served with rice. During the Intifada the eating habits of the population changed because of increasing economic difficulties, extended curfews and strikes. People were obliged to eat more starchy food, which they could store easily and they therefore lacked vitamins and minerals.

7. Children under the Israeli occupation suffer from the violence wherever they are, on the streets, or in kindergartens, classrooms or prisons. They cannot even find shelter in their homes, because soldiers enter houses night and day during army raids. Children experience the helplessness of their parents to protect them and have nowhere to turn for security. '. . . illegal violence has a destructive influence both on the individual and society at large. Therefore, even

if minors recover from the effects of violence, as most of them do, the damage lingers on. Others, who do not recover, will be scarred for the rest of their lives.' (Professor Charlie Greenbaum, Department of Psychology, Hebrew University of Jerusalem, in *Police Violence against Minors – Psychological aspects*, Betselem Information Sheet Update, June–July 1990, p. 5.

8. Next to beatings, tear gas is the second most frequent cause of casualties. Contrary to official directions for their use, tear gas grenades are often fired into homes. In Bureij camp 256 inhabitants were injured by tear gas during the first twenty months of the uprising. In the same period in the Occupied Territories as a whole, 80 persons, mostly young children and elderly people, died of the effects of tear gas, whilst hundreds of women miscarried or lost their babies in premature labour, clearly because of tear gas inhalation (UNRWA data).

9. A large number of young men have been forced into hiding during the Intifada. They are wanted by the Israelis because of so-called 'security offences', such as being politically active, throwing stones and petrol bombs, or having a perceived 'key' role in the Intifada leadership. Some of them are literally trapped. They are not even able to go to the police station and give themselves up because they are not wanted alive. Several *shebab* have been executed on being caught by the Israeli army. In some cases, members of the wanted man's family or his wife are taken as hostages by the army and freed only when the man turns himself in. The *Jerusalem Post* quoted on 24 October 1988 a Reuters report from the day before: 'Security sources said an undercover army unit codename "Cherry" deployed in the West Bank to capture Arabs throwing petrol bombs and rocks, had verbal orders to shoot and kill fugitives "with blood on their hands". . . . Security sources stressed that killings were not the unit's prime task, although it had shot dead several Palestinians in ambushes and undercover operations' (for the source and detailed information on this topic see *Punishing a Nation: Human Rights Violations During the Palestinian Uprising, December 1987–December 1988*, Ramallah, Al-Haq, 1989, p. 37f).

10. Unlike the schools in the West Bank, educational institutions in the Gaza Strip were still officially functioning. But because of daily confrontations between pupils and the army, lengthy periods of curfew (especially in the camps), and army raids on schools one could hardly speak of normal school life.

11. Whilst young children cannot rationalize their fear, adolescents and schoolchildren are able to see their feelings and behaviour in the broader context of the national struggle. 'This perception of themselves as the *Palestinianized self* involves total commitment to one cause, the Intifada and its continuity, in order to achieve freedom. . . . They [the youth] started to appreciate the *unity*, *cohesiveness*, and *thoughtfulness* of their local community' (Nadira Kevorkian, 'Group Work with Adolescents in Refugee Camps: Palestinians during the Intifada', unpublished paper, Jerusalem, 1989). Common suffering and the experience that enables them to survive imprisonment and confrontation with the army give women like Iman and their peers a feeling of empowerment and social responsibility that enables them to cope with their fears.

12. The A-level standard examination which qualifies pupils for university study.

13. The territories occupied by Israel in the Six Day War of 1967, that is, the West Bank and the Gaza Strip.

10. Fifty-three Days' Curfew in Kufr Malik

Suha 'Adi

In winter 1988, during the celebration of the first year of the Intifada, our whole village, Kufr Malik, was declared a closed military area, and nobody was allowed to leave or to enter.[1] A few days later, on 15 November, army jeeps drove through the narrow streets of the village and announced a curfew.[2] This curfew, which was to last until 22 December, is carved into my memory as one of the hardest times I have ever experienced, even though we are used to curfews in Kufr Malik.

The PNC in Algiers and the foundations of a Palestinian state

Like all Palestinians, all the people of our village had followed with interest the Palestine National Council (PNC) session in Algiers. Even when the electricity was cut off in many villages, so that we would not be able to follow on television the foundation of our Palestinian state, we still knew what was going on.

When the Palestinian state was proclaimed on 15 November, the whole village celebrated it. On all the rooftops, on the minaret of the mosque and on electricity poles, Palestinian flags streamed in the wind. The children romped through the streets shouting and singing and we all visited each other from house to house. Kufr Malik is situated in a valley which leads downwards east towards the Jordan valley. We are encircled by Israeli settlements and army posts. The army camp is located on top of the mountain to the west, so they are able to control with ease every movement in the village. On one of the hilltops there is a radar station, and next to it the military camp; southeast on the mountain range are the houses of the Israeli settlement. Luckily there are hardly any problems with the settlers.

When we started celebrating the proclamation of Palestine we knew that we were being watched carefully all the time. But we did not know at that time what was ahead of us. A year later we did not dare to celebrate the first anniversary of our state because we so vividly remembered the suffering from the year before. But on 15 November 1988 we celebrated for the whole day. And the army watched us from their mountain post but did not interfere. The evening hours were quiet as well. The whole village was preparing for the night, when suddenly at ten the first jeeps entered the village. At first it was eerily quiet and all we could hear was the whistles of the *shebab* announcing the arrival of the army. Then the loudspeakers began to scream from all sides '*Man'a itajawal* . . .' (curfew) over and over again. Then soldiers started knocking at doors, they broke into houses and started beating people.

It was the time of the olive harvest, when olives are picked in the daytime and in the night the olive mills work. The army raided the mill houses where people had started their nightwork and started beating everybody inside, men, women, old people and children alike. Everybody was terrified because the soldiers were everywhere and they hit everything that moved. And they did not just hit, they broke bones.

The soldiers also raided the house of one of our neighbours and beat her son. His mother shouted, 'Stop, stop, why are you beating him? He didn't do anything.'

'It is enough that he is a Palestinian,' the soldier answered and continued to beat him.

Meanwhile, hundreds of soldiers surrounded the village like a belt so that nobody could escape into the mountains. The army had brought with them a huge bus to transport the men they planned to arrest. The *shebab* tried to escape into the mountains, but they were caught by army units outside the village.

The first days of curfew

The next day, which was the first day of the curfew, as well as the following day, we were allowed to leave our houses for just one hour. But on the third day and for a whole week after that, we were confined to our homes and not allowed to take one step outside. We were not even permitted to clean outside, to empty the rubbish or to hang out washing. We were used to one or two days of curfew but not to a whole week. We did not have enough food in the house to last us, and there was not enough milk for the babies. The animals too went hungry because hardly any family had more than a few days' fodder. And the animals that were kept away from their owner's house went without food and water for a whole week. At first they craved water and slowly began to starve. The sheep and goats bleated for food. Then they started to die: the newborn lambs first, then the sheep and goats. Their whimpering was hard to bear but we could do nothing.

During the curfew our electricity and water were cut off. We were not permitted to light candles, and if the army patrolling under our windows saw a shimmer of light in the rooms, they would burst in and force us to blow out the candles. The rooms were dark as hell and terribly cold and humid. It was most difficult for mothers with small children. They were unable to heat up milk or babyfood. And soon, everyone's food stocks ran out. Our refrigerators were useless without electricity, and whilst families who had enough gas could at least preserve their food by cooking, others saw it rot in front of their eyes. Usually we would have been able to buy meat, milk and fresh vegetables from the market every day. But this is impossible under curfew. My aunt and I were lucky in that our two-roomed house has an inner courtyard, separated from the street by a high brick wall. Without this wall, which sheltered us from the glances of the soldiers, we would not have been able to use the kitchen and the bathroom, which cannot be entered directly from the living room. Like a lot of other villagers, we would have had to improvise a bathroom and kitchen using a gas cooker and a bucket in the sleeping room. We were not allowed to open the door of the inner courtyard, but within it we could move freely. Friends of mine, Abu Nader's family, who live in the centre of the village, where the houses are built right next to each other so that the soldiers can patrol on the rooftops, could not leave the house to use their toilet without being beaten or shot at. They live next to the school, which had been confiscated by the army and turned into an army camp.[3] Abu Nader's house is overlooked by the main school building, and so they were constantly watched. For twelve days none of them, not even the children, were allowed to leave the house. The whole family, including the three children, had to use a bucket in the sleeping room as a toilet. Imm Nader does not live in Kufr Malik any more. In October 1989 she was deported to Amman.[4]

In the first two days, when we were allowed to leave the house for one hour during the day, I tried to see my relatives and friends. Most of my neighbours and relatives have big families and one hour was not enough to get everything done. I am single and only have to take care of my aunt, so I went from house to house and asked if I could help shopping. The whole village was on the streets. Villagers without food for their animals tried to borrow it from neighbours. People were eager to share their stock of food. At that time nobody thought of the possibility of fifty-three days of curfew. Some of my neighbours have big flocks of sheep, more than fifty animals. These were desperately looking for fodder for their sheep. But soon they started dying in front of our eyes. And because the refrigerators were not working we could not slaughter the animals and store their meat. In our society a sheep is very precious and for most of the villagers sheep raising is the only source of income. A lot of people begged the soldiers to let them buy fodder for the animals, but none got permission. More than 150 sheep died during the curfew. Some families were lucky and had enough fodder, others lost the few sheep they had. My neighbour had only one sheep. One day when she led it to graze during our free hour, a soldier pointed his gun at the sheep and shot it. Just like that.

As I explained, during the first week of the curfew we were not allowed to leave our houses at all, not even to open the windows. During the weeks after that, every day jeeps would drive through the village and announce the time when we were to be allowed out. During this hour the army never left the village and the soldiers stayed in the makeshift camp in the school as well as on the rooftops. Even before the hour was over the jeeps would appear on the streets and chase us back into our homes. Every day it was the same story: 'Curfew, until further notice. Whoever leaves the houses is shot at!'

After a few days, everyone had run out of fresh vegetables, fruit and meat. So we started emptying our stores. Packets of lentils, chickpeas, rice and spaghetti were opened, and we used the dried yoghurt pieces soaked in water. But some families were unable to use their stores. When the soldiers had raided their houses they had emptied all the bottles and containers of food onto the floor. Flour, rice, sesame paste and olive oil, sugar and salt formed a useless mess of foodstuffs in the dirt. My aunt and I were very lucky because of our small household, which is very unusual in Palestinian society. There is a great difference between organizing food for two and organizing food for fifteen. After a short while most families ran out of cooking gas. Normally we rely on bottled gas. Women without cooking gas were unable even to prepare a meal from dried vegetables. Without hot water, dry lentils are completely useless. And people ran out of flour, so they could no longer bake bread, *khubbis*, our basic food. Luckily, we had water. Other villages under long-term curfew had their water supplies cut off, so that they were entirely dependent on wells and natural springs. After the first week of strict curfew was over we could leave the house for an hour a day, but within a few days all the shops were empty. The shopkeepers were not allowed to replenish their stocks. So we began living off very small meals, and at the end we were beginning to starve.

At first, when we were allowed out the kids used to rush out to play in the olive orchards. But soon the playtime was over. When families ran out of cooking gas, the children had to collect wood in the fields. We were freezing. The rooms were cold and damp and except for a few portable gas or oil ovens there is no heating in them. Therefore we had to do the cooking in our free hour outside on the balconies or in the streets. For families with a lot of children it was almost impossible to do all the necessary work in one hour: collect wood, cook the meals for the next day, open the windows and air the house, empty the toilet buckets, feed the animals if there was food (otherwise try to collect some or let them graze), contact the neighbours if they needed help and a lot else.

Extended curfew – adjusting to imprisonment

For the breadwinners of Kufr Malik a curfew means unwished-for free time: they are unable to go to work and earn money. When the Israeli army announces curfew the men working in other West Bank towns or inside the Green Line are warned by phone or, when the phone lines are cut, by the whistles and signals of the *shebab*, not to come back. Most of them do not go back home, they stay outside the village and look for accommodation. This way at least they can continue to work and earn money. Therefore most of the women of Kufr Malik were without their husbands while we endured fifty-three days of curfew. The men who were unable to leave the village in time and were trapped under curfew were worst off. Fathers with eight or nine children were without work and salary for fifty-three days.

One woman living in the village has to care for her eleven children. With so many mouths to feed her stores soon ran out. One day, when we were allowed to leave the house for an hour, she started walking towards the neighbouring village, three miles away. We were strictly prohibited from leaving the village but she must have managed to sneak out. In the village she bought a sack of flour, and pulling it behind her she made her way back to Kufr Malik. But just before she reached our village she heard the jeeps announcing curfew again. She hid the flour between stones and walked back to the neighbouring village. The next day she made her way to the place where she had hidden the flour, waited for the hour we were 'set free' and sneaked into Kufr Malik. Her children had to cope during these twenty-four hours by themselves.

One day we noticed a black Mercedes driving slowly through the streets. Every time it passed our house we ran to the window to find out what this mystery was. It turned out to be a vehicle of the Red Cross. They announced that all sick people should leave their houses and walk to the village clinic to be treated. The black Mercedes was always followed by a military jeep. The soldiers took care that no person other than the sick would even glance out of the houses. Even the dangerously ill had to crawl to the car unaided. My aunt is infected by brucellosis, the Maltese fever. Her treatment is wearisome and complicated and she is illiterate, so until that day I had brought her to the doctor for treatment. She was afraid to go by herself and we were worried that she probably would be unable to explain her treatment to the Red Cross medic. I promised her that I would explain the stage of her treatment and her medication to the Red Cross driver, so that he could explain it to the doctor. But immediately I opened the door of our house and started walking towards the Mercedes, a soldier stopped me. He lifted his truncheon and shouted at me, 'If you open the door any further I'll beat you into a pulp!' I jumped back in panic, and slammed the door behind me, shivering. When my aunt was brought back to the house she told me what had happened to her. The first thing the driver had asked her was why I had opened the door. 'Is she not afraid to get shot?' There was only one doctor at the clinic, and he had no facilities for blood, urine or other laboratory testing. In the opinion of all of us in the village, the Red Cross visit was no more than a symbolic gesture intended for the international press. Now the military government could announce that Kufr Malik was provided with medical care even under curfew.

We helped each other a lot. Everybody gave his last in order that all of us should survive. We ate bread with oil and drank tea. Not more and not less. Bread and oil. But we survived. Though not the animals. The children quickly learned that there was not enough food to eat themselves full. Soon they only wanted to eat in order to survive, not to be satisfied any more.

To feed the babies we thinned milk with camomile or sage tea, to make the milk powder last longer. At the end there was hardly any milk left, even though we had been giving them only barely enough to keep them alive. For me the most difficult thing to bear during the fifty-three days of curfew was the suffering of the children. They had no freedom to run about, they were freezing and they were hungry. The kids said, 'We don't want to eat, we can manage our hunger, but we long to go out.'[5] They kept saying, 'We don't care if there is curfew or not. We want to have our own state to be able to run about.'

A lot of mothers had psychological problems.[6] They were under constant pressure, there was growing tension in the house, a lot of noise from the children who were unable to release their energy running outside. Mothers tried to play games with their children to divert their attention from their imprisonment, but they themselves were suffering from the same tensions and fears.

Communication between houses was difficult, even when it was the only means to exchange food and news. Even at night it was dangerous and difficult to cross the street to neighbours. The army patrolled all over the village and on the rooftops, twenty-four hours a day. If one of us was discovered out on the streets he or she was beaten severely or shot at with tear gas, rubber bullets or even live ammunition. And the soldiers did not differentiate between men and women, adults and children. Anyone arrested violating the curfew was fined 1,000–2,000 Israeli shekel. To make sure that the fines would be paid the identity cards of those arrested were confiscated and only given back when the fine was paid.

When we were in urgent need of something we would try first to contact our immediate neighbour. If they were unable to help they started a chain. For example one of my friends, who lives a few houses away, told me via my neighbour that she urgently needed milk for her children. We were one of the lucky households with a lot of milk because there were only two women in the house. I packed the milk into a plastic bag and handed it over the wall to my neighbour. She passed it on until it reached Umm Mohammed.

Washing clothes took a lot of organization and planning. We were permitted to do washing but not to dry the laundry outside. Therefore we would string a clothesline in the bathroom or the kitchen and hang the laundry up there. But because the rooms were moist and cold the wet clothes took ages to dry and we suffered from the dampness. My neighbour was desperate to dry her laundry and started pegging it out onto the clothesline on her roof. When the soldiers saw it, they immediately tore down the whole lot and started stamping on it in their boots. When they had finished that vandalism, they broke into her house and for four hours turned it upside down.

What particularly heightened tension in the village was not so much the soldiers' disdain of the living but their contempt for the dead as well. When a woman died during the curfew her funeral had to take place with only a few immediate family members attending. Only her son, her two daughters and her husband could bury her. When some other villagers applied for a special permit to help the family to dig the grave, it was denied. This reaction by the military embittered everyone in the village.

The nights were more difficult to bear that the days: freezing cold and pitch dark. In the darkness the presence of the soldiers was even more terrifying than during the day. Army jeeps drove through the empty streets and through their loudspeakers played noisy music or cursed us. Every night the army raided some houses. The soldiers would search every last corner. The cupboards were usually emptied, clothes thrown out on the floor. If members of the family dared to complain, they were shouted at. Sometimes we were made to leave our houses, so we could not know what was happening inside and what was taken. The *shebab* were usually beaten up during these raids. They suffered the most. In the daylight things do not look quite so scary, but because we could not leave the house there was hardly anything to do. Sometimes the pressure was too much to bear and I just sat stiff and cold on a chair, staring into empty space.

Suddenly the Israeli military commander wanted to negotiate with the people of Kufr Malik. Our *mukhtar* was supposed to mediate.[7] But he refused to negotiate with the army, as it would be impossible for him to find a compromise between the demands of the army and those of the *shabibeh*. He would have lost face if he gave in to the demands of the army. How could he have ordered the *shebab* not to protest against the actions of the army, which raided the village every day? We are not cattle to be led to the slaughter without fighting for freedom. We viewed the curfew as an act of collective punishment by the army for our resistance against Israeli colonialism.

I do not know what they expected to gain by the implementation of the curfew. People did not change. But fifty-three days of imprisonment created a readiness for revenge. A lot of families lost their cattle. People were beaten over and over again. Houses were raided, furniture was smashed, and yet the whole action was completely arbitrary. I think it is the arbitrariness which teaches us how to hate. Every day we expect to be put under curfew again.[8] It is becoming part of everyday life that the army can come at any time, and maltreat the people. Their argument is always the same: 'We beat you up, because you have been beating us up.' But this is not true. We do not go to Tel Aviv and beat up the people living there, but they come without reason into our village and club us.

The military zone

Eventually, the curfew was completely lifted, but the whole village was declared a closed military zone. The army stayed in Kufr Malik and bulldozers blocked all the streets with heaps of earth and rocks so that no cars could enter. The women sneaked out through the mountains to buy food for their children, but because they had to carry it back on foot they could not buy enough of all the things they needed. The atmosphere in the village was still very tense. On 22 December we could finally leave Kufr Malik. The men entered the village, rushed to their homes, and families were united again.

I wished that everything were over

I wished that everything were over. But in 1989 everything happened yet again – again and again. Not one house was spared being raided. All of us were affected by the arbitrary actions of the soldiers, time after time. Our village has around 2,000 inhabitants. During the last raid there were 500 soldiers in the village. They were everywhere: in the mountains to catch the *shebab*, in the streets and in the houses. When the soldiers caught a *shebab*, they would break his arms. The Israeli army always argues that it takes care of the injured. That is not true. In our village fifteen people have been injured and two killed. I include only bullet wounds and do not count the injuries of those whose hands were held while their arms were broken. There were a lot more of these injuries. In 1989 we were affected by the tax campaign as well. Tax officials came, guarded by the army, and left tax demands with extraordinarily high tax debts written on them. But I know of nobody who paid these fantastic taxes: the amounts are so high anyhow that no one could pay. Nevertheless we constantly get letters demanding payment.

On 14 October my neighbour was shot and killed by the army. It happened early in the morning, at seven: there was no confrontation at all. But soon afterwards, when the mournful news of his murder became known, the whole of Kufr Malik came onto the streets. We formed a funeral procession to demonstrate our grief and anger and walked towards the house of his mother. Suddenly the army appeared and announced curfew. That night they came to my door. While I was struggling with my nightgown a soldier burst into the room and pointed his machine-gun at my chest. 'Where is the masked man?' he shouted at me. 'Where is the masked man?' I answered him, 'There are no masked men here. We live by ourselves.' 'All of you are liars!' he screamed. 'All of you have masked men in the house and none of you is telling the truth!' He ran through the rooms, searching in vain in every corner, under the mattresses and in the cupboards for his masked phantom. He found my photo album and started interrogating me about all the persons he saw in the pictures, my family and my relatives. I was shivering with fear and when he was completely involved with the photos, I ran out of the house. Only when I was sure that the house was empty again did I carefully go back and start clearing up the chaos he had left. The whole night jeeps roamed through the streets; nobody in the village was able to sleep that night. The next day the army came and deported Munife, her three children and Mohammed Hamdi. He is an old man with a heart problem, but nevertheless they took him. They left him only ten minutes to pack some of his belongings before they deported him. He was not even allowed to say goodbye to his wife. For the soldiers a deportation order is a deportation order: they do not think about the consequences for the victims. I think they deport mothers and children so often because they know if a part of the family is outside already, the father will usually follow soon. Again, one family less.

The Intifada continues. We are still put under curfew. The army enters the village almost daily. I hope the Intifada is bringing us the solution the Palestinian people are longing for so badly, so that finally we can live in peace. Inshallah!

Notes

1. Kufr Malik is a small village, of around 2,000 inhabitants situated twelve miles northeast of Ramallah. Some 300 of its inhabitants currently live in Brazil, as do some members of Suha's family. In search of work, Suha's father left the village in 1961 and travelled to Brazil. His children decided to stay together with their mother in Kufr Malik. At the time of the 1967 Six Day War, Suha's mother lived in constant fear of a massacre by Israeli soldiers. Her fear stemmed from her memory of the Deir Yassin massacre. A few months after the end of the 1967

war, therefore, she left the West Bank and followed her husband to Brazil. Only Suha and her sister stayed in the village. Shortly afterwards her sister married and went to live in Abu Dhabi. Suha now lives with her unmarried aunt in her two-roomed house in Kufr Malik.

2. Meron Benvenisti has described the implementation of curfews, which are legalized by Article 124 of the Emergency Defence Regulations, as 'intended to facilitate the activities of the military government during arrests or searches for suspects.' (Meron Benvenisti, *The West Bank Handbook*, Jerusalem, Jerusalem Post, 1986, p. 85). Hardly implemented until the mid 1970s, curfews became a tool of policy again in 1983. During the Intifada the imposition of curfews as a means to control the population and to isolate population centres became a daily procedure. In the first year of the Intifada (9 December 1987–9 December 1988) the military government in the Occupied Territories imposed at least 1,600 curfews, ranging from a few hours up to forty days. Kufr Malik was one of the villages most affected. During the period surrounding the nineteenth session of the Palestine National Council (PNC) in Algiers and the proclamation of an independent Palestinian state (12–15 November 1988), one million people, including the entire population of the Gaza Strip, were placed under curfew. (*Punishing a Nation: Human Rights Violations during the Palestinian Uprising, December 1987–December 1988*, Ramallah, Al-Haq, 1988, p. 177f.)

3. During the Intifada, when the schools were closed by military order, it became a regular practice of the army to use them as makeshift interrogation centres and army posts. In this respect Kufr Malik is not unusual. The Jerusalem Media and Communication Centre reported that between January and June 1989 thirty-seven schools in the West Bank were occupied by the Israeli military, eleven more than once.

4. Suha is referring to the case of 36-year-old Munifeh Abdel Ghani. On 17 October 1989 she was deported over the bridge to Jordan, together with her children Nader, Lena and two-year-old Mohammed. Munifeh was born in Kufr Malik, and like most Palestinians in the West Bank has a Jordanian passport, but no Israeli-issued identity card. In 1977 she married her cousin Hassan and subsequently she travelled every three months to Jordan to renew her Israeli visa. When she and her husband applied in 1989 for a family reunion (the Israeli authorities allow some exiles to return from abroad and visit their families), they were told it would be issued only if Hassan would collaborate with the military authorities, which he refused to do. On 16 October 1989 the village of Kufr Malik was put under curfew yet again, and all the men were ordered to gather in front of the mosque. Meanwhile Munifeh was taken out of her house, driven to the Civil Administration building in Ramallah and, without being told that she would be deported, put into a taxi heading to the Jordan bridge. Only when she threatened to jump out of the speeding taxi was she brought back to Ramallah, and then to Kufr Malik. She was deported the next day together with her children. (*Senabel Daily Press Bulletin*, 19 October 1989).

5. Based on survey data from 174 Palestinian families in the West Bank and Gaza, Raija-Leena Punamäcki concluded: '. . . that the active and reckless behaviour of children is only part of children's reactions to the cruel and overwhelming situation of occupation. Nearly as often children are suffering from many psychosomatic symptoms, sleeping difficulties and different nervous symptoms, such as restlessness, difficulties in concentration, repeated crying as

well as from paralysing fears.' (Raija-Leena Punamäcki, 'Psychological Factors and Violation of Human Rights', *Human Rights* 1/1983, information bulletin of the League for Human Rights and Freedoms, Helsinki, 1983, pp. 4–26.

6. The Finnish psychologist Raija-Leena Punamäcki writes about the stress among Palestinian women and their modes of coping. 'Stress among Palestinian Women under Occupation', *International Journal of Psychology*, 21, 1986, pp. 445–62.

7. The term *mukhtar* ('the chosen one') refers to an individual selected to represent his village to the central authority and vice versa. The decline of the peasant class throughout the 1970s and 1980s led to a corresponding decline in the power of the village mukhtarship. Some *mukhtars* are still very traditional, others are viewed as collaborators or (as part) of the Israeli presence. Their influence is limited anyway by the Israeli-installed village councils. In the first months of the Intifada these Israeli-appointed councils were the cause of an embittered battle for power between the local popular committees and the army.

8. The interview with Suha was taped in November 1989. Even though we allowed a lot of time for the interview, it turned out to be not enough. We had just finished coffee when the army entered the village and announced a curfew. People in the streets started running. Suha was very scared, hid the tape recorder and tried to convince us to stay and not to take the risk of being shot. But we took the chance of leaving during the first half-hour after the announcement, when the army is usually not so strict. Immediately we were picked up by an army jeep. Obviously the soldiers did not know what to do with two blonde young women. We were told to leave the village by the shortest possible route. While walking through the streets of Kufr Malik in order to reach the main road we were passed several times by jeeps announcing curfew. Passing us they interrupted their announcement only to shout obscene remarks into our direction. 'Go and fuck the Arabs', was the usual beginning of their calls. At the crossroads three miles away from the village we found the Kufr Malik workers, waiting for further developments. This time the villagers were lucky. The curfew was only implemented for a few hours, during which the army sealed one of the houses. The next day we visited Kufr Malik again, dug out the tape recorder and finished our interview.

11. We Don't Pay Taxes Any More in Beit Sahour

Miriam Rishmawi

My name is Miriam Rishmawi and I was born in Beit Sahour.[1] I am sixty-two years old and I have five children. Since the beginning of the Intifada we have not paid taxes in Beit Sahour. We do not want to finance an occupying power which is killing our children; we will pay taxes only to our own government. For almost two years now the whole town has refused to pay. This is our civil disobedience: we want to show the military that we are not willing to live under military occupation any longer. Right from the beginning of the Intifada we lived under the same oppressive regime as all the other West Bank villages, towns and refugee camps. Beit Sahour was frequently under curfew; our schools were closed by military order; day and night the army patrol led through the street, carried out identity checks, arrested people and dragged the men out of their beds in the middle of the night to paint over the newly written graffiti. Once in a while one of our men would be asked to visit the tax office, where they would try to convince him that he should pay taxes, that all the rest of the merchants had paid already. But none of them fell into this trap.

For almost one and a half years it stayed relatively calm like this. But in May 1989 the first tax campaign by the Israeli army started. Beit Sahour was put under curfew and hundreds of soldiers were brought into the city to teach us a lesson in the usual way. But we refused to give in. Instead of paying our taxes we handed over our Israeli-supplied identity cards at the municipality as a sign of protest and started a sit-in.[2] Again we were placed under curfew, our men were arrested and the army tried to beat us into reason. The following month everything returned to 'normal' again.

They came again on 19 September. But already, a week before, the mischief had thrown its shadow ahead. The military started to erect a military camp next to the Shepherds Field. They confiscated the house of my husband's cousin, who is currently working and living with his family in Kuwait. The military camp, which was only a few metres away from our house, turned our life upside down. We hardly had a quiet night any more. The soldiers shouted and laughed twenty-four hours a day, so that we could barely sleep. They ran riot in the neighbourhood, patrolled through our garden and, during the night, around our house. When my son needed to pass the camp on his way to the shops, I had to accompany him. Visitors no longer dared to drop by, because they were afraid to be stopped and searched. Only our neighbours, who had to live under the same circumstances, did not bother about the army.

Sometimes the behaviour of the soldiers was both very rude and troublesome. They did not seem to care at all about our thoughts, feelings and customs. That summer the soldiers once in a while stripped off their clothes completely and bathed naked in the drinking water tanks on the flat roofs of our houses. When women passed by on the streets they made sexually offensive remarks and gestures. Aside from the harassment, nobody wanted to use any more the water that the soldiers had taken their bath in. During the night fires were started in empty barrels in the camp and the jeeps drove with wailing motors night and day through the streets of the town.

One week after the army erected the military camp the whole town was put under curfew. Curfews have had many different purposes during the Intifada. They are imposed to break people's resistance, to punish, or to paralyse the whole town so that the army can raid homes, seal and demolish houses or arrest people. This happened to us during that particular curfew. The army wanted my son. He owns a small sewing shop and like every other merchant he had not paid his taxes. Around three in the afternoon soldiers came and kicked our door open. A few minutes previously they had been in our sewing shop and counted the sewing machines in order to estimate our production and thus our tax debts. Seven soldiers rushed into our house and started searching it from top to bottom. Twenty others encircled the house. The soldiers rushed into every room, flung cupboard doors open and pulled out drawers. Their entire contents were tipped onto the beds and the soldiers started searching them for tax papers and documents. Then they arrested my son for non-payment of taxes. In front of my eyes they loaded him onto the jeep and took him away. During the whole time the search lasted my other two sons were present in the house, unable to do anything. What can we do against an occupying army? But they were not arrested, because the sewing shop is registered in the name of their brother. The whole time our neighbours were watching behind their curtains but there was no way for them to help us. When the jeeps disappeared around the corner they came rushing into the house. I felt terrible, empty and at the same time furious. I had rather they had taken my life than my son.

Here in Beit Sahour we are like a big family. All of us stick together. The origins of the town can be traced back to eight founding fathers, who settled here many hundreds of years ago, and intermarried and had children. I know almost all the families in Beit Sahour, their names and their family histories. We are a city with the solidarity of a village, but with a liberal urban lifestyle. It was not long before the whole city learned about the arrest of my son. A lot of friends came to offer their help and solidarity. I was not left alone. But I was not the only mother whose son had been arrested. They also took twelve other men who had not paid their taxes.

After this wave of arrests we were placed under curfew for another nine days. We could not leave the house. The whole time, telephone lines were cut and I had no way of getting to know the fate of my son. After four days the army lifted the curfew for two hours, so that we could go shopping and exchange news. But we were not permitted to leave the town. This was the prelude to the military siege of Beit Sahour, during which nobody without Beit Sahour residency was allowed to enter the town boundaries. The streets leading out of the town were blocked by piles of rubble and rubbish. The army approached with bulldozers which pushed huge mounds across the streets, then some of these ramparts were guarded by snipers. Whoever wanted to leave the city without interrogation on the spot and the constant risk of arrest had to sneak out along hidden mountain trails.

Four days without an opportunity to go shopping were easy to survive. We in Beit Sahour had been prepared because every day we expected curfew and had stored enough food supplies. When we did become in need of something, as when families with a lot of children ran out of milk or fresh vegetables, we asked our neighbours for help. Everybody helped everybody else and nobody needed to starve.

According to an army announcement, nobody was supposed to leave their house. But the army ran short of soldiers to patrol all the streets. When we wanted to visit neighbours I would leave the house with one of my grandchildren, cross the garden and hide behind the entrance gate. When the coast seemed clear, we would run across the street and sneak into the neighbour's house.

When the curfew was briefly lifted, I thought only of my son. I rushed to the municipality and searched for the mayor. All the other families whose husbands, sons and fathers were jailed flooded in as well. We were a huge group waiting for an answer. The mayor found out that all the men were in the Bassa, the military prison beside the Hebron–Jerusalem road.

When my son returned back home from jail he told me what had happened after his arrest. All the men had been driven to the tax office. The tax official summed up the amount of taxes they owed. But, like the rest of the arrested, he refused to pay. Thereupon they were taken to jail. When we learned their whereabouts all the families tried to bring food into the cells, but in vain. My son told me later what conditions were like in the jail. The men were confined each with up to seventy persons in cells which had been constructed for seven. They were only a few at the beginning but then more and more arrested men were brought into the cell. When the army raided

Beit Sahour not only merchants with tax debts were arrested, but a lot of other men as well. The food was dreadful too. One tomato was distributed between nine men. Tea was served in rusty tins. When the men came to lie down to sleep each of them had to decide first which side he wanted to sleep on, because by no means was there room to turn over in one's sleep.

My son was in jail for seven days, then the Israelis gave him an ultimatum. They said, 'You have a respite until the 2nd of September to decide whether you want to pay the taxes or not. If you don't, you will be imprisoned for two years.'

And then, in the morning of 21 September, the tax raid started. Tax officials went from house to house protected by soldiers. They asked at the doorstep, 'Do you want to pay taxes, yes or no?' All Beit Sahouris gave a single answer: 'No.' Immediately they had got their reply the soldiers invaded each house and started to empty them. Trucks to take the furniture were already parked in front of the houses. The army was well prepared. Everything that was moveable was taken. They took furniture, fridges, ovens, pictures, television sets, stereo players, toys, food and even bottles of alcohol. The soldiers searched the rooms for jewellery and money. My neighbour was asked, 'Where did you hide your gold? We know that Arab women always have gold.' While searching for gold they ripped up the cushions of the people's sofas and armchairs and left a trail of devastation. Food was taken out of refrigerators and destroyed. Machines that were not taken too were often destroyed. When appliances were confiscated and they would not fit through the doors, the soldiers simply hit huge holes in the walls, which the wind still blows through today. The army also entered the homes of people without any tax debts and started to search them. Sitt Kokaly does not even work, so she has no need to pay taxes. When she told this to the tax official he answered, 'From today on you will have to pay taxes.'

When women stepped in the way of the soldiers, they were either pushed aside, beaten or locked into one of the rooms of their home. Regina Hannouna, who is a few years older than I am, suffered a heart attack when the soldiers raided her home. When her daughter-in-law wanted to call an ambulance the soldier ripped the phone out of the wall. Regina is now in the intensive care unit in Makkased Hospital in Jerusalem. Such incidents were many. Too many. They became topics of conversation for the whole town and everybody asked when their turn would come.

On this particular occasion we were exempt from the search of the army. But they came to us on 11 October. On that day all of us were in the fields for the olive harvest. Hardly anyone was in the deserted streets. The army arrived first at the sewing shop of my son and found it closed. My son was on his way back to town after dropping us off in the fields. When they found nobody to open the door of the workshop, the soldiers broke in and smashed the door. Then they started confiscating the sewing machines and loaded them onto a truck ready in front of the building. When my son arrived it was too late to prevent them and he stood helplessly watching. But the sewing machines did not seem to be enough for them. My son in tow, the soldiers went to our home. My sister-in-law lives only a few metres away from us and she always has a spare key. When she saw the army jeeps stopping in front of our house she came with the key so that they would not break a second door. Then they raided the house. But our furniture was not good enough for them. They said to my son, 'This is all old stuff,' and instead of the furniture they loaded him onto the jeep. Since then I have not seen him. He is still in jail.

It was hours later before we got to know what had happened at home. The whole family was picking olives all day and when dusk fell we waited for my son to come and fetch us. But he failed to arrive at the agreed time and when it got later and later I started to worry. Suddenly the figure of my eldest son appeared between the olive trees. Immediately I knew that something had happened. I asked him, 'Did they take your brother?' He caught his breath, asked for a short rest and then told us what had happened. There was no strength left in our hands to continue picking and we left. The olives stayed on the trees. That's where they still are, we have not been there again to finish the work.

A week ago, after forty-one days of detention pending trial, he was sentenced to seventy-five days' imprisonment for tax evasion. The forty-one days of detention pending trial were not taken into account, and the detention officially began on the day of sentence. After these seventy-five days of arrest he will have sixteen months in which to collect all his tax papers and hand them in. If he does not pay taxes by then, he will be sentenced to two years' imprisonment. Our tax debts add up to 2,500 NS (New Shekels) by now.[3] If we were to pay the money he would immediately be set free. But we do not have the money and even if we did, he would not pay.

The day after my son's arrest my second-born son did not go to work in his clinic, but instead stayed at home to decide on a plan of action. The next morning he had to go to work because his patients were waiting. By that time the army had erected a checkpost on the main road out of our town and was controlling all cars and people on their way out and in. This street was now the only exit to the town because all the rest were blocked with rubble barricades. The soldiers had lists of all the Beit Sahouris who did not pay taxes. The line of cars grew longer and longer (this endless waiting became a morning routine for everybody who had to leave the town to go to work). Everybody had to show his identity card and it was checked against two lists. The soldiers called 'bingo' when they found either someone who did not pay taxes or whose name was on the blacklist of the Israeli secret service.

When my son reached the checkpost and showed his ID to the soldiers he was arrested. He travelled back into the town with his hands tied behind his back. They took him to the newly erected army camp just behind our house. Friends of my son had watched his arrest and informed us before the jeeps reached the army camp. My daughter-in-law and I took her four children to a neighbour and ran over to the camp. We both were very worried for my son because he was unwell. In four day's time he was to be operated on for an inflammation in his back. We could see from the roof of our house that he was sitting beside a tent with other prisoners and could hardly hold himself upright. We cooked a meal and carried it over to the camp. But we were refused entry. When I tried to persuade the guard, he pointed his submachine gun at my chest and threatened to kill me. When I retreated he followed me and I had to leave.

For the whole day we stood at the windows of the upper floor of our house and stared over to the camp. My little granddaughter sensed our anxiety and cried all the time for her daddy. Holding her crying daughter by the hand my daughter-in-law again tried to enter through the camp gate. But in vain. Again she was chased away. At four in the afternoon we saw my son being loaded into a jeep. We ran down to the camp and got there just in time to jump in the jeep's path as it was leaving. The driver stopped the car, maybe because he felt sorry for us. He allowed my son to open the window a few inches, and hold his arm out so that his wife and daughter could hold his hand. But just behind the jeep was a car containing army officials. Immediately my granddaughter took her father's hand, the driver started to blow the horn like mad. This was the signal for the driver of the jeep to speed off. Ever since that day my little granddaughter has believed that her father is furious with her. A few times every day she says, 'Daddy is angry at me. He won't talk with me any more.' Her father is the only one of my sons who is married and has children. His four children are always asking for him, which tears my heart apart.

After my son was arrested the neighbours came to visit every day. We drink coffee or tea, but all the old topics of conversation, like children, cooking, fashion and family business, are dead. We talk about the tax campaign, about the military and about our children in jail and detention centres. We know that our problem is the Israeli occupation. As long as we are under occupation we will be unable to solve any of our problems.

Until 31 October 1989 we were under military siege and from 4 p.m. until 6 a.m. we were under curfew. The whole town of Beit Sahour is divided into several districts, in each of which live between thirty and fifty families. Each area has its own committee.[4] This coordinates all the activities in the area, keeps in constant contact with other district committees and organizes help where help is needed. For example, if the head of a family is arrested the family will need food and help. The committee will organize babysitters for the children when the mother is out at work. It distributes food and organizes medical supplies, medical aid, lectures and school classes, counselling on agriculture and household economy and everything that is needed with the shops closed. This is necessary, because almost everything is confiscated anyhow, and because the merchants follow the strike and boycott regulations. I had a few tins of powdered milk, which I did not need. The committee distributed them to needy families who could not provide their children with milk. Women were active in establishing the neighbourhood committees in the first months of the Intifada, and they are still their backbone.

The military siege during the tax campaign brought the people of the town even closer together than before. We had to rely on each other in order to distribute food, medical aid and help equally. All of us had to change our eating habits, and the children had to learn to live without sweets.

During the first nine days, when the curfew had been lifted but Beit Sahour was declared a military zone that nobody was allowed to enter, we got lots of visitors. Most of them tried to avoid the checkposts, drove to Bethlehem and sneaked through courtyards and private gardens into the centre of Beit Sahour. Palestinian women from women's organizations all over the West Bank and Gaza came with solidarity greetings and presents. One group smuggled in gallons of olive oil. They visited the families whose workshops had been stripped of machinery and technical equipment: like the pharmacy of Emily Rishmawi, which was cleared almost completely except for some baby's teething rings which were left on the empty shelves; they also visited Umm Edmond.[5] Her son Edmond was the first person killed in Beit Sahour since the beginning of the Intifada. A soldier on lookout duties on one of the roofs in the centre of Beit Sahour dropped a stone down from the roof. It fell on Edmond's head and killed him immediately. Umm Edmond welcomes her guests with coffee served on the floor because all her furniture was confiscated and sold like all the other furniture by auction in Tel Aviv.[6]

In addition to local and international journalists, fact-finding missions and solidarity groups, a number of Israeli peace activists and journalists visited us as well.[7] One day I saw a group of Israeli visitors pass by our house. I invited them to come in and we drank tea together while soldiers patrolled around the house. Our guests were afraid that they would get us into trouble, so they left their phone numbers and asked for ours. Back home, when they had managed to cross the Green Line, they phoned and asked if everything was okay.

I have had contacts with Israelis for a long time. We buy the materials for our sewing workshop from Israeli commission agents. The first private, rather than business contacts I had was during a funeral three months ago. A young man from Dheisheh refugee camp was killed and his funeral took place in the house of his parents at Beit Sahour. After the ceremony was over, the mourners met back at the house. Among them were a few Israeli women. From the very beginning we did not see them as enemies, but rather as women fighting together with us against oppression and injustice. Israelis who are fighting with us against the occupation policy of their government are very much respected here. They are always welcome as friends. The women had their cameras ready in case the soldiers came. But we were afraid that their cameras would be confiscated and together with my neighbour I hid them. The ice was broken. All this was three months ago. What impressed me most was the story of one of the Jewish women about the arrest of her son in Jerusalem. He was participating in a demonstration against the occupation and was holding a poster proclaiming, 'Stop the Occupation'. Israelis who like us are against the occupation have a difficult time in their own society.

I was never an activist. But once, when I visited my son in prison, he said, 'It's not enough that you come and visit me in jail. You have to do something in Beit Sahour.' This remark ran through my mind for a long time. I kept wondering what I could do apart from work in the neighbourhood committees. Then the idea came to me to write a leaflet and send it outside. I called together all the women whose sons had been arrested and we began formulating it. We thought that through a leaflet we could make our situation known to the outside world and, through the pressure of public opinion, could free our sons – like the pressure from outside later made the military government stop the tax raid and end the military siege. We wanted to explain why we refuse to pay taxes, why our sons are willing to undergo imprisonment for fifty or seventy-five days, and why already our children know what it means not to pay taxes. We will only pay taxes to our own state of Palestine. Because of these considerations all of us women sat down together and drew up the leaflet.

The military siege of Beit Sahour lasted from 19 September until 30 October. That evening, the usual jeep that drove through the streets each night announcing the night curfew failed to show up. The radio announced that the tax campaign would end the next day, and the next evening bulldozers appeared and started pushing the rubble barricades into the gutters. This was a cue for everybody to leave their houses and congregate on the streets. All the inhabitants of Beit Sahour came out. Our neighbours ran out too, of course, and we all started congratulating each other, we fell into one other's arms and happily watched the laughing faces of the children as they ran in the streets. The whole town celebrated until midnight. It was as if we had been forty days imprisoned in a cell and suddenly the door had opened into freedom. I was as relieved as the other people in town, but I could not be so happy because my two sons were still in jail. Then the commanding officer of the whole tax raid operation came into our town and faced the press. Israeli journalists asked him if Beit Sahour had won. He replied, 'This is a difficult question which I am not able to answer.' But the answer was clearly written on his face. We had gained a victory.

On Sunday 5 November the people of the town celebrated its reopening with a big party. The streets were crowded with people. Some of our neighbours had painted placards and the children were singing slogans. The people were to assemble first at the Catholic church, and by the time we arrived, there were already a lot of people there, including a delegation of a hundred Americans. Most of them were Palestinians with American citizenship. Our mayor, Hanna al-Atrash, the head of the Higher Muslim Council from Jerusalem, Sheikh Sa'ad al-Din al-Alami, and an envoy of the former US president Carter were there as well, and each of them made a speech. All spoke of their hope for peace and of the steadfastness of Palestinians of all religions. We were an example that Christians, Muslims and Jews must join ranks in working for peace and that they are able to do so. It was a strange atmosphere. We all felt united and empowered by this openly expressed solidarity from outside, even if not all the guests had made it into Beit Sahour.

Inside the church there were also a lot of journalists and about a dozen Israelis. When the service was over we learned that the Israelis had come to Beit Sahour the day before, because they expected the army to prevent them from reaching the town. And, things happened as they had predicted. The army encircled the town and refused to let more than a handful of people through. More than a hundred journalists and about sixty Israeli peace activists, plus some Christians and Muslims who also were not allowed to enter the town, held a spontaneous meeting in the fields outside the town to protest at the army measures.[8]

After the ceremony at the Catholic church we went to the Greek Orthodox church, and then to the mosque. All the people – we were at least 5,000 – walked to the municipality and then to the Church of the Latin Patriarch. When it had first got underway, the whole march had been silent, but the more people joined it, the more the *shebab* started singing nationalist slogans such as 'PLO–Israel no' and 'Down with the occupation'. It was a demonstration of political and confessional unity.

During the ceremony in the Church of the Latin Patriarch the Americans demonstrated in front of the church. They unrolled trilingual placards against the tax campaign. And the whole crowd sang. Then the army appeared and ordered everyone to leave. Over the loudspeakers they shouted at the Americans, 'Leave this place. This is a closed military area.' Nobody seemed to pay any attention and people sat down on the ground instead. Then the soldiers began to confiscate the placards. They seized cameras from several of the journalists and started beating the demonstrators. The usual army action followed, which left many people bruised and bloody, and others in jail.

We remained steadfast under the military siege, but the end of our struggle is still ahead. We will continue our civil disobedience and we will not pay taxes. Today the streets are open again, but who knows for how long. All over the West Bank and Gaza other streets are blocked instead. Army actions similar to that which took place in Beit Sahour are taking place every day in many obscure villages and camps, whose people do not catch the attention of the foreign press. Only a political solution will put an end to the Intifada and, I hope, bring peace for both our peoples.

Notes

1. Beit Sahour is a small town in the West Bank with 12,000 inhabitants. Close to the road leading from Bethlehem to Herodion, the town is built on the eastern slope of Bethlehem mountain, stretching down to the field where, according to the Bible, the angel first appeared to the shepherds, announcing the birth of Jesus Christ. The majority of the inhabitants of Beit Sahour are Christians, and they live together with their Muslim neighbours in harmony. When the first leaflets (the *bayan*) from the leadership of the Intifada appeared in the streets of Beit Sahour, the Beit Sahouris tried to follow the instructions in them as closely as possible. The agronomist Jad Is'hak developed a programme for the production of food in order to enable the Beit Sahouris to become self-reliant and to produce substitutes for the boycotted Israeli products; when the universities and schools were closed by military order, teachers and parents taught illegally in homes and olive groves; neighbourhood and women's committees built up a network of medical, pedagogic, agricultural and solidarity voluntary groups; the *shebab* every night covered the walls of the city with fresh graffiti, nationalist slogans and the latest political demands, they flew Palestinian flags, organized guards and vigilante groups and stoned Jewish settlers when they sped through the town to their settlement, Tekoa. In September 1989 the united refusal of the whole Beit Sahour population to pay taxes made the Israeli miltary decide to clamp down on the whole town in order to break its resistance. This military siege, and the way the city coped with it, made Beit Sahour known worldwide as a symbol of the civil disobedience that is the Intifada.

2. At the peak of the tax campaign the people of Beit Sahour published a declaration to explain the reason for their refusal to pay taxes. Here is an excerpt: 'You may ask why we don't pay taxes!! – We consider the occupation of one people by another is a clear violation of all international laws and religions, and is against the simplest human rights and democracy. The Israeli policy in collecting taxes contradicts international agreements and especially the Geneva and Hague conventions in this respect. The Israeli authorities, during the twenty-two years of occupation, have not produced any account of what the taxes collected in the West Bank have been spent on. The authorities . . . have created new sorts of taxes which did not exist before, like value added tax (VAT),

and stone tax. . . . Social insurance, houses for the old, or the handicapped or orphans are almost nonexistent . . . there is no free education for our children despite the fact that we are liable for taxes . . . while the state-owned universities in the West Bank and Gaza Strip have been closed for more than two years. . . . Regarding our natural resources the Israeli authorities have taken full control of our water resources and cut the flow of water to us, diverted water to the settlements and sold what was left to us at a very high price. . . . For all these reasons, and as a result of our firm conviction that the money collected as a result of the high taxes levied on us goes towards the purchase of bullets and tear gas to kill our children, we have decided not to pay taxes any more.'

3. About US$1,200.

4. The popular committees emerged after the beginning of the Intifada. Their structures have their roots in the early mass movement in the West Bank and Gaza Strip, in the student, women's and voluntary work movements, and in the trade unions. The popular committees organize together with these organizations many kinds of community work; they keep the Intifada running and facilitate the construction of the infrastructure of the future Palestinian state. According to an Israeli military order of summer 1988 they are illegal, and people can be punished for participation in them with high fines and long jail sentences. This measure had an immediate effect. The work of the committees was rendered more difficult and pushed into secrecy. Under military siege the committees are sometimes the only means of contact between us all and help safeguard the lives of the population.

5. In the pharmacy of Emily and Elias Rishmawi medicines to the value of around US$150,000 were confiscated. During the tax campaign, 120 workshops in Beit Sahour (including some doing traditional mother-of-pearl and olivewood carvings), shops and private houses were affected. According to official Israeli sources, goods and machinery worth around US$2.5 million were confiscated (*Senabel Daily Press Bulletin*, 19 October 1989). The Beit Sahouris themselves put their losses at around US$8 million.

6. A group was formed in Israel which tried to buy the Beit Sahour goods and bring them back to their original owners.

7. Among the Israeli groups which were in solidarity with Beit Sahour were the 21st Year, Campus, Hal-ah Hakibush, the Beita Committee, Kav Yarok and the Beit Sahour Committee. The first contacts between Israeli groups and the people of Beit Sahour started in mid-1988. At the beginning of 1989 a group of 70 Israelis, mostly practising Jews, brought their families to spend Shabbat with families in Beit Sahour. 'In one way . . . it was frightening to many of the Jewish participants: they and their children would be sleeping in an Arab town with the nearest Jew forty or fifty minutes' walk away. But the kids, though often lacking a common language, got together in five minutes.' Maxine Kaufmann Nunn, 'Beit Sahour', *The Other Israel*, No. 39, November–December, 1989, p.3.

12. Deportation and the Principle of Hope

In'am Zaqut

My husband Majed Abdullah Labadi was deported in August 1989. Since then I have not seen him and all my applications for travel documents to enable me to leave the country have been turned down by the Israeli occupation authorities. Our case is not an exceptional one in Palestinian society under occupation – on the contrary. Therefore I want to tell my story.

Growing up under occupation

I am the youngest of eleven children, and I grew up in Shati refugee camp in the Gaza strip.[1] My father supported us by working as a nurse in the United Nations Relief and Works Agency [UNRWA]. When I was five years old, in 1970, the army came with bulldozers and knocked down our house. I remember it very well. It was raining and my father sent us to the house of relatives because he did not want us to see our house demolished. It was the second time that my father had lost his home. The first night in our new, crowded accommodation he told us about our house in Ashdod, which he had had to leave in the 1948 war. It was very difficult for my family, there were six of us at that time, to cope with the demolition.

But this was not the end of my experience of all the misery that life under occupation brings. My brother was killed in 1978 in Lebanon. He was a lieutenant in the Democratic Front for the Liberation of Palestine. His wife was originally from Nablus but she had gone with Bashir to Lebanon. When he died she wanted to return home to her family, but she had lost her identity card and therefore was unable to return. I think she now lives somewhere in Syria. After the death of my brother, the same year, my brother Samir left to study in Havana. He is a dentist by now. He lost his identity card – I don't know how – and because of that the Israeli military authorities are refusing him a *laissez-passer*, so he is not allowed back home. Samir was the first to be banned from his home. In August 1989 my brother Jamal was deported and my brother Baha was jailed.

Majed

I met my husband Majed before I left the Gaza Strip to study at Birzeit University. I was attracted to his whole personality: he is a very active and open man and he constantly talked to me of our situation. I too am very much a child of this country, and grew up with all the pressures of the occupation.

Then I started my studies at Birzeit University and became active in the student council. Majed at that time was a very active trade unionist. I was elected to the student council and usually attended meetings until very late at night. I had to learn a lot of things which in our society are not usually done by a woman: for example, how to speak with a microphone in front of many students, which I had to do many times at meetings. The students had a lot of social and economical problems and we tried to deal with them. But the problem they felt most was the constant pressure from the military authorities and the frequent closure of the universities, which made meaningful study very difficult.[2]

After I felt that I was in love with Majed I many times thought about our future lives. I felt there was a high chance that Majed might be held for a time in jail and that I, as his wife, would have to cope with that. Maybe he would be beaten and harassed or threatened. I was prepared for many eventualities. But all these possibilities failed to make me hesitate because I am very much like Majed. I am not a housewife who spends all her life cooking, cleaning, looking after children and waiting for her husband to come home. I have learned during my life, that I have to be active in my society. I think our problems will not be solved until we work very hard. So I started to work with Majed.

At the end of 1986 Majed and I decided to get married in January 1987. A week before the wedding was scheduled to take place, Majed was served with a renewed town arrest order confining him to Abu Diss. Six months later, in July 1987, the town arrest order was renewed for the fourth time. But we decided despite all the obstacles to marry in October 1987. On 1 October a military order confined me under town arrest to Shati camp. We could not meet for the wedding: Majed was stuck in Abu Diss and I was imprisoned in Shati. We could only talk over the phone with each other – and I had to call him because we had no phone in the house. On 10 January 1988, ten days before the end of his town arrest, Majed was imprisoned. It was the third time he had been jailed (he had already spent fifteen months in prison in 1980, and in 1985 he was held under administrative detention). When he was released ten days later I was under town arrest in Shati. Six months later, on 11 June 1988, we got married. But it was a strange marriage because the bridegroom was absent, and I celebrated our wedding with just a few family members in our house in Shati camp. Majed had to hide because he was wanted. The police considered him to be politically active and a leader of the Intifada. At 10 p.m. Majed sneaked into our hideout and our strange honeymoon started.

Majed's arrest

When I married Majed I thought, if we can live together for two months that will be very good luck. But I did not consider the possibility of deportation. I think the Intifada changed the tactics of the Israeli army. Since the beginning of the Intifada there have been hardly any town arrests. It makes no sense to confine someone to a place which is under curfew half the time anyhow, and where he can be very active. So, during the Intifada there have been only five or six cases of town arrest. During the Intifada the prisons, such as Ansar 3, Dahriyieh or Jneid, deportation and killings or injuries have been used as substitutes for town arrest or punishment.[3] And of course hundreds of persons have been issued special 'green' identity cards prohibiting them from leaving the West Bank or the Gaza Strip.

After we got married, Majed and I lived together in our house at Bir Nabala near Jerusalem for one month. Five weeks after the wedding, on 17 July, the army banged at the door and around thirty soldiers came to take Majed away. At first I failed to realize what had happened. I was as if paralysed; my mind refused to acknowledge that he was no longer in the house. Then it hit me. They had taken Majed, my husband, myself.

After he was arrested and I was left alone in the house I felt that the struggle was going to take on a new dimension for me. It was going to be a struggle not only because I believe in the cause of my people but also because suddenly I was very personally involved. If you are personally affected, that strengthens your readiness to action even more. For me the arrest of Majed was something very special. He is not a husband in the traditional Palestinian sense. Our relationship was already very developed and we were matched intellectually, in our household responsibilities, and in our political and social work. Even when Majed was under arrest and I could only visit him for half an hour at a time because he was under interrogation by Shabak, we did not only talk about private matters.[4] Most of the time we spoke about general problems, though that does not mean that we forgot our private life because of politics.

When we had got married, we had decided not to have children so long as the situation was so uncertain. But had I known what would happen to Majed I would have liked to be pregnant. There would have been someone left for me, a part of my husband. But now, under these circumstances, I think I would have found things very difficult with a child. I can see it in front of my own eyes with Naila, my sister-in-law.[5] Her little boy was born after the deportation of my brother Jamal, her husband, and he has never seen his father, but he asks for him constantly. Especially when he hears his voice over the phone.

The same is happening to the children of my husband's brother Mohammed, who also has been deported, and my sister-in-law Amal. Both children still remember their father well, but their memory of him is fading. It is very difficult for children to understand what deportation means. The children always ask for their father and for their uncle. 'Where are they and when are they going to come back?' But what is the answer? You cannot tell them anything precise, that they are going to come back in a month or two. So we talk about the political situation and try to explain to them why their fathers have been deported: 'There is the Intifada and there are people who have decided that they cannot go on like this anymore and they are fighting for their rights.' After that, they can come back, we tell the children. This morning I went with Khalid, Amal's little boy, to the doctor. He could find nothing physically wrong, though Khalid was feeling very bad; the doctor said Khalid's condition was psychological. There is no medicine for the effects of oppression on people, except a political medicine.

What are probably mostly deeply etched into the children's memories are the prison visits. When their father was in jail before deportation they visited him weekly. Outside his home the only thing that Khalid knows is the prison. He has never been to the seaside or to a park. His father was in jail and his mother was under town arrest for a year. Then the Intifada started. For Khalid the jail was all these things together, the seaside and the park, because there he could see his father and his uncle Majed.

At that time four deportees from Gaza and nine from the West Bank decided to appeal against their expulsion to the Israeli High Court of Justice. We knew that the High Court could do nothing because the Mukkabarat has the files and makes the decisions.[6] There is no law in the West Bank, only military orders.[7] In our view the whole legal procedure is like a charade to give the world the impression that there is legal justice for the Palestinians in the Occupied Territories, even though there is none. We went to the High Court not because we thought there was any chance to stop the deportations but in order to do our best to prevent there being a new list of deportees during the year that the appeal would take. And of course we were able to visit them in jail: there was at least the possibility of seeing each other. There was almost a year between the arrest of Majed and his actual deportation.

A last visit

While Majed was in jail awaiting deportation, I decided to join the committee of families of deportees which had been established in July 1988. We wrote many letters and petitions to the Arab states and to the US, Europe and human rights associations in Israel. We talked with American, British and other consuls to find a way to end the deportation policy. We talked every time about a policy which is dividing families, separating husbands from wives, children from parents. We participated in marches in Tel Aviv and Jerusalem, outside the homes of Yitzhak Shamir and Herzog, and organized demonstrations and sit-ins. But despite the illegality of the deportation policy according to all international laws, it continues.

I learned the exact time of Majed's deportation only on the morning of the day he was to be expelled. Some journalists phoned and told me, 'In two or three hours Majed will be in south Lebanon.' Immediately I decided to go to Jneid prison to see Majed. I went with my mother and my mother-in-law, Fadwa, Ayishe and the children. When we reached the prison we waited for six hours to be allowed in to speak with Majed. After six hours' waiting the guard told us, 'The man you are looking for is not here. He is in Ramleh prison.'

At four in the afternoon we arrived at Ramleh. And this time we were told the truth. Majed was waiting in the prison to be deported and we could visit him for half an hour.

This last visit was very tense, so different from all those we had had in the previous year. I tried hard to convince the soldiers that they should let all of us into the visitors' room to see Majed. It was our last possible visit and our last chance to see him. And we managed to. All the children were allowed in as well. The prison guard led us into a small room. On one side of it were bars. Majed was behind them. There were five soldiers with us in the small room, three on Majed's side and two on my side of the bars. Majed was the only prisoner in the room. 'You are very late,' the soldiers told us. 'The other deportees were visited long ago.'

It was a strange atmosphere. The soldiers seemed to treat us as if we were part of the furniture. They laughed and joked loudly as if we were not there. They seemed not to recognize what the situation meant for us, that we and Majed might be seeing each other for the last time. But immediately I got close to the bars the atmosphere changed. Suddenly as Majed tried to hold us and kiss us through the bars I felt strong and the soldiers suddenly appeared weak and small. Majed and I spoke about what was happening outside the jail. I promised him that we would struggle so that he could come back. And he promised that wherever he was, in south Lebanon, Egypt or elsewhere, he would continue to struggle, in order to hasten the day when he could come back. Seeing his face through the iron bars I had the feeling that he was even stronger than before. Then we spoke about us, about the chances of being able to see each other again, about the experiences of other women activists whom the Israeli military refused to give a *laissez-passer* to leave the country. I told Majed that I would try hard to come to see him soon. I would travel when I was allowed to, but if I could only leave by agreeing to certain conditions, I would never do so. He agreed with me and pressed the hand I had stretched through the bars in support.

I turned towards one of the guards and told him, 'look, this is democracy in Israel. I can't hold my husband, I can't see him and kiss him like husband and wife should. My mother-in-law can't see her son, can't hold him and can't live with him as is the tradition is our society.'

He answered, 'What can I do? The Mukkabarat gave the orders and we have to follow.' I know that there are soldiers who want to refuse, who can grasp what is happening. They must speak out! They have to come into the open!

After half an hour we had to leave the room. This was on Friday. On our way back from the prison in the car, my mind was in a state of confusion. I could think of nothing except that Majed was to be deported. Then I got hold of my rationality again. Tomorrow would be Saturday. Because it is the Jewish Shabbat there would be no deportations. So the earliest day they would deport him was Sunday. That evening I sat down at the table and started writing in order to get rid of the tension in my body and mind. I invented the story of a family but the story was actually my own. Of a family like ours who has a family member outside the country and who cannot get in touch with them. About all the feelings of hopelessness and hope, of the fight in oneself to be strong and not to give in. Of the tension in each of us and how everybody tries to cope with it.

That night I was unable to sleep. At seven I had to go to work. But even there, all I could think about was the deportation.

The day of deportation

On Sunday 27 August I woke up early, at 5 a.m. I had dreamed of Majed. That day, I was unable to work at anything, and to be able to do something and to leave the tension of the house I went to the Red Cross in Jerusalem. One of the representatives told me that the Red Cross is unable to do anything against the deportation policy of the Israeli government and that they are fundamentally against it. The Red Cross is not informed when Palestinians are deported and they get to know details only when the deportees knock at the doors of the Red Cross offices in south Lebanon. I left the Red Cross at noon and back in Abu Diss I started waiting again. All of us were nervous and tense, but there was nothing we could do. Two hours later some journalists phoned and told us that the deportations had started. At 4 p.m. exactly the journalists phoned again and told me that Majed was now in south Lebanon. They knew because they were in a helicopter in front of the soldiers and Majed and the other deportees.

When the phone went dead, we took from a shelf a videotape of the wedding of my brother Jamal and Naila. It was made in December 1986, not such a long time ago, but as we sat together in front of the television and watched this episode of our family history, we recognized for the first time how much had happened since then. Three of the wedding guests had been killed: Muhammed Abu Nasser and my relative Muhammed Zaqut from Nuseirat camp, and Adwe who was killed in Deir Dibsea, near Ramallah. More than ten of the guests were now in prison, including my brothers Walid and Adba. Jamal, my brother, had been deported. My husband Majed and his brother Muhammed had been deported. Three of the women guests had been jailed afterwards and were now abroad. The two years of the Intifada seemed to have been twenty, so many things had happened.

When I saw my mother's face on the videotape I was astonished by how happy she looked. Now the lines of sorrow in her face were much deeper and she looked very, very sad. She had given birth to seven sons and two daughters and now in our big family house there was nobody but her and my father.

After the deportation I moved from our house in Bir Nabala back to the house of my mother-in-law. Here I lived with her, my three sisters-in-law and the two children of Amal and Mohammed. After Majed's deportation a lot of visitors came. Relatives and friends visited me. The women activists of the Palestinian Women's Movement brought news and expressed their solidarity. Members of the Union of Democratic Youth paid a visit. Some teachers from Birzeit University came, as well as some journalists and Israelis. Many friends from Israeli peace groups visited me, from Peace Now, Israeli Women for Political Prisoners, Women in Black, the 21st Year, Dai la Kibbush and others. Most of the activists of these groups were already my friends before Majed's deportation. I have many Jewish Israeli friends and I have learned that they can be both Jewish and my friends. When they come to my house they inform us about their work inside the Green Line.[8] They talk about their political efforts to stop the occupation and the work of small groups of Israeli professionals to document and ease our suffering from collective punishments such as house demolitions and extended curfews.

We have had many meetings and have talked a lot about Israeli policy in West Bank and Gaza. Everyone who has come agreed that the deportation policy is a violation of every law in the world and of the Fourth Geneva Convention, that it was banned by the Nuremberg Military Tribunal and is unjust for Majed and the others.[9] We consider the deportation policy to be an attempt to force more and more Palestinians to leave the country. Deportation of one individual is *de facto* deportation of the whole family because where she can the wife will follow her husband into exile with their children. The supporters of the transfer policy want to deport all Palestinians, to empty the Promised Land for Jewish settlers.

Life is a struggle – we must go on

In October 1989 I filled in the application form for a *laisser passer*. Until now I have received no answer. I consider this reaction of the administration to be a refusal. I hope that I will be able one day to see Majed. But I hope I can see him for as long as I want, where I want and at the time I want to see him. I would refuse to sign a paper that set conditions on my leave to travel, like 'go for two years or not at all'. I would refuse because I would be convinced that they wanted to deport me like they deported Majed. I wait for the day when we get our rights because I know that this will be the day I can see my husband again: when we have a Palestinian state alongside the Israeli state. I think after several years of Intifada our people have decided to struggle even harder than before, until we win our liberation, our identity cards, our state. We have reached the limit of our endurance of the Israeli occupation. There is no way back, we have to go on.

The deportation of Majed pushed me to struggle even harder than before. I constantly push myself to be more and more active on all possible levels: at the universities, for women and for changes in my society. One of my activities is the group of families of deportees. We were only five women when we founded the committee: Naila, Amal, Lina Tbeile from Nablus, the wife of Mohammed M'tour and I.[10] We saw our activities as not only for the deportees but as a struggle against the overall occupation policy of Israel.

There are three deportees in my family, and when I look into the faces of my mother and mother-in-law, I can read what they feel in their eyes. They have made the decision that they are going to see their sons in their homeland. That they must struggle and struggle and struggle. They have nothing left but their struggle. They are willing to do everything they can do at their age. Like my mother-in-law, who wrote an appeal.[11] They go to every sit-in in front of the Red Cross that is concerned with imprisonment or deportations. They make solidarity visits to the families of women whose sons have been killed. They visit the injured whose houses are in reach.

Even though we are two families that have been hit hard by the Israeli occupation, I do not think we are an exception. There are many families who have lost a member, whose homes have been demolished or whose children or fathers have been deported. Most Palestinian families are split in one way or another. In the last few months there have been a lot of cases in which women with children have been deported from their villages because they did not have an Israeli-issued identity card.[12] They deport a lot of women in such cases now, and we in the deportation committee want to follow them up. We have visited several women who live in fear that they might be deported any night and who no longer dare sleep in their houses.

The constant threat of deportation is also affecting women activists who apply for a *lamshamel* (family reunion) but until now unsuccessfully.[13] I know one example in Dura camp, near Ramallah. Three months ago a woman from Dura who is very active in the Intifada was picked up by soldiers in the streets of Ramallah. They took her to the police station and asked for her identity card. She told them that she had a Jordanian passport and was married to a man from Kaddura camp. Two days later soldiers and the Mukhabarat came to her house and deported her over the bridge to Jordan. A politically active woman who has relatives without identity cards or who is without residency herself must be very cautious, and even stop being active and going out into the streets. As well, a lot of husbands order wives without identity cards to stay at home in order not to take the risk of being deported.

When I speak with women who are in hiding because of the threat of deportation, I can see clearly that my case is not at all a special one. Then I feel stronger – and this strength is much needed. Without it we will not survive. I am still in a constant emotional struggle: sometimes I know that I have to fight here and work to help our people to achieve liberation, and sometimes I want to be with Majed so much I long for him with all my senses and it takes a lot of effort to switch back to rational thinking and everyday life. I hope with all my heart that our efforts and suffering are not in vain and that we will one day live secure and peaceful in a Palestinian state alongside the state of Israel. And I hope that this day and the day I see Majed back home again are not too far away.

Umm Mohammed's appeal

I am a Palestinian mother in mourning. My two only sons are in Jneid prison waiting for Israel to carry out their execution – 'execution' because for Palestinians to be expelled from their homeland and separated by force from their families is a sentence of death, a pain as deep as the loss forever of someone dear.

I am a woman in my sixties. I know that I may not live to see my sons again in this house, where they have lived all their lives, the house that they themselves helped to build with their own hands and hard work. I grieve not only for myself but for the young families they will leave behind, their devoted and long-suffering wives and their small children who, I fear, will no longer know the loving arms of their father. We know that their lives in exile will be miserable, as ours will be without them.

But I am very proud of both sons. They are strong in spirit and dedicated, above all else, to peace and freedom for their people and their country. What crime is this, to fight against the chains that bind our people? To fight without weapons, not to cause harm to others, but to end the occupation they have lived under all their lives.

They can take my sons away from me, away from their wives and children, away from their country and people, but will this bring peace closer? When their bulldozers uproot our olive trees, and dynamite blows up our houses, does this bring peace closer? If every mother loses her sons and daughters, will this bring peace closer? If they empty the land of Palestinians, will this bring peace closer?

I am a Palestinian mother in mourning for my sons. But even this bitterest of sacrifices I will undergo with my head high, for their sake and for the sake of those who will be deported in future. I feel my people's tragedy through the uprooting of my sons. And I know that adding to the suffering we have all undergone over the years of occupation does not make us want freedom any less.

I appeal to the mothers of this world, mothers who understand oppression and who also understand the love of children and of homeland, to raise their voices with mine against the unjust and inhuman expulsion of Palestinians, my two sons and all the other sons of mothers like me.

Umm Mohammed
Mother of Mohammed and Majed Labad
Abu Diss, West Bank, 26 August 1988

Notes

1. Shati camp is the local name for the Beach camp. It lies along a sandy stretch of the Mediterranean coast to the north of Gaza town. It was established after the 1948 Arab–Israeli war to give shelter to 23,000 refugees from Lydda, Jaffa, Bersheeba and the southern coastal plain. Some 8,000 refugees have moved out of the camp and resettled in the nearby Israeli government housing project of Sheikh Radwan. Today Beach camp has a registered population of some 42,000 people. In the first twenty months of the Intifada 4,300 people from the camp were injured and 17 killed. (UNRWA, Palestine refugee camps information sheet.)

2. The University of Birzeit was especially hard hit by closures. Between 1973 (one year before Birzeit was upgraded to a university) and 1987 the university was closed fifteen times for relatively long periods (varying between two and four months). Finally it was closed from January 1988.

3. Under the emergency regulations the military government is authorized to issue a deportation order 'whenever necessary or desirable to preserve public security, defend the area, secure public order, or to put down sedition, revolt or riots'. Since 1967 nearly 2,000 people have been deported from the Occupied Territories. After a long period, 1980–1985, during which no deportations were carried out, the military government reinstated the measure in August 1985 at the beginning of the 'iron fist policy'. By February 1986, thirty-five people had been deported to Jordan. (Meron Benvenisti, *The West Bank Handbook*, Jerusalem, Jerusalem Post 1986, pp. 86–7). During the Intifada, fifty-nine Palestinians were deported. (Database Project on Palestinian Human Rights.)

4. Shabak is the Israeli secret service.

5. Naila 'Ayesh Zaqut is twenty-eight years old. Born in Ramallah, she studied in Bulgaria. In 1986, after her return to the Occupied Territories, she married Jamal Zaqut. On 15 February 1987 she was arrested by the Israeli army and brought to the Russian Compound detention centre in Jerusalem, where she was interrogated about her activities in Bulgaria. The usual methods of interrogation continued despite the fact that she was pregnant. She lost her baby in jail and was only afterwards transferred to a hospital for examination. She confessed in court to having been a member of a Marxist student group in Bulgaria, but she declared later that the confession was extracted under torture. The court case is still pending. In February 1988, two weeks before their baby boy was born, her husband Jamal was arrested and accused of being a leader of the Intifada; later he was deported to Lebanon. On 3 October 1988 Naila was arrested by the army and brought to Hasharon prison. She was accused of distributing leaflets of the Democratic Front for the Liberation of Palestine. After the intervention of the Women's Organization for Political Prisoners and other human rights organizations her baby was allowed to stay with her while she served six months' administrative detention in jail. The Israeli defence minister rejected a petition signed by hundreds of Israelis calling for her immediate release. Subsequently, Naila was given a special identity card to mark her status as a released prisoner and, despite her legal papers, was refused permission to leave the country to see her husband.

6. Mukhabarat is the Arabic name for the Israeli secret service.

7. The Emergency Defence Regulations of 1945 were enacted by the British high commissioner to fight the Jewish underground movements. They give the administration the broadest authority to infringe upon the basic rights of the population. Despite the fact that the Knesset has defined the regulations as 'undemocratic', they together with more than 2,000 military orders (1,200 in the West Bank, 900 in Gaza), are part of the existing law in the Occupied Territories. The regulations provide the legal basis for an extensive series of individual and collective punishment such as expulsion, curfew, demolition of houses, house arrest, closing off areas, preventive and administrative detention, and censorship. Characteristic of the security enactments is that people can be punished for holding opinions or for refusing to inform on their friends, rather than only for acts which they themselves have committed. (Benvenisti, p.77.)

8. In July 1990 Women for Coexistence (WFO) began a campaign on behalf of In'am, who is still being denied a permit to leave the country by the military government (WFO, c/o Zigelmann, 18 Zecharia Street, Tel Aviv 62592).

9. In'am refers to the charter of the Nuremberg Military Tribunal of 1945,

which in Article 6 defines the practice of deportation as a 'war crime' and a 'crime against humanity'.

10. In early 1990 Naila was allowed to leave after signing a paper committing herself not to reenter the country for two years.

11. Umm Mohammed's appeal is added at the end of this text.

12. Between mid-September 1989 and the end of the year more than 150 Palestinian women and their children were deported from the Occupied Territories. In the Israeli press this procedure has been called the 'Rabin transfer'. The military authorities refuse to give resident status to women who marry Palestinian residents or to the children born to them if the women themselves are born in West Bank villages (but who for example were outside the country in the 1967 census). At a special meeting of the Tel Aviv group Women in Black, Beth Goldring, an editor of the Senabel Press Service which is documenting the deportations, described the procedure: 'Soldiers raid the villages and impose a curfew, order all men to gather in the school yard or village centre, collect taxes and arrest wanted youth; while the men are thus occupied the women are taken from their homes. In many cases the women are not allowed to take all of their children with them, in others, even children registered as residents on their father's identity cards are deported and their documents are destroyed. . . . Now that Jordan has officially disengaged from the Territories it is still unclear what happens to the women after they are deported.' (Rayna Moss and Adam Keller, 'Deportation of Women', *The Other Israel*, November–December 1989, No. 39.)

13. 'Lamshamel' is the Arabic expression for family reunion. Between June and September 1967 some 200,000 people left the West Bank in addition to residents who at the time of the 1967 war were out of the country. Approximately 140,000 of them have since submitted applications to return and reunite their families. During the first year after the 1967 war 45,000 were allowed to return, and at the beginning of the 1980s between 900 and 1,200 applications per year were approved. In 1985 the authorities curtailed approval drastically and only a few dozen persons were admitted. Despite the limited number of family reunification permits issued, they serve as a reward for cooperation with the miliary government and during the Intifada became a highly political issue. (Benvenisti, p. 89.)

13. Women's Activities in Popular Committees during the Intifada

Rana Salibi[1]

Collective action and popular work

When in January 1988 the United Leadership of the Uprising (UNLU) called in its leaflets for mass participation by Palestinians in national and popular committees, neighbourhood committees were organized by activists of the women's committees and by the youth. The leftist factions had already started organizing the people in grassroots committees because for a long time they had believed in mass organization. The Communist Party, for example, had seen the organization of a mass movement as vital since 1974. The Nationalist Front, too, had started organizing, and the other leftist factions followed. The different priorities of the four main women's committees were evident in the neighbourhood committees as well. The communist women, for example, mainly organized working women.

So, when the Intifada made collective action necessary, the idea and the structures of mass organizations were there already and people started organizing themselves. It was a fantastic time and atmosphere. The women's movement played the most important role in the organization of the popular committees. In my town they were the only group actively organizing. The men had no committee, the student movement was relatively passive and the intellectuals talked a lot but seemed less able, or willing, to become active. I am a member of one of the leftist women's committees and we started organizing where organization was needed.

When the merchants began their commercial strike, people were afraid that the closure of the shops would last for a long time, and they started cultivating their plots of land to grow vegetables. The women of the refugee camps were especially active in the agricultural committees. But most of them lacked agricultural knowledge. One task of the women's committees was therefore to find teachers and arrange lectures. Most of us had experience in voluntary work and on this basis we tried to introduce new ways of teaching. It became directly related to our immediate needs and very pragmatic. Everybody who had knowledge or experience in planting, plant propagation, food preservation, household organization, writing, medical care or anything else useful taught it. We learned from each other and from our mistakes. From the beginning there was competition between individuals but it was inspiring rather than limiting. We became known as the best teaching committee in the area. What fascinated me most was our solidarity and our spirit of working together. The women themselves were very enthusiastic and wanted to help. They saw that other women participated and wanted to do the same. It was like a chain reaction. The men participated only as audiences. Some of them wanted to take part in our weekly meetings, but we refused to let them. During the previous years of community work we had experience of men taking over as soon as projects became successful and we wanted to avoid a repetition of that. Most of the men were not able to understand our rejection of their involvement.

When the Israelis closed down schools in the West Bank, we became involved in teaching children too. Whilst most classes in the West Bank are gender-segregated, in the neighbourhood classes we often taught boys and girls together in one room. Some parents complained, but in general they were simply happy that their children were getting some schooling. The children liked the classes a lot, but because the school closures lasted so long and because our teaching was not regular they found it increasingly difficult to concentrate.

To organize the people in neighbourhood committees, we had to learn their needs. We therefore went from house to house, and spoke with their occupants. We talked about their needs and about our concept of organization. Only after we had the necessary information did we collect money and buy things, for example flour, to distribute to families in need. To coordinate activities we would arrange a weekly meeting with all the active women in a neighbourhood. Like every activity, the meetings had to take place in private houses, there was nowhere else we could go. During the early months, the entire neighbourhood became my house. I would have breakfast here, a cup of tea or lunch there; I felt that the people were my family. Whilst some women participated in our activities, others did not, but still I had the feeling that the oppression of women by men was not so much in evidence at that time.

The Intifada affected even traditional women, and men came increasingly under pressure from neighbours and activists to let their women become involved, but nevertheless many women I worked with believed that their only duty was to care for their family. They said that they wanted to do nothing that could harm their family, that they had too many household responsibilities. And because the Intifada makes life more difficult anyway, women do not want tension in the house too. The easiest way, therefore, is to do what your husband wants you to do. 'The best wife is a woman who obeys her husband.' Thus a lot of women were willing to offer us a room in their house to meet in, but when their husband disagreed most of them were not willing to fight the issue through. And it needs time to change the traditional attitudes. Many women feel, if they can struggle in front of their house, okay, but they would not leave the home for four hours. Thus women become pacifists, without the spirit to fight. One example concerns the mothers of martyrs. Whenever a Palestinian man, woman, or child is killed during the Intifada the local women's and popular committees mobilize the neighbourhood and even women from other places in the Occupied Territories for solidarity and condolence visits. These visits are important actions which strengthen the bonds of solidarity between people. The bereaved women wanted to show their gratitude but in some cases were unable to do so. They said, 'I want to reciprocate what the people did to help me, but I cannot defy my husband.' At the beginning of the Intifada, the national idea was able to break this barrier. Feminist demands have only recently come up and are put forward by intellectuals and by activists who are limited in their work by their families.

One activity initiated by the women's movement worked very well from the beginning: the knitting of pullovers for detainees. This was something women could do at home. Either their husbands did not see them doing it or they accepted it, because the women were doing something for the cause without leaving the house and their household responsibilities.

In camps and villages women participate more than in the cities. The main difference is the amount women face the soldiers. In the camps, demonstrations are mostly led by women, usually young, unmarried girls, and women take part in the actual fighting against the soldiers. Of course, city women participate in demonstrations as well, but not to the same extent as camp women. Even though I have most experience of working with women in the cities, I found camp women easier to work with. They are more sceptical, feel a need for organization much more and face the soldiers on a daily basis. Camp society is in general more conservative than the towns, but the enormous pressure on the camps makes women's participation necessary. At the beginning the Intifada was mainly a movement of the working class and the semi-working class, and this is what most of the people in the camps are. I believe that middle-class women are more difficult to mobilize because they rely on the money of their husbands and have more to lose! I was annoyed sometimes when women who had never participated in anything invited us for a cup of tea, simply in order to make their neighbours jealous.

The mobilization of women is such a difficult task, with such a lot of setbacks, that I lost patience with it and started working mainly with youth.[2] They are much more open to change, and want to challenge the traditional structures. Anyhow, I think the Intifada gets its momentum from the Palestinian youth, both male and female. Apart from old women, who have a special role in the uprising, the most active females are girls and unmarried women below the age of twenty-five. Activism in the Intifada needs a lot of commitment, and only young women and girls are not tied down by family responsibilities.

Working with the young boys and girls is wonderful. The popular committees in a way substitute for social activities at schools, which are closed by military order. Schools and the committees are an important recruiting ground for girls: they are the only way they can get to know the activists. If they are courageous enough, they are recruited into one of the factions. As members of these, they will hear lectures, participate in the faction's activities and learn techniques of organization.

One of the first things I tried to teach my local children was that men and women are equal. We had long discussions on that topic. I tried to give examples from their immediate environment, pointing to the participation of girls in blocking the streets, burning tyres and patrolling areas. Once, one of my children had an argument with his religious teacher about equality and would not give in. I was happy! Afterwards we sat down together again and this time we talked about the reaction of his teacher. But sometimes my work with the children depresses me a lot. Currently two of the children I work with are in jail, and two were killed just a few days ago. This was something I was always afraid would happen. The children themselves know the dangers they face every day. They are scared but they hide their fear with the words '*Yaqdah thauriyeh*' ('revolutionary awareness'), which means, if you are strong enough, the soldiers will not get you. Despite their fear, the girls have gained self-confidence. When they are imprisoned, they no longer afterwards tell their parents everything that happened. They are afraid they might be prevented from being active. This is a qualitative change in behaviour and, I think, a big step forward. Some of the girls face confrontation with their families in order to be able to participate in one of the committees, and some come secretly, defying their parents.

In some ways it is easier to talk with children about gender relations than with women. In the women's groups we never talk about these issues directly and we cannot interfere in these delicate matters. We try to speak with neighbours when there are problems in a particular family. We have had cases in which politically active and progressive men would not allow female members of their family to leave the house. Though politically progressive, these men had very traditional ideas on social issues and felt threatened by their women's demands to participate in Intifada activities. I think that even if, deep down, such a man is convinced that women have a role to play beside the traditional one, he is afraid that the neighbours will gossip and ruin his reputation.

Our activities with women in their neighbourhoods did not only focus on charity, emergency and teaching tasks, we tried to raise the social consciousness of the women, and political issues as well. This last task turned out to be in many aspects the most difficult. Many Palestinian women believe politics to be dangerous, and for a lot of them one lecture was too much. But to understand the complexity of politics takes times, and many lectures. A second difficulty was that we had to keep these discussions secret, not only because of the army but also because of the women's husbands, who were not supposed to know that their women were listening to political ideas. A third problem was the factionalism in the women's movement. Political lectures are linked to the factions and women who want to get information about politics but are afraid of becoming identified with one of the factions are alienated.

The banning of the popular committees

The spirit of solidarity and collective resistance that had prevailed during the first months of the Intifada was broken in August 1988 when Israel made the popular committees illegal. Anyone involved in the organization of any cultural or educational activity could face prosecution and up to ten years' imprisonment. As a result, many women were afraid to participate in activities and committees. It became difficult to find houses in which to hold meetings and classes for women and children. Though a lot of mothers, especially middle-class women, were willing to send their children into other people's homes for lessons, they refused to host classes in their own homes. Their fear was understandable because the soldiers started to break into houses, disrupt classes, and beat and arrest teachers and students.

The factionalism in the women's movement also increased after the outlawing of the popular committees. At the beginning we had cooperated and coordinated a lot, but now each women's group started to recruit women separately. One reason for the growing factionalism was the increasing problem of space. We could not meet in private houses any more because the soldiers raided them frequently. Once again, the women's committees had to rely solely on their own facilities, such as kindergartens and clinics. That our work had to go underground affected our relationship with the community as well. Before, activities were done in the open under the eyes of everybody, but now the gossip started again, limiting women's ability to go out.

Factionalism is a big problem for me and really hinders me in my work. I believe that we must educate our youth in democracy and freedom, but the secrecy and illegality we have to work under are in the long run counterproductive and foster both factionalism and fundamentalism. To teach and learn democracy when the demand for your legitimate rights and freedom is already considered a crime are almost impossible tasks – but the only way left open to us.

Notes

1. This is a pseudonym.
2. The Palestinian Federation of Women's Action Committees conducted a study on the participation of children in the Intifada. According to their findings, regionally the largest participation by children is in refugee camps, followed by villages and finally by cities. Female participation is slightly less (10 per cent) than male participation. Girls between thirteen and sixteen participate in violent actions, while young girls do not. Female participation is highest in the refugee camps. 'The Uprising and the Palestinian Child: participation of children in the Intifada and its social dimensions', Tantur Conference, Jerusalem, April 1989.

14. Fear of Sexual Harassment: Palestinian Adolescent Girls in the Intifada

Nadira Shalhoub Kevorkian

The fear of sexual harassment and actual sexual harassment by the Israeli occupation forces have become serious problems in the occupied Palestinian territories. Definitions and perceptions of social problems vary across time and with changing circumstances. In this case study, I intend to analyse the social perceptions of sexual harassment and the social reaction towards it in Palestinian society, a society in transition, in the specific context of the Israeli occupation and the Intifada. I shall attempt to show how the victims of sexual assault or harassment perceive and cope with these threatening yet delicate problems.

The problem of female victimization has been revealed to be universal. The recent increase in awareness and concern about this issue, especially over the past decade, is the result mainly of work by the feminist movement. Verbal harassment at one end of the spectrum of men's behaviour towards women, and brutal rape, wife-battering and all forms of threatening and violent conduct at the other, are all reminders to women of their vulnerability. Young and old, rich and poor, working women and housewives, none are immune to these forms of intimidation.

Having to be constantly on guard does not constitute paranoid behaviour for women: it is reasonable caution. From childhood, girls are taught to beware male strangers; many actually experience sexual abuse, from relatives or strangers. Adolescence is the most critical time for young females in their learning of what it means to have to be constantly on guard. With the onset of puberty, they become aware of changes in the attitudes of men towards them. Adolescent girls start to experience comments, glances, whistles and admiration of the visible development of their sexuality. Within her immediate social circle and among peers, the young woman learns that she cannot always control the sexual nature of encounters with men. She also learns that if anything 'happens', she will be the one blamed. Throughout her life, she learns survival strategies in order to preserve herself physically, socially and emotionally. She lives in the knowledge that to be considered respectable a woman must avoid men's sexual and physical exploitation. Women come to perceive themselves as potential victims of sexual and physical assault by men.

There are, of course, differences between societies, cultures and religions with regards to women's status, the boundaries of permissible behaviour, expectations, sexuality, etcetera. Traditional societies differ from modern society, Christians differ from Moslems, etcetera. Values, beliefs and practices pertaining to all aspects of sexuality change over time. Particular behaviour may be defined as immoral, later as criminal and still later, as psychopathological. Of course, the boundaries are not clear-cut, and alternative viewpoints do coexist. However, there is usually a predominant attitude in a particular society at any specific point in history.

Sexuality and the role of the woman in Arab Muslim culture

In Arab Moslem tradition and culture, the subject of sexuality is taboo. The Arab woman has started to participate in the labour force, in politics, education, etcetera, and the way she is perceived socially is beginning to change, but a very hard struggle still lies ahead. Women in the Arab world are perceived and treated as second-class citizens: there is no such thing as equal rights with men, neither in the large perspective, in terms of similar opportunities in education, the labour market, or professional advancement, nor in the near perspective of the family regarding the raising of children, life as a marriage partner, rights in divorce, etcetera. Islamic law discriminates between women's and men's rights. It sees the woman as powerless, dominated by her sexuality, which must be controlled and protected by the powerful and mentally, physically and socially superior man. Sexuality is viewed as the weakest part of the woman. Arab women do not talk about and are not allowed to learn about their sexuality. The role of the woman is to keep her sexuality secret and to protect it. She knows that if she somehow fails in this duty, she will be blamed. The destiny of any woman found to be engaged in a sexual or even a close emotional relationship with a man outside wedlock is death. The perceived need to protect the woman from her own weakness causes her to be forced to marry at a very young age, so that she becomes trapped in the cycle of marriage and the duties of mother and wife. The Arab woman has to be very careful in every step she takes: she lives in constant fear lest she incur the slightest suspicion that she does not conform to the traditional and cultural role expected of her. The price of infringement of the norms is high: the honour and the good name of her family, including the extended family. Ultimately, it can cost her her life. The most frequent reason for the murder of women in Arab society is rape or adultery.

The role of women in the Intifada

As a result of recent political developments in the Occupied Territories of the West Bank and the Gaza Strip, Palestinian women have started to participate actively in the political struggle and in protecting their families, husbands and children from the enemy. This has had the effect of raising the Palestinian woman's self-esteem. She has become increasingly aware of her essential role in preserving her children, family, society and nation. But this same situation has placed women in the situation of defining themselves in relation to two contradictory roles. On the one hand, there is the traditional role of staying at home, raising children, and preserving and protecting the family honour; on the other hand, the woman's new political role requires her to get out and contribute to the political struggle of her nation. Although this dilemma has existed since the Israeli occupation began, it has become more pressing since the Intifada began.

The study

In recent years, criminal justice and social science research has found that adolescents are the victims and perpetrators of a considerable amount of sexual violence and abuse.[1] This study focuses on the perceptions of female Palestinian adolescents regarding feelings of being threatened and their fears, based on information from their peers, concerning the sexual exploitation of Palestinian women by the Israeli occupation forces. I have thus tried to arrive at some understanding of the self-perceptions, thoughts, beliefs and values of young Palestinian girls during the Intifada. The aim of this study, which was sponsored by Bethlehem University, was to reach Palestinian adolescents in refugee camps, to listen to them, share their feelings and try to share with them the difficulties and dilemmas experienced by them in this harsh period.

Weekly meetings were held with two groups of young Palestinian girls in two refugee camps.[2] The declared aim was to work with these girls to help them to cope with the stressful events and situations experienced by them during the Intifada. This approach was based on the rationale that sharing and communicating such experiences with others (ventilation) is beneficial. The most frequently mentioned fear raised by the female adolescents was *Iskat*. This term was used by them to refer to girls being drugged, gagged, physically assaulted and raped by soldiers intent on breaking their honour and their political determination and obtaining information about the activities of their relatives and friends.

The phenomenon of *Iskat* provides the focus of this analysis. Despite the limitations of this small study,[3] it is important to raise awareness about this phenomenon, to assess the perception of female adolescents and to describe the victims' or potential victims' reactions to sexual harassment and exploitation, reactions which are based mainly on subjective perceptions, rather than actual experience of sexual assault.

Problems of definition

The definition of the sexual abuse of children and adolescents, in general, is fraught with difficulties, for all definitions are culture- and time-bound. They are not based on rigorous scientific inquiry, but on the values and beliefs of individuals, professional organizations and society at large. The term 'sexual abuse' is not universally accepted and is frequently used interchangeably with 'sexual exploitation', 'sexual misuse' and 'sexual assault'. The term 'sexual abuse' may mean anything from being kissed by a stranger to exhibitionism, genital manipulation, intercourse or pornography. Within the legal frame of reference, sexual abuse is classified by criminal acts such as rape, incest, sodomy. Medically, the definition may become confused with consequences such as genital injury, venereal disease, or pregnancy. Both the legal and the medical frameworks fail to consider the psychological and interactive aspects of sexual experience. The definition of sexual abuse and harassment in this study is less restrictive: the degree of fear or threat of being raped or sexually exploited, the cultural context of the potential victim, the development stage of the victim and the effect on her mental, social, emotional and physical well-being define whether what occurs is sexual abuse, or harassment, or not.

The experience of working with this particular group of adolescents has shown the necessity to re-define the terms sexual abuse and sexual harassment. The study pinpoints the effects simply of hearing the story of a girl who has been raped or sexually abused. The effect on such hearsay is especially pronounced in a society that forbids talking about such cases and that places all blame on the sexuality of the female. It is clear that the threat of abuse, and the conspiracy of silence that surrounds it, terrifies such girls. Awareness of their vulnerability makes them unable to think about more constructive matters. This suggests that the fear of victimization is almost as bad as the actual experience of it. Another unique and very important element in the Palestinian situation is the change that the meaning and perception of 'sexual harassment' has undergone during the Intifada, due to the fact that the potential offender is a political enemy. This change has raised new ways of dealing with the phenomenon, not only by the victims and potential victims, but also by Palestinian society at large.

Sexual harassment

The following example serves to illustrate the sense of doom and of being out of control felt by a young girl who participated in the study:

> I am afraid. I am left feeling helpless . . . sick . . . upset . . . angry. I can't talk about it. . . . I don't know whom to talk to about it. I am frustrated and depressed . . . but I shouldn't be. . . . I cry alone at night . . . but I shouldn't.

The girls were very much concerned about sexual abuse and assault, the so-called *Iskat*. Although sexual abuse might be assumed to be a minor complaint in Palestinian society in comparison to all the other hardships being suffered during the Intifada, it has a significant effect on female adolescents.

> I spent all night thinking about the story that our neighbour told my mother. . . . She told us that the Jewish people rape girls when they are imprisoned. . . . They do it violently and aggressively. . . . Our neighbour said that they want to damage our honour and humiliate us.

Such stories preoccupy adolescent girls: they talk about the physical, mental and emotional hardships that face young Palestinian girls in prison. Fourteen-year-old girls express this in the following way:

> What can we do? . . . What can we do? . . . We are helpless. . . . They master our lives . . . as an Arab proverb says . . . 'With them it is the war or struggle, and they are the enemies and the judges'.[4]

The girls reported that during interrogation following arrest, female interrogators make girls take off their clothes and stay in their underwear, and then allow male soldiers to pass through the interrogation room. To a Palestinian girl this type of incident is extremely humiliating.

Stories were told of girls who were drugged and photographed naked in order to blackmail them for information on the political activities of family members, relatives or neighbours. The form of the harassment varies widely, but the pattern of the behaviour and its effect represent a serious violation of the female's personal integrity: she feels as if she is no longer a human being, that her value is not in her social function and contribution, and that she is transformed into a sexual object. This transformation affects her self-evaluation and confidence and even has negative repercussions on her school performance.

Knowing that they might become victims of such abuse has a cumulative effect on adolescent girls. The girls reported becoming nervous and irritable. They felt threatened and helpless. Many developed techniques to protect themselves, such as not walking alone in the camp, and avoiding the market, visits to relatives, or participation in demonstrations. Perhaps the most frustrating issue for the girls was that if anything did happen to them, they would come up against cultural traditions and stereotypes. One girl expressed her feelings of fear, anger and depression thus:

> I don't feel safe in my own home . . . soldiers might come in and rape me. I have nightmares about the enemy abusing my sister and my mother in front of me.

One unfortunate girl who was raped and surrendered information lived for a while alone with this nightmare, afraid to tell anybody about her ordeal. In the end, after writing a full confession of what had happened to her, she committed suicide. This confession is available to anyone who wishes to read the details. This example will give the reader an idea of the psychological state of these young teenage girls when they think that they might have to face such a fate. A young girl told me:

> I am terrified of leaving the house, even to go shopping or visit a friend, for fear of being taken away by the Israeli army. They might take indecent pictures of me, by force, or by drugging me as they have done to some of my friends, and use such pictures to blackmail me or my family in order to obtain information.

Another moving example is the story told by a mother who was threatened by three soldiers. One, already holding her nine-month-old baby girl in his arms, talked about raping the little girls if the mother refused to tell him where her son was hiding. The soldier made crude movements, as if to show that he was not joking.

Sexual harassment and sexual abuse are not everyday occurrences in the Occupied Territories, but they do exist and they inflict psychological havoc on young girls. Girls attempt to cope with the stress and the horror in various ways. For instance, I was told the story of a young girl whom the Israelis raped in Gaza prison in order to obtain information. The girls who told me the story emphasized that even in a society as conservative as theirs, in which a girl can be killed for having sexual relations with a man, and in which this raped girl's experience was known to everyone, she still has had many offers of marriage. The girls explained to me, in detail, how people respected the rape victim and helped her to overcome the trauma of rape. There are many similar stories, and whether true or not, they are subconscious ways of coping with the anxiety and horrors of the Israeli repression of the Intifada. A sixteen-year-old girl said, 'They can rape a girl but they cannot rape a nation.'

Implications

To live an illusion, not knowing the truth, is the most dangerous of all things for human beings, women or men, because it deprives them of their most important weapon in the struggle for freedom, emancipation and control of their own lives and futures. To be conscious that you are still living under occupation is the first step on the road to emancipation.

Nawal El-Saadawi

In general it can be said that females assess their perceptions and even their experience of male violence from a male perspective. The omnipresence of male violence seems so overwhelming that sometimes it is easier for women to hope that they will be protected by men, the law or something else rather than to confront the illusion of protection. This line of argument is pertinent if we are referring to sexual assault or harassment in normal life conditions: it is neither applicable nor relevant in the situation of living in an area of political conflict. The Intifada has created new, problematic and frightening issues, which threaten the physical, social, and mental well-being of female adolescents. As if it were not enough for a Palestinian female to be a part of the Arab world, in which the status of women is still very low, she now faces an enemy who exploits the traditional cultural codes and stereotypes for his own political purposes.

Recovery from sexual or physical assault can be an extremely lengthy process, sometimes lasting a lifetime. Women, especially the young, tend to blame themselves for the abuse, and this guilt often intensifies with time as they gain a clearer understanding of cultural norms and taboos.[5] Anxiety and extreme levels of fear are frequently mentioned consequences of sexual abuse among both children and adults.[6] The threat and the fear, as noted in my case study, caused girls to experience problems in concentrating on tasks. The girls felt powerless, out of control, and some of them developed a 'victim' mentality which affected them in other situations too. Some tried to master and control the trauma, some by defining themselves as 'war injured'. As we know from the literature, parental responses to their children's victimization, such as reassurance, support and emotional security immediately after the abuse, help to offset trauma in both the short and the long term.[7]

In general terms, in cases of sexual abuse the victim, whether child or adult, is usually afraid to talk to anyone about her experience. It is kept hidden. Increased social awareness, especially in the last decade, and the development of the caring professions have made it easier for victims to talk out and seek help, whether from formal institutions such as the police, the courts and welfare services, or from informal set-ups such as the telephone hotlines that have been created especially for this purpose.

The Palestinian case differs in that before the Intifada there was no social awareness of the need for intervention in such instances. The only way of dealing with sexual victimization was the traditional–cultural way, in which the female was inevitably blamed for having provoked or precipitated the sexual abuse: by being in the wrong place at the wrong time, or by wearing unsuitable clothing, etcetera. Hence, she was presumed guilty, and had to be punished, sometimes by death.

This attitude obviously deters the girls from talking about their victimization and so they tend to keep it secret, not sharing it with anyone, thereby perpetuating the period of trauma. In some cases, girls have committed suicide in order to put an end to their suffering. Furthermore, according to tradition, a female should be a virgin when she gets married; if not, it is legitimate to have her killed for having brought shame on the family. Thus, a girl who has been raped might prefer to kill herself rather than tell her family that she has lost her virginity or wait for her husband to discover it. All these factors compound the problem.

The political situation has created other problems. Whilst teenaged and adult women have participated actively in the Intifada, on the other hand it seems that this active participation, and public awareness of women's key role, has made the enemy conscious of a need to devalue this new status of women. In searching for appropriate ways to achieve this end, the Israelis are using the traditional code of conduct and the traditional view of sexuality for their own ends. This analysis is based on the girls' perceptions of the causes, reasons for and results of the problem.

When I talk about men here, I talk about their power as males and, added to this power, their political power as an enemy. I talk about fear on the part of the victims, still young and lacking in knowledge and experience with regard to survival techniques. I talk about the normal fears prevailing among women of male stereotypes and beliefs about women and their sexuality. I talk about the fear of a political enemy. The sum total of all these fears looms large.

In the long term, this situation may either increase the vulnerability of women, or increase their will to resist and find new ways of resolving the problem of sexual harassment. Both of these possibilities were in evidence among the girls in the two groups. It is not possible at this stage, however, to predict the direction of change. Moreover, other developments, such as the return to religious fundamentalism and the demand that women readopt the traditional, modest garb, coupled with the fact that the most usual age for females to get married is still between fourteen and sixteen, have a dynamic of their own.

Notes

1. US Congress, 1977; US Department of Justice, 1980; McCahill, Meyer and Fischmann, 1979; Katz and Mazur, 1979.
2. Twenty-three in number.
3. There is an absence of exact statistical data on the incidence and frequency of sexual assault; the girls' fears are largely based on hearsay evidence.
4. In Arabic, *Fika al-Chisan wa ant alhasm wa al-hakam.*
5. Rosenfeld et al., 1979.
6. Adams-Tucker, 1981; Braut and Tisza, 1977.
7. De Francis, 1979; Peters, 1974.

References

Adams-Tucker, C. (1981). 'A Socioclinical Overview of 28 Sex-abused Children', *Child Abuse and Neglect*, 5, pp. 361–7.
Adams-Tucker, C. (1982). 'Proximate Effects of Sexual Abuse in Childhood: a report on 28 children', *American Journal of Psychiatry*, 139, pp. 1,252–6.
Ageton, S. S. (1983). *Sexual Assaults among Adolescents*, Lexington Books, Toronto.
Braut, R. and Tisza, V. (1977). 'The sexually missued child', *American Journal of Orthopsychiatry*, 47, pp. 80–90.
De Francis, V. (1979). *Protecting the Child Victim of Sex Crimes Committed by Adults*, Denver, American Human Association.
Katz, S. and Mazur, M. A. (1979). *Understanding the Rape Victim: a synthesis of research findings*, New York, John Wiley.
McCahill, T. W., Meyer, L. C. and Fischmann, A. M. (1979). *The Aftermath of Rape*, Lexington, Mass.: Lexington Books, DC Health and Company.
Peters, J. J. (1974). 'The Psychological Effects of Childhood Rape', *World Journal of Psychosynthesis*, 6 (5), pp. 11–14.
US Congress Senate Committee on the Judiciary (1977). *Challenge for the Third Century: education in a safe environment – final report on the nature and prevention of school violence and vandalism.* Subcommittee on juvenile delinquency, 95th Cong. 1st Sess. Washington, DC, US Government Printing Office.
US Department of Justice (1980). *Criminal Victimization in the United States, 1978.* Bureau of Justice Statistics. National Crime Survey Report NCS-N-17, NCJ-66480. Washington, DC, US Government Printing Office.

15. Women on the Hilltop

Hannan Mikha'il-Ashrawi

The Gold Snake[1]

I pick up a stone. Clutching it tightly in my fist, I raise my arm. The impulse to hurl it with all my strength rises in my body, through my veins, like a viscous substance – cold and deliberate. The mid-morning sun reflects the bracelet on my wrist and the blinding glare freezes all motion. A gold snake, its scales worn out by years of scrubbing and cleaning, of embracing and releasing, of dressing and undressing, stares at me blindly with two ruby eyes.

I was only fourteen when the snake, with new scratchy scales, was wound around my wrist as part of my dowry – the *mahr* in partial payment of the bride price. Along with it came a heavy *halabi* (from Aleppo) gold chain from which dangled an intriciate *lozeh*,[2] the filigreed almond which was even bigger than the one my mother wore hanging from her neck in between her wrinkled breasts. Both almonds were empty. On my other wrist, a thick coin bracelet with genuine Osmali and Inglizi[3] coins completed my engagement gear. I felt rich and cherished then, entering the mysterious cult of womanhood fully adorned in the tradition of my sex and race. The coin bracelet was the first to go in that year of drought, when the olive harvest failed and our grapevines withered in early summer. Next the *lozeh* went to pay for Walid's schooling – Walid, my only born, the joy of my life, the hope of my future – while he lived.

But the snake remained. I wore it on my wrist all those nineteen years until it wore me, winding itself around my thickening flesh, its tail meeting its head in a tightening double circle that refused to slacken. Not all the soap or oil greasing my hand could slip it off my wrist, until I stopped noticing its existence. We became one.

Those same ruby eyes stared coldly at me on my wedding night, as I clutched the bedpost frantically praying for the pain to stop and bit my lips with a fierce determination not to scream, whilst the sheet turned ruby red with the blood of my twice torn body. It was my duty, my fate and pride as a virgin bride, I was told. But no one warned me or armed me against the pain. On that same bed Walid was born. At fifteen I watched my body being taken away from me again as the dayeh[4] poked and prodded between my thighs and kneaded my swollen stomach like leavened dough with a calculated impersonality that was even more terrifying than my pain. For a whole day and night my body refused to give up its inhabitant, while I prayed and prayed for a boy in order to spare this unknown child a woman's fate. I cursed my husband then for his unbidden foray inside my body, and my mother for her forbidden secrets which she never divulged. 'You'll forget,' she had said. 'All women do, or the race will end.' I never forgot. And as the screams welled up from the depth of my stomach through my parched throat, I froze at the dispassionate glare of the ruby eyes, and in silence and blood gave birth to Walid. At fifteen I became Imm Walid,[5] and Abu Walid strutted about with the pride of fatherhood, having sired a son, while I silently cursed my fertility and worshipped its fruit. That was eighteen years ago.

Walid's eyes were open when I got to him. Staring blindly into an empty sky, they did not recognize me. With all my pent-up pain and the million silent screams I could not release, I pressed my palm to open the gash which the bullet had made in its passage through his head. Blood and brains mingled as I cradled his head on my lap and drenched my *thawb*[6] with a warm thick liquid that seeped through to my breasts and thighs. I knew that the bracelet was uncomfortable in its cold hardness and I tried to remove it from beneath his head. But he felt nothing. I wrapped his tortured head with the *hatta* (scarf) he had worn around his neck ('It's our national symbol, Yamma') and cried searing hot tears, silently, gently singing a broken lullaby, 'Nam ya habibi nam'.[7]

Abu Walid, the *waled*, (the father) now stares into space; no longer a father, he fingers his beads and murmurs 'la illaha illa Allah'.[8] I am the *waledah*; (the mother) having once given birth, I claim my right over life and death. The pain of the latter, I swear, is greater and more unforgivable. The soldiers appear, and the snake coiled around my wrist glitters wickedly like an obscene signal. With my free hand I pull at it, twist it back and forth, but it refuses to let go. I pick up a stone; resting my wrist on a rock, I strike at the snake with almost insane strength. My wrist is bloody, but I feel no pain. The snake breaks off. With my mangled hand I grasp the stone damp with blood and with all my strength hurl it at the pointing guns.

A Pair of Shoes

I cannot remember where I left my shoes. I remember taking them off – spike heels, patent leather, Italian imports – and carrying them in my hand as we climbed the hill through a cloud of tear gas. My stockinged feet are torn and bleeding, my sheer French hose are a mess, but never mind. Strange, this delicious sensation of freedom, to be able to wiggle my toes and feel the roughness of the earth, the sharpness of the stones through the soles of my bare feet. I pick up those same stones now, rough and heavy, and pile them up deliberately, with uneven thuds, onto the makeshift barrier. My soft hands are blistering, blessed beautiful bubbles that will turn into rough calluses. My husband had spared no expense to preserve the cool smoothness of my hands – a dishwasher, a maid, expensive hand and body lotions. These hands now hauling rocks were trained to do nothing more arduous than arrange on a silver tray the appetizing *kubbeh* and delicate spinach *fatayer*[9] that the guests at our bridge parties used to enjoy so much.[10] Sami always made a point of complimenting me on the delicacy of my ringed hands as well as on my aesthetic abilities in the preparation of *mezzeh*[10] trays. I always made a point of smiling back, dutifully, mechanically, like the cherished and pampered wife I was, basking in the glow of my husband's pride of possession. Our guests would smile back, looking knowingly at one another (how lucky Leila was), secretly envious of my (his) good fortune.

A captive of this chain of painted smiles, as words floated like colourful balloons over the green baize-covered bridge table, I turned inwards and accused myself of an ungracious lack of gratitude. A strange and heavy sensation like a cumbersome rock settled on my chest until I could hardly breathe. Sisyphus rolled his rock uphill in an exercise in futility, while I harboured mine inside, an ever-increasing heaviness that only I could feel.

I reach for a rock too heavy to lift. Najwa sees me and quickly comes to my side – in her faded jeans and sensible shoes – and helps me roll it, then pile it on the rising barricade. We exchange knowing, somewhat conspiratorial smiles, and I feel a lightness of spirit, a sensation of breathlessness like a delicate silk thread weaving a safe and warm cocoon of recognition to engulf us. How I used to envy her, with a sulky, sullen, deliberate silence as Sami and 'our friends' spitefully gossiped about her. She dared to live alone, openly flaunting her single state (bachelorhood, she called it), wearing unfashionable clothes (even trousers and jeans for work), unashamedly educated (A PhD scared potential suitors) and clearly oblivious to the dictates of social ritual and decorum (being conspicuously absent from weddings, funerals and bridge parties). I used to look down at the ruffled front of my silk shirt, ever on the lookout for that slovenly wrinkle or spot that might betray me, passionately resenting all the 'dry clean only' labels on the designer outfits with which my husband's export-import (mainly import) business supplied me. Particularly her shoes: how I longed – with the hidden desire of the physically deprived – for the indulgence, the pleasure, of sensible shoes to walk in. Not the leather vice and stilts that my husband found 'so very sexy' but those soft, firm walking shoes that would enable a women to stride confidently and surely on her way to a specific destination. My shoes made me hesitant, tentative, and ever so feminine in my husband's eyes; and I never walked anywhere.

Which is why he blamed me for Lina's beating. 'It's all your fault,' he said 'You should have taken her to school and back every day like I told you.' But how could I know that it would be that one fateful day, the one time I gave in to her constant entreaties to let her walk home from school with her friends, to release her from the mechanical prison which transported her from one confinement (at home) to another (in school) without the joy of sunshine and fresh air? I knew about the Intifada and the soldier's bone-breaking brutality, bullets and tear gas – more than my husband ever dreamt I knew – and yet I dared release my ten-year-old butterfly for a few minutes of freedom. I drove behind them, schoolgirls growing wings, and in that split second between seeing the raised truncheon in the soldier's hand and braking and opening the car door, I lived through an infinity of terror. I wobbled on my high heels and clutched her to my breast, blood and streaming hair, taking the blows on my arms and shoulders, shielding that precious, vulnerable head with an obstinate imperviousness to pain that can transform a mother into a rock.

For two days and one night I sat up by her hospital bed, holding her hand, staring at the closed eyes beneath the bandaged head, willing her with all my might to live. She lived, my Lina with the hair of brown silk; my Lina, who always used to start her drawings with a rainbow and a smiling sun, now draws a Palestinian flag, below which a young girl faces a gigantic figure in uniform brandishing a blood-stained club. Her laughter is not a giggle any more, but reverberates with a knowledge way beyond her years.

It is this knowledge that I share with Najwa now. On top of the hill behind the barricades (Sami does not know where I am), I look down at the soldiers who look like the armed robots that Lina used to play with, and I laugh. I don't give a damn about my lost shoes.

Notes

1. The following two short stories appeared first in the Palestinian weekly *Al-Fajr*, 6 March 1989. Reprint with the permission of the author. The two stories belong together. They describe the experience of two different women in the turmoil of the Intifada and can be symbolic for the experience of most of the Palestinian women in today's West Bank and Gaza.

2. 'Loz' is the Arabic word for almond.

3. Ottoman dinars and English Elizabethan gold coins are used as finery of the *shakkeh*, the headcover of country women. They are perforated and sewn onto the *shakkeh*.

4. Midwife.

5. Women are usually named after their firstborn son. Imm Walid means mother of Walid. The same is due to men. A father is called after his firstborn son. Abu Walid means father of Walid.

6. The traditional long embroidered Palestinian dress, worn mostly by the peasant women is called 'thawb'.

7. 'Yamma' locally for mother. This lullaby is known to every Palestinian child. 'Good night my darling good night.'

8. 'There is no God than God.'

9. *Kubbeh* is a small ship-shaped Lebanese fried speciality made with minced lamb, spices and pinenuts and covered with burghul. *Fatayer* is the term for all kinds of sweet and salty pastries. They can be filled with spinach, white cheese and sugared nuts, or baked with oil and thyme (*sata*) on top.

10. *Mezzeh* is the term for all kinds of hors d'oeuvres: salads, dips, kebabs and specialities such as *kubbeh* and *fatayer*. They are served on a tray and usually eaten with a drink of arak.

16. Political Detainees in the Russian Compound in Jerusalem: Overview and Testimonies

Collected by the Women's Organization for Political Prisoners, Jerusalem[1]

Introduction

Palestinian women political prisoners

In numerical terms, Palestinian women in the West Bank, Gaza Strip and East Jerusalem are less affected by punitive measures such as arrest, administrative detention, house arrest and deportation than Palestinian men. From June 1967 until the end of 1986, 1,875 men, compared with 32 women, were deported from the Occupied Territories.[2] These 32 deportees were well known for their political activity. In 1988, 15 women were issued with six-month administrative detention without trial orders, some of them twice consecutively. Of them, 11 were members of one or other of the four women's committees in the Occupied Territories.[3]

This Israeli focus only on top-level political activists seems to have changed during the Intifada, when thousands of women took to the streets to protest at the Israeli occupation. Although the numbers of Palestinian men in prisons and detention centres still by far outnumbered that of women, the latter's numbers increased dramatically. Whilst the average number of Palestinian women political prisoners before the Intifada almost never exceeded 18, in July 1988 more than 90 women were in jail.[4] From December 1987 until August 1989, an estimated 50,000 persons were arrested, approximately 1,000 of them women.[5]

As the number of arrested women and girls increased, the prisons ran out of space in which to hold them. Until mid-1988, the Neve Tertsa women's prison, with a capacity of around thirty-five to forty prisoners, was the only conventional women's prison. Because of lack of space most women were therefore held in the three detention centres, Kishon (Jalameh) near Haifa, Abu-Kbir near Tel Aviv and the Russian Compound (Moskobieh) in Jerusalem. In July 1988 the new women's prison, Hasharon or Telmond, was opened after Palestinian prisoners went on strike against the prison conditions in Neve Tertsa.[6] Meron Benvenisti had already commented in 1986 that 'the concentration of thousands of security offenders in the jails turns imprisonment into a sort of training ground for the struggle against Israeli occupation'.[7] This is true as well for the women Palestinian detainees in Israeli prisons and detention centres. Two former women political prisoners, released in the May 1985 prisoner exchange, declared in 1986 in the weekly newspaper *Al-Fajr*: 'We turned the prison into a school, graduating hundreds of strong women. As we said from the beginning, we cannot separate the national struggle from struggle in prison.'[8]

Those Palestinian women political prisoners who are sentenced to years of imprisonment for their political activity are usually highly politicized and can cope with their imprisonment much better than the majority of Palestinian women, and especially the large number of minors arrested during the Intifada. Miriam, active in one of the women's committees, was arrested in February 1989 and underwent interrogation in the Russian Compound before being transferred to one of the women's prisons:

> I am thirty years old but some of the girls were under sixteen. I felt strong. I know that I have to pay a price for my activities. My aim is to achieve independence for my people and to achieve this, I am willing to pay the price. But the young girls really suffered. They were arrested during a demonstration in Jerusalem and they started crying. We tried to calm them down and help them, but I think the older you are and the more experience you have and the more committed you are, the better you can cope with imprisonment.[9]

The increasing number of women detained during the Intifada is the result of increased participation by women in Intifada activities and the Israeli practice of indiscriminate arrest of thousands of Palestinians.[10] Most of the women and girls arrested during the Intifada are picked up on demonstrations, during clashes with the army, on their way to school or in the streets. They are kept for interrogation for a few hours, days or weeks, accused of throwing stones, swearing at soldiers, participating in demonstrations, writing graffiti etcetera, released on high bail (ranging from a few hundred to thousands of US dollars) and later heavily fined. A lot of minors are kept for interrogation. WOFPP counted 164 women detainees in the Russian Compound between 1 December 1988 and December 1989. Of these 72, that is, 44 per cent of the detainees, were minors between the ages of twelve to eighteen. Many minors are facing arrest for the first time. They have probably never spent a single night outside their home. Suddenly they are left alone, they have to spend nights under interrogation or in overcrowded cells, with no protection from the violence and often sexual intimidation and threats they are facing.

The B'tselem report of July 1990 gathered extensive information 'on violence and humiliation of the children on the part of police and General

Security Service (Shin Bet) investigators and on conditions of imprisonment which do not meet minimal standards of human imprisonment'.[11] Professor Greenbaum of the Department of Psychology at the Hebrew University of Jerusalem analysed the consequences of police violence on minors, but sadly his conclusions are in many ways valid for adults as well:

> The immediate effect on the victim is that of trauma, characterised by fears, an exaggerated reaction to any circumstance reminiscent of the conditions suffered during detention and, sometimes, a loss of the ability to function. An additional effect is that of a sense of guilt, especially if the minor feels that he turned somebody else in, or admitted to doing things he never did. In the long term, post-traumatic stress may set in; this condition incorporates some of the preliminary signs of stress, but can linger for years afterwards. Another consequence is hatred towards the authorities and the nation they represent. We must take into account that many detainees are innocent of any crime but are released only after a very trying period of confinement; thus the victimized minor will infer that there is no advantage of behaving as a 'good' child, since both the guilty and the innocent are punished. The circle of hatred spreads out and encompasses the friends and the family, so that illegal violence has a destructive influence both on the individual and on the society at large. Therefore, even if minors recover from the effect of the violence, as most of them do, the damage lingers on. Others, who do not recover, will be scarred for the rest of their lives.[12]

Whilst women political prisoners who are sentenced or under administrative detention are subject to a regime of inadequate health care, bad food, overcrowded cells and harassment from Israeli criminal prisoners, women under interrogation have to rely completely on the mercy of their interrogators: 'there is no way of ascertaining what happened to the detainee from the day of his arrest'.[13] Throughout interrogation, women detainees are kept in complete isolation, under extremely unhygienic conditions; they are not supplied with toilet paper or sanitary towels and are subjected to various kinds of torture.[14]

Methods used to extract a confession include: 'solitary confinement, transfer of the detainee from place to place in order to undermine his self-confidence, cold showers in the winter and at night, the arrest of relatives to put pressure on the suspect, threats, verbal abuse, and forcing the detainee to stand for long periods of time'.[15] This practised 'arrest of relatives' includes the arrest of women and children to extract confessions from their husbands and fathers. The suspect is threatened that his wife will be tortured in his hearing in the jail if he refuses to confess. This was the case with twenty-year-old Majdolen Abu Atwan. On 28 April 1989, in the eighth month of pregnancy, she was arrested while crossing the bridge from Amman. In Jerusalem, she recalled later:

> I was taken to a regular cell, and the following day I was interrogated again. I could hear my husband's voice in the other room saying that I was his wife. They allowed me to see him. Later, my husband told me that the interrogator had threatened him that they would beat and torture me until I lost my baby, unless he confessed.[16]

To put pressure on wanted activists to give themselves up, the Israeli military forces frequently arrest members of their family, wives, mothers or children, as hostages. In the case of the wanted Jamoos Alawi, in the afternoon of 12 August 1989 Israeli soldiers arrested eleven mostly female members of the Alawi family, including Jamoos's fiancé, his mother, his sister and her children. The hostages were kept without food, drink or access to a toilet, under the staircase of the headquarters of the Israeli military administration in Nablus, until they were released the following day at noon. Jamoos's sister was kept for an additional three days.[17]

'It has been found that in addition to torture and humiliation, physical abuse and beatings, the Palestinian women detainees also suffer systematic and consistent sexual harassment.'[18] While there are very few cases of actual rape by soldiers or policemen during interrogation, threats of rape, sexual assaults, insults and harassment are reported frequently. The Intifada has accelerated changes in social attitudes towards women prisoners. Preservation of national honour is increasingly being seen as more important than personal honour (*'ira*), that is, the preservation of the sexual integrity of women. Women who undergo sexual harassment are no longer seen as the one responsible for it, if the assailant is an enemy soldier, interrogator or collaborator.

Politically active and experienced women are usually more prepared to talk about sexual harassment during interrogation. But most of the young women and minors feel deeply ashamed, and if they are willing to report it do so 'hesitantly, shyly and very mild'.[19] How delicate the issues of both sexual harassment by the occupation forces as well as violence and sexual assault inside Palestinian society are is demonstrated by the careful design of projects on these issues by the Palestinian women's movement, and by the way the Palestinian media deal with sexual harassment. For example, the daily newspaper *Al Nahar* printed an interview with members of WOFPP on 14 March 1989, dedicating an entire page, including photographs, to this subject. Every issue raised by the activists, even the description of physical attacks and humiliation, was quoted directly, without editing or rewriting, but all mention of sexual harassment was left out, which made the whole article unclear.[20]

This ambivalent attitude within Palestinian society in the West Bank, Gaza Strip and East Jerusalem makes it difficult for women to develop a clear stand towards the suffering they have gone through, and to speak out.[21] Women and girls who participate in Intifada activities are afraid that the publication of such 'delicate' facts will lead to their being locked in their homes by their families or being married off as soon as possible after their release from jail. As a result, they would be unable to participate in the liberation struggle any more. The policy of sexual harassment would have achieved its goal of paralysing politically active women in a bid to quell the Intifada.

Below we present the testimonies of two women detainees held in the Russian Compound in Jerusalem. Laila is one of the seventy-two minors who were detained in the Russian Compound in 1989. Her case is exemplary of the experiences of many other schoolgirls who were arrested on their way to their classrooms, on demonstrations or shopping on the Jerusalem shopping street Salah al-Din Street. The Israeli Egged bus number 23, which passes through Salah al-Din Street, in Arab east Jerusalem, is a favourite target of stone-throwing youths and the street itself is the battlefield for daily clashes between the ever-present Israeli soldiers and policemen and Palestinian youth.

Hiba is one of ten women between the ages of forty and seventy-five who were detained in the Russian Compound in 1989. Her life and experience are representative of those of many other mothers in the Occupied Territories today. She has eight children, three of whom were jailed at the same time as she. She has experienced soldiers coming in the middle of the night, and has learned not to trust their words, she has had to cope with her worries and fears for her sons while being in the TZINOK herself, and she still has enough courage left to declare solidarity with other women detainees.

Political detainees in the Russian Compound in Jerusalem: conditions of detention[22]

The Russian Compound in Jerusalem (the Moskobieh) is the detention centre used for holding the majority of women arrested on political grounds in Jerusalem and the central and southern part of the Occupied Territories. Since the beginning of the Intifada, the number of Palestinian women transferred to the Russian Compound because of suspected violations of security and public order has increased enormously.

Among the detainees are fourteen-year-old girls, young women, breastfeeding mothers, as well as adult and old women arrested in various places of work, on the bridges leading to Jordan, or in their homes. They are brought to the Russian Compound for interrogation and detention. Some of these women are detained as hostages, so that their husbands or sons will give themselves in to the police. There are mothers arrested because they do not have the money to pay the fine imposed on their child for throwing a stone, or because they verbally confronted security forces arresting their children.

Some detainees are held in a police station, interrogation branch, or cell for hours or days only; others are kept there for months. Children and babies arrive at the Russian Compound with their mothers, but are separated from them – even those who are still being breastfed – and handed over to a relative or the *mukhtar* of the village called to the prison by the police. Sometimes it happens that the detainee's family does not know about her arrest at all, because the police informs families only sporadically, and only in cases concerning Jerusalem residents.

The detention centre in the Russian Compound is known for its extremely harsh conditions. Within the same building there is a separate section for interrogations by the Shabak (general security service), which is managed independently from the police and the detention centre authorities. Frequently a detainee disappears, after her presence in the Russian Compound has already been confirmed. This means that she has been transferred either to the security branch in the Russian Compound or to the security service branch in another town, without her lawyer and family being notified. When the lawyer requests information in order to find her, he receives no answer.

The interrogation tries to extract a confession from the detainee condemning herself and/or others. Attacks and torture push the women into quick confessions. Sometimes the physical condition of the interrogated detainee deteriorates to a degree requiring immediate hospital treatment.

Beatings and assaults, sexual harassment and insults, and even threats of rape are frequent measures from the moment a suspect is arrested and brought to the Russian Compound. They are applied during interrogations in the police station or in the Shabak branch. Many of the suspects experience systematic beatings about their head or neck and long hours of standing, often on one leg, with their hands on their head, with the other leg tied to a door handle. The women are also exposed to swearing and obscene gestures from the prison staff.

All registration and writing during interrogation is done in Hebrew. The interrogator translates orally the content of the document, which the detainee is requested to sign. There is no way to investigate detainees' recurrent complaints that interrogators tell them that they are signing a denial of accusations which is really a confession.

The detention centre authorities possess full autonomy in decisions concerning all the conditions of detention. Constant changes of procedure and regulations are the result. This situation opens the gate to the arbitrariness of the guards. Political detainees are the main victims of arbitrary assault in the Russian Compound. The Jewish criminal detainees kept in an adjacent cell enjoy better conditions and treatment. The constant, arbitrary changes of procedure facilitate oppression against the detainee and leave little possibility for proof and criticism. Everything happens behind closed doors. Concerning a detainee's condition during interrogation – when she finds herself in the hands of the Shabak – there is no controlling body, not even the police, that can be addressed and held accountable to the public, as long as it remains possible to prohibit visits by the lawyer. Thus, it is completely impossible to bar the illegal methods of pressure, threats and torture applied in obtaining confessions from detainees.

The testimony of Hiba A. Shweiki (a 45-year-old widow)

When I returned home, I noticed that the glass of one of the windows had been broken. Neighbours told me that soldiers had come, knocked on the doors violently, and smashed the windows. As I was very afraid, I went to tell my daughter what had happened. Upon my return I found an order pinned to the door ordering me to report to the police. Since the note was written in Hebrew, someone had to translate it for me.

I did not report to the police, but went to sleep. At 11 p.m. soldiers knocked on the door. I said, 'Excuse us, it's a mistake,' and they left. However, five minutes later they returned, more than ten men and one woman soldier, led by Captain Salim. He ordered me to put on my clothes and to come for interrogation. He promised that I would be asked a few questions only, that it would take only a few hours, and that I could return home afterwards.

Captain Salim is the person who had detained my son a month earlier. He told me then too that he merely wanted to ask a few questions, but my son has not returned since then. When I reminded Salim of this, he shouted at me, 'If you refuse to come, I will tell the woman soldier to do what she has to do.' The house was surrounded by soldiers and I could not get dressed in privacy, so I just wrapped myself in a bedcover. Then I was put onto the back seat of a private car. In it with me were two soldiers, one man and one woman.

When we arrived at the Russian Compound, I was registered. Then I was taken into a room, and a policewoman entered and ordered me to undress completely. When I asked her why, she said, 'This is my job.' She made me turn out every piece of clothing I took off, including my underwear. Before she left, she told me to get dressed; but she left the door open, so that everybody could see me.

The policewoman came back with a policeman and they took me to a tiny cell, hardly bigger than the mattress on the floor. The mattress was bare and made of rubber. A hole in the floor served as a toilet, and it was flooding the room. Near the hole was a pile of garbage, leftover food. Above the hole, very low and close by was a water pipe for washing and drinking. Sometimes the pipe supplied water, sometimes not. The room had no windows, except a hole in the ceiling, which was covered by an iron grid. On the floor I saw pieces of clothing which I identified as the clothes of my three sons who had been detained earlier [one son was detained wounded in the hospital]. They served me food: a loaf of bread stuffed with a boiled egg, jam or sardines and tomatoes. The food was disgusting. I could not eat it and was forced to throw it away. When I asked for a bag to collect the garbage scattered in the room they just laughed at me.

During the first three days in solitary confinement, nobody talked to me or explained why I was there. On the third day I was transferred to another cell for another spell of solitary confinement; I spent about one day there. I began to feel weak and dizzy, my stomach ached and I was about to faint. In the tiny cell next to me, a man had a terrible fit and then suddenly went silent. I heard people in other cells saying that they were afraid something had happened to him. They called the guard and told him that two people had fainted, the man and I. I asked the guard if I could see a doctor. He agreed, and took me to interrogation. The interrogator, Abu Nihad, began by saying: 'Ahlan, Umm Shahid!' [Welcome, mother of the martyr.] He was referring to my wounded son who had been taken from the hospital. When I asked Abu Nihad what he meant by that he did not answer. Then he ordered me to remain silent and to listen to him.

For approximately one hour, Abu Nihad talked about the charges against me. I said that as far as I was concerned, there was no point in talking, since he would not believe me. But he insisted that I talk. When I told him that there was no truth in his words, he called me a liar.

When I rejected his suggestion that I should have something to eat and drink, he left, and I remained alone for about twelve hours. I was not handcuffed, but I was locked inside. Finally Abu Nihad returned and ordered the policeman to take me back to the tiny cell I had occupied previously. I lay down on the mattress and almost fell asleep, but was woken by two detainees talking in the adjacent cell. Their voices passed through the pipe in the shower. I asked them to stop talking, because I did not feel well. After a while the two men were removed. I felt very bad. I felt a pain in my stomach and I was about to faint. I started to shout and to call the policeman. But nobody came. A little later a doctor, a male nurse and a policeman arrived. As far as I understood, the doctor scolded the guard for not calling him. I was suffering from falling blood pressure, and it was very difficult for me to walk to the clinic; I could walk only by supporting myself on the wall. In the clinic the doctor examined me, gave me a pill, and I felt better. Then he phoned Abu Nihad, but I do not know what he said.

Later Abu Nihad and the policeman wanted to return me to solitary confinement. But I told them that I would rather be shot dead than enter that cell again. I refused to enter, so Abu Nihad took me to another tiny cell. I stayed there for two days in complete isolation. Nobody came in, nobody talked to me.

In the morning of the third day I was taken for interrogation. When I refused to confess, Abu Nihad started to shout at me, 'In-al-dinik!' [Damn you and your religion!] He slammed his fist on the table and threatened that unless I confessed, he would order the detention of my twelve-year-old daughter Intisar. He picked up the telephone and ordered Intisar's arrest. Five more interrogators entered the room. The first rested his foot on the empty chair in front of me and slapped my right cheek. He said, 'You are a liar, you must confess!' Then they all gathered around me, repeating, 'Confess! There are others who have confessed already. They named you, so you had better confess!' They continued shouting at me, and I kept answering that I felt ill and in need of a doctor. Abu Nihad answered, 'If you confess, we will take care of you!'

I became desperate, and said, 'Okay, prepare the confession you want.' He showed me a text written in Hebrew and demanded that I sign it. I refused. I told him I would not sign, since I do not know how to read and write, and I was not going to sign something I could not understand. They continued, saying that people had incriminated me. So I told them. 'Bring them here, and I will clarify things with them.'

Later, I was informed that at precisely the same time my sixteen-year-old son Jamal was being interrogated next door. He heard me saying, 'Bring them', and recognized my voice. At the end of the interrogation I was taken to another cell for solitary confinement. In the adjacent cell there was a man who told me he was from Bethlehem. Suddenly I heard the door open, and someone cried, 'Mother, mother!' This was my son Jamal. We cried together. He asked me what I was doing there and I told him that I had been arrested. He begged me to eat and drink, even though the food was disgusting. He told me to close my eyes while eating, and he managed to convince me. Then he said that he had an idea that they would come and take one of us soon. And indeed, five minutes later they took me to another cell.

During my second day in this cell, another woman was brought in, and on the next day, a third woman joined us. We were together the whole day. When they came to count us, they noticed that there were three of us in this tiny cell, so they took us to a larger cell. I was put alone in a *tzinok* [tiny cell] containing four beds on two levels. This cell was cleaner, and it had a sink. Throughout all this time I was unable to take a shower, and received neither toilet paper, nor a towel, soap, or change of clothes. I was constantly afraid that I would get my period, because there was nothing I could have used except for a woollen blanket.

On the second day I was taken to court so that my detention could be extended. My lawyer failed to arrive. When the charge sheet was translated to me, I was shocked to hear what I was accused of. The judge told me that he would prolong my detention by sixty days, and asked 'What do you request from the court?' I asked to be released on bail. The judge said he was prepared to prolong my detention only by thirty days, and he told me to ask my lawyer to request my release on bail. I answered that I had no way to contact my lawyer. After the trial I was placed in solitary confinement for one night, and the following day I was transferred to an ordinary cell.

When I arrived at the cell I took a shower for the first time since my arrest and changed my clothes. Three days later I met attorney Lea Tsemel and a Red Cross representative. Until then I had not seen a lawyer, nor officials from the Red Cross. The next day I met my lawyer's assistant. While in solitary confinement I received a parcel from the Women's Organization For Political Prisoners.

I remember the time when the Jewish criminal women detainees started to sing loudly. We called the policewoman to ask them to lower their voices, but she refused. So we also started to sing. A few minutes later about twenty soldiers and two civilians entered, holding clubs and gas grenades in their hands. They screamed at us, 'Who is the one singing national songs?' When we answered that the criminals had started the singing, they shouted and threatened to throw the gas grenades into the cell if we continued. Then they left.

The next day, they came for a woman detainee in order to take her fingerprints, despite the fact that they had already done so. The policewoman returning her asked for her name. The detainee answered, 'You know my name, and besides my name is written in the file.' The policewoman shouted that she had to answer, and from then on she was not allowed to walk outside.

We were thirteen women in the cell. When this detainee told us what had happened, we decided collectively to refuse exercise. I told the policeman that none of us would go outside unless the punished woman was also granted exercise. A policewoman separated us and announced that I was being punished: no visitors, no walks, no cigarettes. I stayed in solitary confinement the whole day. When I was returned to the cell the Red Cross representative informed us that we were on collective punishment. In response to the punishment, all the women decided to go on hunger-strike. Two days later, following eighteen days of detention, I was released on bail.

Testimony of Laila[23]

[Laila is sixteen and a half years old. She is from El-Azaria near Jerusalem, and was arrested on 13 February 1989. She was accused of throwing stones at a bus on Salah al-Din Street. She was detained until her trial, and sentenced on 7 July 1989 to one year in jail and eighteen months imprisonment suspended. Due to her young age, her sentence was reduced by three months. Her testimony was given to her lawyer while she was detained in the Russian Compound.]

I was standing on a side road, when I saw several girls running and four civilians carrying pistols chasing them. I was afraid and started to run too, but I fell. I was caught and put in a car, where I met a girlfriend from school who had been caught just before me. In the car the men ordered us to open our legs, and they beat us between our legs; they even tried to penetrate me with their clubs. When I resisted, they tore the zipper off my pants. One of the soldiers had a metal wire. He bent the edge and placed the wire around our necks, pulling our heads back and forth. During interrogation my hands and my legs were put in handcuffs, and my wrists started to bleed. When I refused to sign a form written in Hebrew, the contents of which were not translated to me, a woman interrogator named Marcelle hit my fingers with a metal ruler until they bled.

One day, while I was held in a regular cell, my friend was removed. After a while we began to worry, and asked a policewoman called Ruhama what had happened to her. Ruhama told us our friend had died. We continued to ask her, until she took me to a dining room. My feet were cuffed, and my hands were tied to an iron railing above my head, my face touching the wall. Rumaha and a number of policemen beat me violently.

The night before my trial. I was taken into a small room. Three men threatened to rape me, unless I confessed to throwing stones. They brought a metal wire and threatened to insert it into my vagina, unless I confessed. On the day of the trial, while we were walking along the corridor to the detention centre, one of the soldiers tripped me. When I fell down he started to 'ride' on top of me.

Notes

1. The Women's Organization for Political Prisoners (WOFPP) consists of Israeli women, both Jewish and Palestinian, united in their resistance against occupation. Their aim is to defend the 'human and democratic rights of Palestinian and Israeli women imprisoned because of their social and political activity in the legitimate struggle against occupation'. WOFPP's first group was established in Tel Aviv in May 1988 in reaction to the increased repression that accompanied the outbreak of the Intifada, which included an increasing number of arrests and incidents of harassment of women. The WOFPP Jerusalem group

was founded in 1989, concentrating on the city's Russian Compound as the largest detention centre for women from Jerusalem and the West Bank. WOFPP members are present at the Russian Compound every day, where they meet detainees' families and try to assist them. The group provides assistance to prisoners, delivers food parcels to them and tries to arrange legal representation. WOFPP believes its important achievement to be its existence as a 'public eye', therewith 'countering the prevailing indifference towards the negation of political prisoners' basic rights'.

The two affidavits that follow the introduction (both names are pseudonyms), are taken with permission from WOFPP's 1990 Information Booklet, WOFPP, PO Box 8537, Jerusalem, Israel 91083.

2. *Al Mobadun Al Filastiniun*, Acre, Dar Al Aswar, April 1986, p. 116; Meron Benvenisti, *The West Bank Handbook*, Jerusalem, Jerusalem Post, 1986, pp. 86–7.

3. *List of Palestinian Women issued Six-Month Detention without Trial*, Jerusalem, PHRIC, 1989.

4. *Al-Fajr*, 31 July 1988, p. 2.

5. The Database Project on Palestinian Human Rights, *Summary Data: December 9, 1987 through August 31, 1989*, Jerusalem, 1989.

6. See *Punishing a Nation*, Ramallah, Al-Haq, 1988, p. 250f.: and Benvenisti,* p. 176.

7. Benvenisti.

8. Nura Maklouf and Haifa Abu Halib (pseudonyms), 'Women Political Prisoners Emerge Stronger', *Al-Fajr*, 7 March 1986, p. 6.

9. Interview with Miriam (a pseudonym), Jerusalem, 26 June 1989.

10. The B'tselem Report of November 1989 concludes: 'The first [conclusion] is the considerable injustice caused on a routine basis by an overwhelming propensity towards inefficiency, indifference, and neglect, which degrade not only defendants and their attorneys, but also the judges, prosecutors, and soldiers working within the judicial system. . . . In this atmosphere of neglect, commotion, and utter chaos, hundreds of people are sentenced to months and years in prison. . . . In these circumstances, the court changes from an arbiter of guilt and innocence to a tribunal whose primary purpose is to fix the date for terminating punishment of no predetermined length, served prior to any formal conviction.' B'tselem – the Israeli Information Centre for Human Rights in the Occupied Territories, 18 Keren Hayasod St, Jerusalem 92149, *Information Sheet: Update May 1990, The Military Judicial System in the West Bank, Followup Report*, p. 4.

11. *Violence against minors in Police Detention*. Information sheet published in cooperation with Aid to Imprisoned Minors. Jerusalem, B'tselem, July 1990.

12. Prof. Charlie Greenbaum, 'Police Violence Against Minors – Psychological Aspects', in *Violence Against Minors in Police Detention*, Jerusalem, B'tselem 1990, p. 7.

13. Benvenisti, p. 59.

14. *WOFPP Report 1990*, pp. 7–8.

15. Benvenisti, p. 59.

16. *WOFPP Report 1990*, p. 22.

17. *WOFPP Newsletter*, August 1989, p. 2.

18. Matzpen, April 1989, translated by Prof. Israel Shahak, quoted from *WOFPP Information Paper 1989*, Jerusalem, 1989.

19. Ibid.
20. Ibid.
21. See Chapter 16.
22. This section is quoted directly from the *WOFPP Report 1990* (pp. 6–7, 10–11), and gives the background information necessary to put the two testimonies into context.
23. According to Israeli police statistics, between January 1989 and May 1990 a total of 1,744 minors (thirteen – eighteen years old) were detained in the Russian Compound and in the Kishle police station. A total of 833 of them were charged with specific offences. (*Violence against Minors in Police Detention*, tables 1 and 2.)

Bibliography

Abu Dhaleb, Nuha, 'Palestinian Women and Their Role in the Revolution', *Peuples mediterranées*, No. 5, 1978, pp. 35–48.

'A Dual Challenge: women and activism in the Gaza Strip', *Spare Rib*, No. 183, October 1987, pp. 10–11.

Antonius, Soraya, 'Fighting on Two Fronts: conversation with Palestinian women', *Journal of Palestine Studies*, Vol. 8, No. 3, Spring 1979, pp. 26–45.

―― 'Fighting on Two Fronts: Palestinian women', *Al-Fajr*, 8–14 March 1981, pp. 8, 14.

―― 'Prisoners for Palestine: a list of women political prisoners', *Journal of Palestine Studies* Vol. IX, No. 3, Spring 1980.

―― 'Women's Struggle and National Liberation: Third World Women speak out', in Miranda Davis (ed.), *Third World – Second Sex*, London, Zed Books 1983.

Ashrawi, Hannan Mikha'il, *From Intifada to Independence: a Palestinian woman speaks out*, Netherlands, Palestine Information Office and Arab League.

Ata, Ibrahim, 'Prospects and Retrospects on the Role of Moslem Arab Women at Present: trends and tendencies', *Islamic Culture*, Vol. LV, No. 4, 1981.

―― *The West Bank Palestinian Family*, KPI, London, 1986.

Atieh, I., *Palestinian Women on the Move: activities and organisations*, Jerusalem, Arab Studies Society, 1985.

al-Bahr, Z., 'Living in the Camps', *Middle East International*, No. 296, 20 March 1987.

―― 'Women in the Camps: a special way of life', *Middle East International*, No. 296, 1987.

Barzilai, S. and Davies, A. M., 'Personality and Social Aspects of Mental Health Disease in Jerusalem Women', in *International Journal of Social Psychology* No. 18, 1972, pp. 22–8.

Bendt, Ingela and Downing, James, *We Shall Return; women of Palestine*,

London and Westport, 1982.

Brait, Nabila, 'Women in the Palestinian Economy', *Al-Fajr*, 2–8 August 1981, pp. 8–9.

Canaan, T., 'Unwritten Laws Affecting the Arab Palestinian Women of Palestine', *Journal of the Palestine Oriental Society*, Vol. 11, 1931, pp. 172–203.

Dajani, S., *Surif Women's Cooperative for Handicraft: a case study prepared for the UN Decade for Women Forum*, Jerusalem, 1985.

Davies, Miranda, *Third World – Second Sex*, London, Zed Books, 1987. Includes an interview with Sirham Barghouti, pp. 94–6.

Debus, B. and Spieker, M., 'We Do Not Only Want a Liberated Land: Palestinian women's movements in the West Bank', unpublished paper, 1984.

Doumani, Beshara and Johnson, Penny, 'Two Families', *Merip*, Vol. 17, No. 3, May–June 1987, pp. 15–18.

Ehrlich, Avishai, 'Zionism, Demography and Women's Work', *Khamsin*, No. 7, 1980, pp. 87–105.

Elhadi, Musoun, 'The Women's Movement in Palestine Since the Beginning of the Twentieth Century', paper presented at the Palestinian–Italian Friendship Conference, Jerusalem, 25–26 August.

Fawri, Didar, 'Palestinian Women in Palestine', in Monique Gadant (ed.), *Women of the Mediterranean*, London, Zed Books, 1986, pp. 59–71.

Fawzia, Fawzia, 'Palestine: women and the revolution', in: *Sisterhood is Global*.

Fishman, Alex, 'Palestinian Women and the Intifada', *New Outlook: Women in Action*, June–July 1989, p. 7.

Fitch, Florence, *The Daughter of Abu Salem: the story of a peasant woman of Palestine*, Boston, Badger, 1930.

Friedlander, Dov and Eisenbach, Zwi, 'Modernization Patterns and Family Change: the Arab population of Israel' *Population Studies* 33, 29, pp. 239–54.

Giacaman, Rita, 'Development a Key Problem for Palestinians in the Israeli occupied West Bank', *Listen Real Loud*, Vol. 6, No. 2, Spring 1985.

—— *Life and Health in Three Palestinian Villages*, Jerusalem Study Series 14, London, 1988.

—— *Palestinian Women and Development in the West Bank*, Birzeit University, 1982.

—— 'Palestinian Women in the Uprising: from followers to leaders', *Journal of Refugee Studies*, Vol. 2, No. 1, 1989, special issue *Palestinian Refugees and Non-refugees in the West Bank and Gaza Strip*, pp. 139–46.

—— 'Unhealthy Attitudes', *Jerusalem Post*, 21 March 1982, p. 8.

—— and Johnson, Penny, 'Building Barricades and Breaking Barriers', in Z. Lockman and J. Beinin (eds.), *Intifada: the Palestinian uprising against*

Israeli occupation, Boston, South End Press, 1989, pp. 155–170.

Giacaman, Rita and Muna Odeh, 'The Palestinian Women's Movement in the Israeli Occupied West Bank and Gaza Strip', in Toubia Nahid (ed.), *Women of the Arab World*, London, 1988, pp. 57–68.

Haddad, Yvonne, 'Palestinian Women: patterns of legitimation and domination', in Khalil Nakhleh and Elia Zureik (eds.), *The Sociology of the Palestinians*, London, 1980.

Halabi, Rafik, *Die Westbank Story: Stirb für dein Land und die Ehre deiner Schwester*, Koenigstein, 1981.

Hamad, Saida, 'Intifada Transforms Palestinian Society, Especially the Role of Women', in: *Al-Fajr*, 13 March 1989, pp. 8–9.

al-Hamadi, L., 'Palestinian Women in Prison', in Khamsin, *Women in the Middle East*, London, Zed Books, 1987.

Hammami, Rema, 'Women, the Hijab and the Intifada', *Merip Report*, May–August 1990, Nos. 164–5, pp. 24–8.

——— (ed.), *Annotated Bibliography on Palestinian Women* (compiled by Pari Baumann), Jerusalem, Arab Thought Forum, 1989. Includes literature on the women's committees, and a bibliography on Middle Eastern Women.

al-Helo, Nehaiya and Lende, Karen, 'Women's Activism in the West Bank and Gaza', *Al-Fajr*, 7 March 1986, pp. 8–9, 15.

Hiltermann, Joost, 'Before the Uprising: the organization and mobilization of Palestinian workers and women in the Israeli-occupied West Bank and Gaza Strip', PhD thesis, Dept of Sociology, University of California Santa Cruz, June 1988.

——— 'Organising under Occupation', *Middle East International*, No. 296, 1987.

——— 'Sustaining Movement, Creating Space: trade unions and women's committees', *Merip Report*, May–August 1990, Nos. 164–5, pp. 32–6.

Husseini, Salim F., *Women and Abortion in the West Bank of Jordan: a pilot study*, Jerusalem, Jordan Family Planning and Protection Association, 1981.

'Intifada', *Spare Rib*, No. 194, September 1988. Interviews with three Palestinian women activists.

'It is Possible to Agree on Principles, an interview with Hannan Mikhail-Ashrawi', *New Outlook, Women in Action*, June–July 1989, p. 7.

Jad, Islah, 'From Salons to the Popular Committees: Palestinian women, 1919–89', in Jamal R. Nassar and Roger Heacock (eds.), *Intifada: Palestine at the crossroads*, New York/Westport/London, Praegar, 1990, pp. 125–42.

Janho, Souhaila, 'Women's Participation in Rural Development: a case study of two West Bank Palestinian villages', unpublished MA thesis, Institute of Social Studies, Den Haag, 1983.

'June Days in Nablus', *New Outlook*, Vol. 15, No. 6, (134), July–August 1972.

Kamal, Assad, 'Women under Town Restriction', *Al-Fajr*, 22–28 March 1981, p. 7.

Karmi, G., 'Palestinian Women: a force for liberation', *Palestinian Digest*, Vol. 8, 4 July 1978.

Kazi, H., 'Palestinian Women and the National Liberation Movement: a social perspective', in Khamsin, *Women in the Middle East*, London, Zed Books, 1987.

—— 'A Perspective of Social Change among Palestinian Muslim Women on the West Bank', unpublished thesis, London School of Economics, London, 1986.

Khaled, Leila, *Mein Volk soll leben* (My people shall live), Munich, 1974.

Khalid, Usama, 'A Palestinian History of Women's Struggle', *Al-Fajr*, 8 March 1985 (Part One) and 15 March 1985 (Part Two).

Khalifa, I., *Women and the Palestine Question*, Cairo, 1974 (in Arabic).

Khalifa, Sahar, 'Stories of Daughters: our fate, our house', *Merip Report*, May–August 1990, Nos. 164–5, pp. 29–30.

—— *Der Feigenkaktus* (Wild Thorns), Zürich, 1983.

—— *Die Sonnenblume* (The Sunflower), Zürich, 1986.

Khalili, Ghazi, *Palestinian Women and the Revolution*, Acre, Dar-al Aswar, 1981/77, (in Arabic).

Khass, Mary, 'The Effects of Occupation on Women and Young People – Some Examples', *Journal of Refugee Studies*, Vol. 2, No. 1, 1989, pp. 147–9.

Kossman, Ingeborg and Scharenberg, Lukrezia (eds.), *Palästinenische Frauen – der alltägliche Kampf*, Berlin, 1982.

Lahav, Hadas and Schwartz, Michal, 'One Valiant Woman' (interview with Zahira Kamal), *Al-Fajr*, 29 March 1985, pp. 10, 15.

Landon, Meryl, 'Women's Issues Don't Change the Status Quo', *Al-Fajr*, 21 March 1986, p. 6.

Maklouf, Nura and Abu Halib, Haifa 'Women Political Prisoners Emerge Stronger', *Al-Fajr*, 7 March 1986, p. 6.

Mansour, Sylvie, 'Identity among Palestinian Youth: male and female differentials', *Journal of Palestine Studies*, Vol. VI, No. 4, Summer 77.

Masri Asa'ad, Nawal, 'Women in the Labour Market in the West Bank after 1967', paper presented at the Conference on the New International Division of Labour and the Middle East, Amsterdam, Holland, 28–30 January 1988.

Mikha'il Ashrawi, Hannan, *From Intifada to Independence: a Palestinian woman speaks out*, Netherlands, Palestine Information Office and Arab League.

Mogannam, Matiel, *Arab Women and the Palestine Problem*, London, 1937.

Moors, Annelies, *Gender, Economy and Kinship: rural women on the West Bank*, Birzeit University and Amsterdam University.

—— *Gender Hierarchy and Social Relations in a Palestinian Village*, Amsterdam, 1985.

Mothers and IUDs, Jerusalem, Family Planning and Protection Association (West Bank), 1989.

Natour, Salman, 'A Bride on the Road', *Al-Fajr*, 28 October 1983, p. 11.

Nazzal, Laila Ahes, 'The Role of Shame in Social Transformation among Palestinian Women in the West Bank', unpublished PhD thesis, University of Michigan, Ann Arbor, 1986.

'Palestinian Democratic Women Struggle for 1. Independence, 2. Peace, 3. Equality of Rights', paper to the First Conference of the Union of Palestinian Committees for Women Workers in the West Bank and the Gaza Strip, Jerusalem, 13 February 1983 (in Arabic).

'Palestinian Women – Triple Burden, Single Struggle', *Peuples mediterranées*, No. 44–5, July–December 1988, pp. 247–68.

Pallis, E., 'Women of the West Bank', *Middle East International*, 10 October 1980.

Papps, I. 'The Role and Determinants of Bride Price: the case of a Palestinian village', *Current Anthropology*, Vol. 24, April 1983.

Pesa, Flavia, 'Between Dreams and Slogans: the straitjacket of sex and class', *Al-Fajr*, 8 March, 1985.

—— 'The Image of Women in Palestinian Literature', *Al-Fajr*, 15 March 1985, p. 11.

—— '*Super-exploitation in the Sewing Industry*', *Al-Fajr*, 19 April 1989, pp. 8–9, 15.

Peteet, Julia, 'No Going Back: Palestinian women in Lebanon', *Middle East Report* (Merip), January–February 1986.

—— 'Women and National Politics – the Palestinian case', unpublished PhD thesis, University of Michigan, Ann Arbor, 1985.

—— 'Women and the Palestinian Movement: no going back?', *Middle East Report* (Merip), No. 138, January–February 1986.

Pollock, Alex, 'Realistic Methodology and the Articulation of Modes of Production: Peasant houshold production in the North Jordan Valley of the Occupied West Bank', unpublished PhD thesis, University of Strathclyde, Glasgow.

Punamäcki, Raija-Leena, 'Psychological Stress Responses of Palestinian Mothers and Their Children in Conditions of Military Occupation and Political Violence', *Quarterly Newsletter of the Laboratory of Comparative Human Cognition*, Vol. 9, No. 2, April 1987.

—— 'Stress among Palestinian Women under Occupation', *International Journal of Psychology* 21, 1986, pp. 445–62.

Rahbek Pedersen, Birgitte, 'Oppressive and Liberating Elements in the

Situation of Palestinian Women', in Bo Utas (ed.), *Women in Islamic Societies*, London and Malmoe, 1983, pp. 172–91.

Rishmawi, Mona, 'The Legal Status of Palestinian Women in the Occupied Territories', in Nahid Toubia (ed.), *Women of the Arab World*, London, 1988, pp. 79–92.

Rockwell, Susan, 'Palestinian Women Workers in the Israeli-occupied Gaza Strip', *Journal of Palestine Studies*, Vol. XIV, No. 2, Winter 1985.

—— 'A Study of Palestinian Women Workers in the Israeli Occupied Gaza Strip', unpublished essay, April 1984.

Ronen, Ya'el, 'Since That Interrogation', *HaAretz* Friday supplement, 23 December 1988.

Rouhana, Kate, 'West Bank Women Overcoming Obstacles to Education', *Al-Fajr*, 15 March 1985, pp. 7, 10.

Said, Manar, 'Maternity: high risk in the West Bank', *Al-Fajr*, 8 March 1985, p. 10.

Salah, Rima and Ghada Hashem Talhami, 'The Movement Should Try to Erect Bridges Between Palestinian Women,' *Al-Fajr*, 5 July 1987, pp. 8–9.

Samed, Amal, 'Arab Palestinian Women: entering the proletariat', *Journal of Palestine Studies*, Vol. 6, No. 1, Autumn 1976, pp. 159–68.

—— 'The Proletarianization of Palestinian Women in Israel', *Merip Report*, No. 50, 1976.

Sayeh, Mai, 'Choosing the Revolution', in M. Gadant (ed.), *Women of the Mediterranean*, London, Zed Books, 1986, pp. 86–91.

Sayigh, R., 'Choosing the Revolution', in M. Gadant (ed.) *Women in the Mediterranean*, London, Zed Books, 1986.

—— 'Encounter with Palestinian Women under Occupation', *Journal of Palestine Studies*, Vol. X, No. 4, Summer 1981, pp. 3–26.

—— 'Femmes palestiniennes: une histoire en quête d'historiens', *Revue d'études palestiniennes*, pp. 13–32.

—— 'The Mukhabarat State: a Palestinian woman's testimony', *Journal of Palestine Studies*, Vol. XIV, No. 3, Spring 1985.

—— 'Palestinian Women: triple burden, single struggle', *Peuples mediterranées* 44–45, July–December 1988, pp. 247–68.

—— 'Roles and Functions of Arab Women: a reappraisal', *Arab Studies Quarterly*, Vol. 3, No. 3, Autumn 1981, pp. 258–74.

—— 'Women in Struggle: Palestine', *Third World Quarterly*, Vol. 5, No. 5, October 1983.

—— 'Women's Struggle in the PMR: a critique', *Al-Fajr*, 22 March 1985, pp. 7, 15.

—— and Peteet, Julie, 'Between Two Fires: Palestinian women in Lebanon', in Rosemary Ridd and Helen Callaway (eds.), *Women and Political Conflict: portraits of struggle in times of conflict*, New York, 1987, pp. 106–37.

Seoudi, Mona (ed.), *In Time of War: children testify (drawings by Palestinian children)*, Beirut, 1970.

Simha, Ethia (Advocate Advisor on the Status of Women), *The Status of Women in Judea, Samaria and the Gaza Strip*, Jerusalem, July 1984.

Siniora, Randa George, 'Palestinian Labor in a Dependent Economy: the case of women in the sub-contracting clothing industry in the West Bank', unpublished MA thesis, American University at Cairo, 1987.

Sus, Nura, 'Woman Power in Palestine: Women's Committee for Social Action', *Al-Fajr*, 21 March 1984, p. 16.

Talhami, Ghada, 'Palestinian women: the case of political liberation', *Arab Perspectives*, 4 January 1984, p. 6.

―――― 'Women in Movement: their long, uncelebrated history', *Al-Fajr*, 30 March 1986, pp. 8–9.

Tawil, Raymonda, *My Home, My Prison*, London, Zed Books Ltd, 1983.

―――― 'Return and Reminiscence of a Palestinian Woman', *New Outlook* 15, November–December 1971, pp. 29–35.

Taylor, Shami, 'Palestinian Women Workers Face Discrimination – on two fronts', *Al-Fajr*, 10 May 1983, pp. 8–9.

United Nations, *The Situation of Women and Children Living in the Occupied Arab Territories and Other Occupied Territories*, UN Secretary General, October 1984.

Wolf, Elsbeth, *Palestinian Women's Health Care and Well-being*, Working Group on Development Studies, University of Amsterdam, November 1986.

'Women in Palestinian History', *Al-Fajr*, 11–17 May 1980, p. 5.

'Women of Palestine International Women's Year 1975', *American Near East Refugee Aid Newsletter*, No. 33, May–June 1975.

'The Women's Committees and the Intifada (One Aspect of The Palestinian Women's Movement)', *Intifada, Year 1*, special issue of *Children of Stones*, No. 5, ICCP, Geneva, 1988.

Women under Occupation, Palestine Liberation Organization, Department of Information, Tunis, 1989.

Woodsmall, Ruth Francis, *Moslem Women Enter a New World*, New York, 1975 (1936). See the chapter entitled 'The New Area of Girl's Education in Palestine and Transjordan', and 'A Modern Health Programme in Syria, Palestine and Transjordan'.

Working Paper of the Union of Palestinian Committees for Working Women in the West Bank and Gaza Strip to the Nairobi Conference on the UN Decade for Women, July 1985.

Zarour, Miriam, 'Ramallah: my home town', *Middle East Journal*, Vol. 7, No. 4, Autumn 1953, pp. 430–39.

Zinaida, Frederica, 'Our Host the Palestinian Women', *Women of the World*, No. 3, 1973, pp. 20–23.

Index